your
PERSONAL
GUIDE to
Wellness

Taking Control of Your Health

Jamie McManus, M.D.

your PERSONAL GUIDE to Wellness

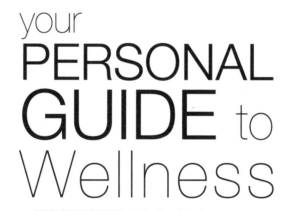

Taking Control of Your Health

with
Dorothy Casper
&
Vicki Spackman

NEW HORIZON
COMMUNICATIONS

ISBN: 1-55517-742-5

e.1

Published by Cedar Fort Inc.

www.cedarfort.com

Distributed by:

Cover design by Nicole Shaffer

Cover design © 2004 by Lyle Mortimer

Printed in the United States of America

10 9 8 7 6 5 4 3 2 1

Printed on acid-free paper

WITH SPECIAL THANKS...

Growing up in a small town in Northern California as one of six children brought me to adulthood with a great sense of family and a somewhat naive view of my abilities to "reshape the world." My dad is an engineer who believes we all have a responsibility to do something meaningful with our lives. When I was only six or seven years old, I remember having conversations with him about what I would become. Because I liked science and enjoyed people, I thought I should be a doctor. No family member had been remotely involved in medicine, but it seemed like a noble profession. My dear father instilled in me a desire to succeed and a belief in my ability to do so.

My mother was always there whenever I needed her, ready to listen with her heart. She raised six great kids in the turbulent '60s and '70s, and never failed to go the extra miles for each of us. My five siblings (Michael, Cynthia, Brian, Milissa, and Alison) and I remain close and have great gatherings with our large extended family, now spread up and down the West Coast.

The greatest joy of my life—my most treasured "accomplishment— is motherhood. My handsome son Adam and my beautiful daughter Heather are the lights of my life. To me, my single most important responsibility is to be a role model of a healthy and joyful life. They inspire me on a daily basis to be true to my inner self and follow a path that brings happiness and contentment.

I am grateful for the opportunity to be a physician. I have loved every minute of being a doctor. I appreciate each and every patient that has ever entered my exam rooms (from Roseville, California to Mukilteo, Washington) over my 15 years as a practicing family physician. My patients taught me to listen intently and to focus on the entire person in the context of his or her life. They taught me to be open-minded and creative and to challenge established and traditional approaches. They also taught me that it is their body and life; and they inspired me to work with them to create a treatment plan that they could put into effect after they walked out my office door.

As a practicing physician, I saw a need to help people understand that health is their responsibility (in partnership with their physician). Because of the importance of this concept, it was a natural transition to focus on bringing the message to an audience outside my exam rooms. Doctors are simply too busy to devote the necessary time to each and every patient: to give advice on diet and weight loss, to illustrate stress management techniques, and to outline personalized exercise regimes so that each patient has the best chance to stay healthy. We have become a treatment-oriented, disease-supporting medical system with little time to spend on the prevention of disease and promotion of health. We recommend appropriate screenings, but spend precious little time talking about what can be done to preserve health. Most physicians just don't have the time to learn about all the possible alternative approaches to consider assisting in the management of a particular condition.

To counteract the terrible diets that many of my patients seemed to practice, I have always recommended the use of supplements. I have taken at least a multivitamin since my early twenties; and, due to the prevalence of cancer in my family, I also began to add antioxidants as research began to unfold on antioxidants reducing the risk of cancer. When my friend John suggested in 1990 that I try Herbalife supplements, little did I know that the use of these products would change my life so dramatically. Not only did I experience great health benefits from these products, but, through Herbalife, I was also able to ultimately pursue a professional dream—to share my philosophy of health preservation through lifestyle and dietary changes on a worldwide platform. This has been a joy, an honor, and a responsibility that I do not take lightly.

I am so grateful to John for being a great support and for pushing me to explore my professional options. He encouraged me to open a door that has allowed me to develop skills as a speaker, a television host, and a writer, enabling me to meet people all over the world who really want good health and vitality. I want to express sincere appreciation to all I have met, spoken with, and worked with as I have traveled the globe for Herbalife. I send big hugs to my friends and colleagues around the world.

This book is the realization of a dream for me. My greatest professional joy has been inspiring people to take control of their health, and to improve their health and their chance of living an energetic and fulfilling life. This book provides a larger venue to do just that.

Very few things in life are a "one man/or woman show," and this book was certainly not one of them. I appreciate James J. Barber, M.D. (Dr. Jim) for encouraging me to write a book, sharing my philosophy of wellness.

I am especially grateful to my co-authors, Dorothy Casper and Vicki Spackman. They have not only brought their creativity and writing expertise to this project, but they have also brought their encouragement. They supported me through the inevitable delays and challenges and helped me to persevere. They were willing to rewrite, rework, and redo until this book was something we could all be proud of.

I am also grateful to you, my readers. Thank you for your confidence and trust, and for allowing me to share my wellness philosophy with you. I promise that as you put these principles of health into practice, your lives will change for the better.

Good reading and, most importantly, good health.

Dr. Jamie

aka Jamie F. McManus, M.D., FAAFP

I am a middle-aged mother, wife, and career woman. As a result, I am stressed out, maxed out, and on the edge. So is my overworked, al-ways-seems-to-have-another-patient-waiting doctor. Even though I am certain she is doing the best she can, the truth of the matter is she has only five minutes to spend with me once a year for my annual physical. She does the bare minimum in testing, and then, on her way out the door and without looking back, she asks, "Everything else OK?"

To which I reply (to the back of her head), "Other than the grape-fruit-size lump growing in the middle of my back, everything is great."

She can't hear me. She is already in the next examining room. The worrisome thing about this situation is I know that if she did have time, she could tell me things that could possibly save my life.

Because of the realities of medical care today, I am the one account-able for my health, not my doctor. Today, I must educate myself and practice the daily disciplines required to remain healthy.

However, the education process can be daunting. Hundreds of books, publications, websites, friends, not to mention my mother, have advice, all of which is often contradictory. Thankfully, Dr. Jamie McMa-nus (aka Dr. Jamie) wrote *Your Personal Guide to Wellness*.

I love how this book educates us in a non-condescending fashion about modern medicine and health challenges of the 21st century. Ad-mittedly, when I first saw the manuscript, I went straight to the chapter entitled "Healthful Aging," but each and every chapter got my attention and contained information beneficial to me, my family, and friends. For instance, despite the limitations of today's medical care, Dr. Jamie knows that doctors are vital in our health process, so she devoted one chapter to "Making Your Physician a Partner in Your Health Journey."

She knows that parents play a critical role in their children's health habits, so she wrote another chapter entitled, "Legacy for Our Children," where she points out ways for parents to teach and pattern healthy habits to give their children long, healthy, disease-free lives.

She knows that women today have new questions regarding their health, so she provides answers in a chapter called, "New Hormone Challenges for the 21st Century Woman." In *Your Personal Guide to Wellness*, Dr. Jamie doesn't just inform us about a condition, but helps resolve our personal health issues through a "Follow-up Preventive Prescription" at the end of every chapter. Her education and expertise as a doctor is evident in this book, but she also writes with the humor and empathy of a fellow human being who lets us know she understands what we are going through.

In the last chapter, Dr. Jamie gently reminds us that wellness is not just about physical health, but mental and spiritual as well. She guides us through a list of health goals to set for ourselves, then has us specify how to accomplish our goals. This interactive approach helps us make long-lasting change in our lives.

I recommend you read this book with a highlighter pen and a pencil close by. You will want to highlight key phrases that you should act on. You'll also feel like jotting down ideas to include in your own personal wellness plan.

I met Dr. Jamie seven years ago at an Herbalife training session. Her smart and practical advice rang true. I loved her preventive approach. She has never ceased to amaze me because, despite her worldwide travel schedule and devotion to her family, she has always found time to answer my health questions and the questions of thousands of others. So many people around the world said, "You should write a book!" and she finally did. She will be thrilled when people take what they have learned from her book and change their lives through better health.

Thanks, Jamie,

Leslie Stanford

TABLE OF CONTENTS

CHAPTER 1

WELLNESS
A Winning Life Strategy

points to ponder as you read:

- ✓ What is wellness?
- ✓ What is the cost of illness?
- ✓ How can I improve my odds of avoiding a major illness or disease?
- ✓ Who is ultimately responsible for my health?

Two years before I started medical school, I watched my favorite grandmother die of colon cancer at age 61. This was a horrifying, yet enlightening, experience for me. Watching her die made me realize that treatment doesn't always work, that there must be a better way to deal with disease. This realization colored everything I learned during my medical school studies. In each of my classes, as I studied the many ways the human body can break down, from normal aging to the progression of disease, I was always thinking in reverse, trying to discover how to prevent that degeneration, premature aging, or disease from happening. In fact, I ultimately chose family practice because I wanted to work in a branch of medicine where I would have the opportunity to intervene before disease began, thus making a difference in the lives of my patients.

Later, as a family practice physician, I observed in my patients the progression of disease, health challenges, and a poor day-today quality of life. I saw patients who were struggling because they did not feel their best. They would battle with a variety of symptoms that didn't conform to a specific medical diagnosis. Some of these patients would become very frustrated at the lack of answers for their lingering ailments and spend an inordinate amount of time flitting from doctor to doctor, trying to find the one who could write the magical prescription to restore their health and vitality.

What they were actually looking for was a prescription for wellness. They wanted to be free from illness and disease, and they wanted to feel good. They wanted to have the necessary stamina to keep up with their daily activities and meet the challenges of job and family. They wanted the vitality and energy to enjoy life.

From my 22 years as a doctor, I have determined that the lack of wellness may be the greatest loss experienced in America, as well as in other industrialized countries around the world. Illness in all its varieties, from chronic low-grade daily health problems to the development of life-threatening disease, has major implications in our society. A lack of health, energy, and vitality are at the core of poor job performance, accidents, family and marital stresses, inferior school performance, and a sub-standard quality of life. Sickness isn't just costly in terms of social ramifications, but also in actual dollars and cents.

Hundreds of dollars are added to every American's tax bill annually to offset the expenses of Medicare. Countless billions of dollars are spent needlessly each year on medical treatments for preventable illness. It is estimated that 95 billion dollars is spent annually on just obesity and its related diseases.

An Arabian proverb says, "He who has health, has hope, and he who has hope, has everything." Good health is the most important treasure we can secure in this life. If you don't have good health, it really doesn't matter what else you do have. All the fame, fortune, and prestige in the world cannot be enjoyed and utilized in the midst of sickness and disease. A lack of wellness hinders the ability to keep up with the demands of life. A lack of wellness saps energy and restricts activities. A lack of wellness ultimately limits the ability to fully enjoy life and to make the most of you.

The good news is that wellness is not only a standard to strive for, but a goal that can be achieved. Scientific research has clearly shown a definite link between health challenges/diseases and lifestyle factors, such as eating habits, weight, activity levels, smoking, sleep habits, and how stress is managed. The personal risk for developing major diseases and severe health problems is 20% genetics and 80% lifestyle. This is the really good news, 80%—not 50 or even 75%, but 80%—of your future health is determined by you!

This was validated for me through the lives of my two grandmothers. My dad's mother died of colon cancer at the age of 61. She was overweight, smoked heavily, and ate a high-fat diet. My maternal grandmother lived to be 96. She ate well and maintained a healthy weight throughout her life. She didn't smoke, walked every day, and got plenty of sleep every night. She also managed her stress levels by always saying whatever was on her mind. (While that may not have always had a positive impact on the stress levels of those around her, it certainly worked for her!)

The level of wellness that my 96-year-old grandmother enjoyed is available to all. For the past seven years, I have traveled around the world teaching such principles of wellness.

Realize that by changing diet and lifestyle, adding fiber, utilizing supplements, cutting back calories, losing excess weight, and exercising consistently, the trend of today's ill health can literally be reversed and potential future disease prevented.

When walking out of the doctor's office, make sure you have the information needed to take control of your health, to turn around health challenges, and to maintain the best level of health possible. You should feel empowered and have the ability to literally change the quality of your life for the better.

I love being a doctor, and I have a passion for helping people learn to be healthy. I know the compensation that comes from helping sick patients, but I far prefer assisting people to be well. It's much more rewarding to educate, inspire, and motivate people to take control of their health, thereby controlling their destiny.

Hippocrates, the father of modern medicine, said, "Health is the greatest of human blessings." Through *Your Personal Guide to Wellness*, you will gain information and knowledge to secure the "greatest of human blessings" and to apply this life strategy to your own life. Read this book straight through, but also keep it as a reference for yourself, spouse, and family to provide the information to help you take control.

FOLLOW-UP PREVENTIVE PERSCRIPTION:

WELLNESS CHECKLIST

On a piece of paper, number 1 to 25 down the left-hand side. After reading each of the following 25 statements, record next to the corresponding number on your paper whether that statement would apply to you: Always, Somtimes, Never, or I Don't Know.

1. I drink six to eight, eight-ounce glasses of water each day.
2. I eat a minimum of seven servings of fruits and vegetables each day.
3. I eat a low-fat diet, with fat calories being less than 20% of total calories consumed.
4. I limit the amount of red meat I consume.
5. I avoid fast food.
6. I stock my kitchen with healthy food choices.
7. I cook my food using methods to maximize nutritional value.
8. I exercise a minimum of 30 minutes a day, three times

a week.

9. I have a fitness regimen that includes aerobic, resistance, and flexibility exercises.
10. I do not smoke or use drugs.
11. I limit my intake of caffeine and alcohol.
12. I get eight hours of sleep per night.
13. Besides participating in an exercise program, I lead an active lifestyle that includes such activities as walking, hiking, bicycling, swimming, sports participation, gardening, etc.
14. My weight falls in the ideal range for someone of my age and body type.
15. I use antioxidant supplementation.
16. I am free from symptoms of depression or anxiety.
17. I know how to relax and utilize stress management techniques on a daily basis.
18. I make a point of getting adequate fiber in my diet.
19. I avoid processed foods as much as possible.
20. I know vital numbers associated with my health, such as blood pressure, cholesterol levels, etc.
21. I see my physician for preventive care—pap smears, physicals, etc.—as recommended for my age.
22. I understand the advantages of alternative health care, such as chiropractic care and massage therapy.
23. I am familiar with the medical history of my family, can identify those illnesses for which I have a genetic predisposition, and actively utilize necessary preventive measures.
24. I have a good relationship with my primary health care provider and feel comfortable asking questions and seeking advice to foster my own personal wellness.
25. I accept responsibility for my health and take effective steps to safeguard my future.

Count up the number of statements you answered with Always, Sometimes, Never, and I don't know.

If you answered even one statement with "I don't know," keep reading.

Needed information to educate you on accepting responsibility for your health care is found in the following chapters.

If you answered up to five statements with "Never," keep reading.

Important information, pointing out necessary steps to care for your health, is found in the following chapters.

If you answered up to seven statements with "Sometimes," keep reading.

Motivating information to inspire you to the next level of self healthcare is found in the following chapters.

If you answered any statements with anything other than "Always," keep reading.

The latest, up-to-date information you need for taking control of your health is found in the following chapters.

Even if you answered all statements with "Always," keep reading. Cutting edge, ultimate wellness information is found in the following chapters to verify you are on the right track and to help keep you there.

CHAPTER 2

WE ARE LIVING LONGER
but are we Living Better?

points to ponder as you read:

✓ What is today's predicted average life span?

✓ Why have the number of health problems and diseases seemed to increase over the last couple of decades?

✓ What two major factors have been proven to affect health & disease development?

✓ What are the health implications of obesity?

Looking back in time we can see the average life expectancy has shifted remarkably. It took millions of years for humans to reach the milestone of living just under 30 years. The average life span for a human being living during the Roman Empire was 28 years. Two thousand years later, at the beginning of the 20th Century, the life span for humans had jumped to 49 years. Remarkably, a little girl born today will likely live to be 85 years or older. (Life expectancy for males lags behind females by an average of six years in most developed countries; but, men, read on, and you may catch up with us!)

Ironically, because life expectancy has increased dramatically over the past 100 years, people are at risk for health problems that were of almost no concern prior to the 20th Century. The top four causes of death in America and, essentially, in every developed country around the world, are cardiovascular disease, cancer, stroke, and diabetes. Because of increased life expectancy, these health problems are not only the major cause of death, but they have also become the main challenges of life. These diseases not only taken their toll in human suffering, but also have an incredible financial impact upon every country's (and every individual's) budget. The medical costs of supporting disease through surgeries, drugs, nursing homes, home health nurses, hospital stays, etc. for millions of afflicted individuals is astronomical. Each of us is paying higher insurance premiums and higher taxes due to the cost of supporting disease—disease that is largely preventable with simple lifestyle modifications!

Today, because we are living longer, we are beginning to look differently at the concept of aging. We are becoming sophisticated enough in our scientific abilities to look beyond the treatment of disease and become more focused on the maintenance of good health and vitality for as long as possible. We now have a huge world population reaching their mid-forties to mid-fifties, who are definitely interested in not having gray hair or wrinkles. This generation of "Baby Boomers" (people born between 1945 and 1960) is a significant percentage of the U.S. population today, possessing a major portion of the expendable income. They (myself included) are spending billions of dollars on plastic surgery, gym memberships, spas, nutritional supplements, etc. Baby Boomers want more than the absence of disease. More than any generation before them, they want optimal health.

In his book, *The Wellness Revolution,* Paul Zane Pilzer writes, "Boomers are refusing to passively accept the aging process. Their desire to continue feeling and looking well has set the stage for a huge surge in the wellness industry."

With scientific studies now elucidating various anti-aging strategies and validating the benefits of antioxidants and lifestyle choices in slowing aging and aging-related diseases, we have just begun to see the financial impact of Baby Boomers in their quest for graceful aging and unflagging vitality. Companies will be established and fortunes made by serving the aging Baby Boomers with products and services directed at helping them stay healthy, fit, and youthful.

Most of us reaching mid-life are intrigued by the thought that it is possible to maintain a youthful appearance with a high energy level. We want the vitality to participate in favorite activities, whether traveling around the world, hiking up mountains, gardening, family activities, or shopping 'til we drop. Today, we are willing to use our increased expendable income to look for solutions to preserve our health and to prevent the development of the top health challenges listed above.

Two dramatic factors of the past few decades, proven to affect health and disease development, are diet and physical activity. In the past 30 years, a nutrient-poor diet has led to a spiraling increase in the number of those suffering from being overweight to obese. In upcoming chapters, we will explore needed dietary changes, including limiting the consumption of fast food, to help achieve and maintain a healthy weight. In addition, we will explore the role specific nutrients play in disease prevention. As we are living longer, it is imperative to make dietary changes that will enable us to stay healthy and minimize our risk of disease, especially diseases that are 100% preventable, such as Type 2 diabetes.

The second significant factor—physical activity—has declined rather dramatically over the past 50 years. This is a significant problem not only for adults, but also for children. We are watching more TV and spending more time in front of the computer. Our children spend countless hours watching television and playing computer and video games. Numerous studies have directly linked the number of hours spent watching TV with being overweight to obese. We are walking and moving less. There is a subset of people determined to be more physically active, but overall statistics show that the industrialized world population in general is more urbanized. We are taking buses and trains and driving cars in lieu of walking, jogging, or cycling. Whereas we may have intermittent physical activity, we are failing to participate in regular physical activity, including muscle toning and development exercises that can preserve health. Later in the book, we will delve into the elements of exercise and the specific changes needed to reverse the problems associated with a sedentary lifestyle.

Because we are consuming more calories in our diet and expending less calories in our activities, there has been a dramatic spike in staggering and alarming statistics. In 1980, one-third of America's population was overweight to obese with about 18% suffering from obesity. In the U.S. Surgeon General's report published in December of 2002, 62% of Americans are now overweight to obese with approximately 38% of Americans—almost four out of every 10 Americans—being obese.

The implication of obesity is very significant in the medical arena. If you are obese, you have a much higher risk of developing cardiovascular disease or suffering a stroke. If obese, you are setting yourself up for an increased risk of developing a variety of cancers. You also have an extremely high risk of developing Type 2 diabetes, which increases the risk of premature death from heart attack and stroke, as well as multiplying the likelihood of below-the-knee amputations, blindness, and kidney failure. Type 2 diabetes today is a global epidemic, increasing at an exponential rate in America and every country around the world, including Africa and India. Wherever America has installed fast food restaurants, we see an increasing occurrence of our Western diet-associated diseases.

The sad truth is that Americans (and the world population) are getting sicker and sicker. We have an increased life expectancy, but a decreased quality of life. We are experiencing a rise in diagnoses of life-threatening conditions. While more people are surviving cancer, heart attacks, and strokes, we are also living with the limitations of these diseases—the financial burden and the reduced quality of life that is the ultimate price. We are living longer—but are we living better?

The good news is that no one has to be a part of these gloomy statistics. There are specific lifestyle changes that can be made and steps to take to change these trends and statistics. I firmly believe that we can have a healthier America and ultimately, a healthier world. The United States sets the trends which many countries follow—but we are not leading the health trends. Currently, many countries in Europe have significantly longer life expectancies, better maternal-baby statistics, and lower rates of many chronic diseases. This book is about taking control of your life. It will give the needed information to make necessary changes in your life, and, hopefully, the inspiration to persevere in successfully incorporating healthful attitudes and activities, resulting in a healthier you! You only get one life; live each day to the fullest.

FOLLOW-UP PREVENTIVE PERSCIPTION:

PERSONAL PATHWAY TO HEALTH & VITALITY

Welcome to a journey to health. Below is a graphic that illustrates my philosophy of wellness. Here is up-to-date, scientifically-founded information to place your feet firmly on the personal pathway to health and vitality. Review this graphic and contemplate your own life. What are the areas where you need to make changes? What might be a good starting point for you?

PERSONAL PATHWAY TO
HEALTH AND VITALITY

W E L L N E S S

All five elements continuously flow together,
creating a Life of Wellness

NUTRITION

Healthy Food + Supplements = Nutritional Assurance

Complete, proper nutrition makes weight control
easier and provides the fuel needed for regular
exercise.

WEIGHT MANAGEMENT

Achieving & Maintaining
a Healthy Weight

The better physical
shape, the easier to keep
up with an exercise
program.

COMMUNITY

Family, Friends, Professional,
and Spiritual Involvement

Community involvement
and spiritual develop-
ment strengthen positive
self-esteem, which, in turn,
encourages good self care,
which starts with good
nutrition.

FITNESS

Active Lifestyle
—MOVE MORE

Exercise produces
endorphins, which
help relieve stress.

STRESS MANAGEMENT

Relaxation and Learning to
Reduce Stressors

Managed stress encourages
involvement with others.

CHAPTER 3

THE FAILURE OF MODERN MEDICINE
to Address the Health Challenges of the 21st Century

Points to ponder as you read:

- ✓ Why are doctor visits so short today?
- ✓ What is a holistic approach to medicine, and why do most primary care physicians fail to offer it?
- ✓ What are some beneficial alternative treatment approaches?
- ✓ How can this book help you in dealing with your doctor?

When I was 13 years old, I was the catcher on our eighth grade girl's softball team. During the first month of the season, my left shoulder began to hurt, and, as I continued to play, the pain worsened. Finally, the pain was intense enough that my mother took me to an orthopedist. He wasn't overly concerned by the pain I was experiencing and said I probably had tendonitis due to overuse from my being the team catcher. The doctor was ready to send me home, but my mother wasn't ready for us to go. She insisted that the doctor x-ray my shoulder and upper arm. He was resistant, but finally went ahead and performed the x-ray as requested. When he brought the x-ray back into the room, his face was as white as his coat. The x-ray showed a growth on the bone of my upper arm (the humerus). He was concerned enough to x-ray my arm again a month later. This time the x-ray showed that the growth had slightly changed, and I was scheduled for surgery two weeks later, the week after I graduated from eighth grade.

My doctor never really allowed me to talk about my concerns. I was secretly terrified that they would find cancer, and that I would have to have an amputation. Fortunately, the surgery was completely successful, proving that my tumor was benign; and I've never had any trouble since.

From this experience, I learned two things that have changed my life. First, I learned that I would rather be behind the stethoscope than in front of it, which inspired me to pursue a career as a medical doctor. But, I not only wanted to be a doctor, I wanted to be an *effective* one. From my orthopedist, I had received a first-hand lesson on how *not* to communicate with your patients. I discovered that one of the most important attributes a physician can have is to be a good communicator. To me, this is the "art" of medicine, and not the "science." I have always prided myself on being an excellent physician, but I am also fully aware that *far* more is needed than my diagnostic acumen and my knowledge of human anatomy and the latest medical advances. If I do not put my patient at ease, allowing him to tell me his problem, if I do not explain my reasoning as I send him out for a particular test, if I am not clear in explaining what is wrong with him, or if I fail to make him a *partner* in his health process, then I have not done my job. Physicians must be teachers, counselors, and coaches, in addition to being diagnosticians.

Another important lesson I learned, which is the actual basis for this book, is that it is necessary to take personal responsibility for your health care. Many years ago, my mother took personal responsibility for my health care in my orthopedist's office. She insisted on the x-ray of my arm because she knew her daughter tended to be stoic. She wasn't leaving that doctor's office until the x-ray that she and my dad considered necessary was done! This willingness to take personal responsibility for your health care is even more necessary now. The fact is that today your health care dollar isn't going as far as it used to. You're not really getting as much "bang for the buck" from a visit to your doctor as you once did.

Doctors today have extreme time constraints upon them. In 1980, the average primary care doctor saw approximately 22 patients per day. In 2004, primary care physicians are now treat 35-45 patients per day, along with expending countless hours each week on insurance and administrative matters. (Doctors spent only a few hours a month on these matters until the "managed care" era of medicine began in California in the late 1980s.) These primary care physicians are the ones who should be able to (and at one time did) fully discuss your medical condition with you. Primary care physicians should be able to give you more than just an evaluation of the specific issue that brought you into their office on a certain day. Ideally, they should provide you with an overall treatment plan, incorporating not just a prescription, but all the modalities that may help your condition, whether it's massage therapy for chronic back pain or omega-3 fatty acids for recurrent migraines.

With the time constraints most doctors are working under today, it is not surprising that many do not have the time to fully diagnose your condition, let alone do a complete wellness evaluation to determine what dietary changes you need to make, what is the best exercise plan for you, and whether or not you need to lose weight (and, if so, how to do it safely and effectively). It takes time for a doctor to discuss a health situation, giving all the information needed to improve the one condition you came in for, let alone put together a "Winning Life Strategy for Overall Good Health" specifically designed for you!

It is also important to realize that conventional medicine tends to have a particular mindset. Most medical practioners know about ordering tests, evaluating the results, and prescribing medicine, because that is what they were taught in medical school. They understand pharmaceuticals and how to prescribe them, adjust medications, deal with side effects, etc.

The pharmaceutical industry is one of the most powerful industries in America and consequently, much of the scientific research performed over the last 50 years has been on the treatment of disease, rather than on its prevention. And, in all honesty, that is exactly what the research should focused on. Many lives have been spared because of the incredible advances science has made. People rarely die of pneumonia due to the development of antibiotics. CT and MRI scans diagnose tumors early enough for them to be cured surgically. There are numerous other examples of how lives have been spared because of medical advances in the treatment of disease.

With the development of immunizations, however, we started to be able to *prevent* certain infectious diseases (like diphtheria, tetanus, polio, etc). And now, in the early years of the 21st Century, it is clear that we in the medical community must shift our paradigm from treatment to prevention. We need to spend research billions on preventing the diseases that now plague our society, such as Type 2 diabetes. It is shocking to realize that Type 2 diabetes and other health plagues today could largely be prevented if doctors and the medical system could successfully help people lose weight and eat more healthfully. What is even more stunning, however, is that doctors do not learn how to help people lose weight as part of their medical school education. As of 2001, only one-third of medical schools in the United States had a core course on nutrition in the curriculum for medical students. Nutrition and weight control are the basis of health, the basis of human function, and yet, in medical schools there is no mandatory courses in these subjects for doctors-in-training. Consequently, disease prevention is getting short-changed in the medical community.

The goal of the powerful pharmaceutical industry is *not* prevention of disease. The pharmaceutical industry's main two-fold goal is to get consumers to buy more pharmaceuticals and to get doctors to prescribe more drugs. Just 20 years ago, there were three prescription medicines for diabetes and now there are over sixteen. Articles in the latest medical journals tout the newest drug that can help decrease insulin resistance, without once mentioning the need for weight loss or lifestyle modification. The next time you watch TV, there will probably be more than one commercial for a prescription medication. Listen carefully to the last few seconds of the ad and notice the list of possible side effects associated with the use of the medicine. The numerous negative effects described will help you realize that medicine alone is usually not the answer.

In 1998, a study was published in the Journal of the American Medical Association that must have made the pharmaceutical industry sweat. Perhaps this is why there was *no* publicity about this study, and there has been no significant follow-up. The study examined hospitalized patients and concluded that in the United States in 1994, there were between 76,000 and 137,000 deaths from adverse drug reactions. This would make pharmaceutical complications approximately the fifth leading cause of death in the United States! While this may not have been a perfect study, it definitely raises the specter of concern. Because the pharmaceutical industry is so powerful, no one is tracking any overall statistics. The pharmaceutical industry doesn't want anyone to know the potential, and real, risks of prescription medication.

Please understand that my goal is not to criticize the medical profession. I am proud to be a physician and know that the overwhelming majority of physicians truly care about their patients and give them as much time as they possibly can. They read their journals, attend CME conferences, and do an outstanding job of staying current in the rapidly changing world of medical science. But, I would call upon physicians, the academic and research community, and even the federal government to commit the time, thought, and monetary resources needed to generate studies to elucidate and validate the information, tools, supplements, alternative therapies, and techniques needed to help people lose weight, improve their nutrition, understand the importance of exercise and stress management, and manage–or better yet, *prevent*–disease. The result of this joint effort would be *fewer* individuals diagnosed with Type 2 diabetes, *fewer* women having lumpectomies and mastectomies, and *fewer* open heart surgeries. In turn, this would free up *more* money for the education of inner-city children, *more* money to clean up our precious environment, and *more* money to fund programs to improve the quality of life for all of us!

And, if about now you are thinking, "Okay, Dr. Jamie, time to get off the soapbox," you are probably right. But, for the future health of our nation, I hope that what I have detailed above is not a pipe dream, but a future reality. To date, the medical industry and the medical profession are missing the real goal of health care. They are very good at supporting disease, but they have a dismal record with prevention. Most doctors are not overly comfortable or well trained in the area of nutrition, herbs, and the myriad complimentary approaches to disease or condition management. They don't know how to help people lose weight. They are skeptical about chiropractors. They think that massage, meditation, and yoga are voodoo. Most doctors today are more comfortable in prescribing drugs and performing surgery than in discussing the approaches listed above, even though research shows that lifestyle adjustments and weight loss can produce positive health results, without the risks and side effects inherent in surgery and pharmaceuticals.

Here is an example of a non–pharmaceutical, non–surgical preventive approach. D. Russell Crane, director of Brigham Young University's Family Studies Center, examined "high utilizers" of health care—people who made four or more trips to a doctor during a six-month period. His research showed that members of that group who were prescribed marriage and family therapy, reduced their visits to the doctor by 53%. Crane said patients benefit from therapy in two ways. First, improved marital and family relationships reduce stress, which can lead to or exacerbate physical problems. Second, therapy results in increased support for patients from family members.

Crane's results do not surprise Dr. Michael Rhodes, director of the family medicine residency program at Utah Valley Regional Medical Center. "Patients are individuals, more than just a combination of physical symptoms," Rhodes said. He emphasizes, however, that most doctors aren't trained to look for mental-health issues or to recommend counseling.

The good news is that the tide is turning. Ever so slowly, various medical centers throughout the United States are providing the integrated care that is needed. Such centers are providing training for physicians who are interested in developing a holistic approach to medicine. This type of approach meets all the facets of a patient's health— physical, mental, and emotional. Physicians using this approach see a person as part of a family and society, factors that can and do play a significant role in an individual's health.

These medical centers are also the facilities that have developed wellness centers, which offer aid and information on topics ranging from cooking with tofu to how to stop smoking. These facilities focus on individual patients, offering assistance to make needed lifestyle or behavioral changes.

As previously stated, my purpose is not to criticize doctors or the health care industry. I love being a doctor and truly have enjoyed the practice of medicine. However, because I understand the realities of medicine today and the time constraints under which most doctors practice, my goal is to provide you, as an individual, with an additional resource for information. I want to help you understand the difference between a disease and a con-

dition. I want to inform you of the symptoms of body dysfunction. I want to arm you with facts that will allow you to approach
your primary care physician with intelligent questions that will
net you needed information to improve your health. I want to
give you the knowledge and suggestions you require to make
informed decisions for yourself.

Epictetus once said, "Only the educated are free." The goal of
this book is to educate you in health matters your doctor doesn't
have time to discuss. After you leave your doctor's office, I want
you to have access to information that will free you to make
choices that can truly be life-changing.

FOLLOW-UP PREVENTIVE PERSCIPTION

PREPARING FOR YOUR NEXT DOCTOR VISIT.

To get the most "bang" for your "medical buck" the next time
you go to the doctor, be prepared. Think through and/or write
down your answers to the following questions. If you are taking
an older parent or child to the doctor, ask the following questions in advance.

1. When did the condition start?
2. What are the exact symptoms? (be specific)
3. Does the condition seem to worsen at certain times of
   the day? (i.e. morning or night)
4. Have you had this before?
5. Has something like this occurred in other family
   members?
6. What medication(s) are you currently using?
7. What supplements do you take?
8. Have you ever had a reaction to a medication or
   treatment?

Also, take a list of the following questions, and be prepared to discuss them with the doctor. Take notes.

1. How long should this condition last?
2. Is bed rest advisable?
3. Are treatment options available besides medication?
4. Are there nutritional supplements that would help with this condition?
5. Should diet be modified for this condition?
6. Are there lifestyle factors that could be contributing to the development of this condition?
7. Is this condition contagious? If so, what are suggestions for containing the condition?
8. Do hereditary factors contribute to this condition?
9. If medication is prescribed, what are the possible side effects and advisories?
10. Where can I go to find out more information about my condition?

In addition, keep track of important health information for yourself, spouse, children, and even your parents, if you are their caretaker. Below are some important facts to know for you and your loved ones.

Women

- Age you began menstruating
- Number of pregnancies, deliveries, abortions, or miscarriages, etc.
- Age you reached menopause (stopped menstruating or had a hysterectomy)
- Date of last mammogram
- Date of last pap smear; abnormal paps, and, if any, diagnosis and treatment, if required

Men

- Date of last Prostate Specific Antigen (PSA) test and results

Everyone

- Family history
- Date and results of last cholesterol tests (HDL, LDL, total, etc.)
- Date and results of last fasting blood sugar test
- If over age 50, date and results of last colonoscopy and stool test

Children

- Immunization dates

CHAPTER 4

DIETARY EXCESSES AND DEFICIENCIES
and the Insidious Onset of Disease

Points to ponder as you read:

- ✓ How can Americans have dietary deficiencies in "the land of plenty?"

- ✓ How do dietary deficiencies affect how well the body works?

- ✓ How has fast food become such an integral part of Americans' diets?

- ✓ What problems occur with a constant consumption of fast food?

- ✓ What specific diseases have been linked to obesity and high-fat diets?

- ✓ What diseases and health challenges are linked to deficiencies in our modern diets?

A sports car enthusiast, 40 years old, married with four children, bought a Porsche. This was the realization of a long-held dream and the car was given great care. It held a place of honor in the garage, corner spot, even temperature, away from doorways where family members would be walking. Children were allowed to look at the car, but were instructed not to touch—especially with sticky fingers. When bicycles were ridden into the garage and dropped on the floor, it was on the side of the garage away from the Porsche. When not being driven, the car was lovingly protected with a custom car cover. And, of course, this car received the best maintenance possible. It had its own personal mechanic, who gave it frequent checkups; and only products befitting a Porsche were used on it. One thing this Porsche owner was especially careful about was the fuel used in his car. A machine of *that* caliber deserved only the best; no cheap bargain fuel for this car.

Not everyone owns a Porsche (or Mercedes), but each one of us possesses an even more valuable machine, deserving of the finest possible care. The machine I am referring to is the human body with all its built-in control systems—systems that keep the heart pumping at just the right rate, the brain processing experiences, the muscles firing into action, the immune system fighting potential invaders, etc.

How do you care for your body? Are you giving your machine the same careful and meticulous care you would lavish on an expensive car? It can be frustrating and inconvenient to have a car stop running correctly and break down. But, it can truly be devastating when the body stops running well and breaks down because of the onset of disease. A car can be traded in, but you've only got one body. If you are concerned with what you feed your vehicle, how much greater care should be given to what you feed yourself.

Since research has shown that the fuel we put into our bodies, what we eat day in and day out, has a direct correlation to the development of disease. We will examine the connection between excesses and deficiencies in the diet to disease development.

First and foremost, it is important to note that the most common conditions that plague our country (and our world) today are directly linked to simply eating too much! The Surgeon General's last report on the health of the nation carried the shocking statistic that 62% of Americans are overweight to obese—up from 38% in 1980. The rising prevalence of obesity is now seen around the world in industrialized countries that have westernized their diets. Scientific studies have clearly validated the connection between the consumption of high-fat, high-calorie diets with coronary artery disease, many types of cancer, stroke, hypertension, and Type 2 diabetes. These diseases are clearly more common in people who are obese. Walk through any shopping mall in America to realize that it is not just adults who are suffering from weight-related problems. It is sadly apparent that teens and children are also becoming increasingly overweight and even obese (See Chapters 6 and 17).

The connection between obesity and the excessive intake of saturated fat, refined carbohydrates, salt, and total calories to both early mortality (premature death) as well as disability (living with heart disease, Type 2 diabetes, hypertension, etc.) is well understood by doctors and the general population. But, is our understanding of this connection leading us to make necessary dietary changes, or are we just accepting these conditions as a way of life?

In 2002, 1.2 million Americans died of coronary artery disease. It is estimated that at least 50% of these deaths were related to being overweight and eating "the typical American diet." That means that 600,000 people died needlessly!

There are an estimated 25 million Americans who live with heart disease, worrying about when their next heart attack will occur. They have higher doctor and pharmacy bills, spend more time at the doctor's office, and deal with the side effects of medications that may affect their sex drive or sexual performance, leaving them with a chronic cough, or produce liver damage.

We have made tremendous advances in the early detection of cancer and have developed many new and more effective types of cancer therapies. More and more Americans are living many years after an initial cancer diagnosis. While this is wonderful news, we now know that many cancers could be prevented if people would simply eat the five to nine servings of fruits and vegetables per day that the American Cancer Society and essentially *all* cancer experts recommend. It is estimated that 50-70% of all cancers are attributable to diet and lifestyle (including smoking). When the monetary cost of cancer therapy is calculated (that is ultimately shared by all of us), as well as the emotional and physical burden of this disease, it is easy to see the immediate and essential need for dietary changes.

When we examine what is driving this obesity epidemic and the resultant increases in obesity-related diseases, we realize there are *three* main factors:

1. the easy availability of fast foods, convenience foods, and take-out meals;
2. a reduction in physical activity over the past two decades;
3. dietary deficiencies leading to out-of-control eating patterns.

Having grown up in the 1960s, I remember my parents taking us to a drive-in for hamburgers, fries, and milkshakes. This was an "event," a big treat, which occurred, at most, once a month. My mother was a stay-at-home mom (which was essential with *six* children), and we ate breakfasts and dinners together at our kitchen table the majority of the time. Today, families eat more than 60% of their meals away from home or bring home take-out foods. The family meal is often a rushed one in the charming, intimate atmosphere of the local McDonald's or Taco Bell!

The office of the Minnesota Attorney General did research on the fast food industry and came up with these fast food facts. There are more than 300,000 fast food restaurants in the United States. Fast food has become a popular part of the busy American lifestyle because (1) as the name implies, it is fast (no need to wait for dinner to be prepared), (2) it is convenient (no need to prepare dinner), and (3) it is predictable (be honest now – how many of you have already memorized the available selections on the drive-thru menu?).

Let's examine some basic fast food meals and see how they stack up nutritionally.

Burger

Quarter-Pounder with cheese, large fries, 16-ounce soda (McDonald's)

This meal:	Recommended daily intake:
1,166 calories	1,500-2,500 calories
51 g fat	No more than 50-80 g
95 mg cholesterol	No more than 300 mg
1,450 mg sodium	Approximately 2,000 mg
49 g sugar	Less than 60% of total daily calories

Pizza

4 slices sausage and mushroom pizza, 16-ounce soda (Domino's)

This meal:	Recommended daily intake:
1,000 calories	1,500-2,500 calories
28 g fat	No more than 50-80 g
62 mg cholesterol	No more than 300 mg
2,302 mg sodium	Approximately 2,000 mg
54 g sugar	Less than 60% of total daily calories

Chicken

2 pieces fried chicken (breast and wing), buttermilk biscuit, mashed potatoes and gravy, corn-on-the-cob, 16-ounce soda (KFC)

This meal:	Recommended daily intake:
1,232 calories	1,500-2,500 calories
57 g fat	No more than 50-80 g
157 mg cholesterol	No more than 300 mg
2,276 mg sodium	Approximately 2,000 mg
46 g sugar	Less than 60% of total daily calories

Taco

Taco Salad, 16-ounce soda (Taco Bell)

This meal:	Recommended daily intake:
1,057 calories	1,500-2,500 calories
55 g fat	No more than 50-80 g
80 mg cholesterol	No more than 300 mg
1,620 mg sodium	Approximately 2,000 mg
52 g sugar	Less than 60% of total daily calories

The fast food meals shown above provide what I call "double negative nutrition." They offer the negative health effects associated with the consumption of excessive saturated fat, salt, sugar, and calories, while they consist of foods devoid of micronutrients and fiber. This results in a toxic, two-fold attack on our nutritional status.

The availability and relatively low cost of fast food, coupled with slick marketing techniques, have drawn Americans to fast food restaurants in droves, which has doubled the percentage of overweight children in America in just 10 short years (1991–2001). This does not mean that you can never eat fast food; but it does mean that it should be a small and infrequent part of an overall balanced, healthy diet. I, personally, cannot tell you the last time I ate anything from a fast food restaurant, but I can tell you that I frequent such establishments less than five times a year.

Keeping the above fast food charts in mind, review the following facts regarding calories, fat, cholesterol, salt, and sugar.

CALORIES

On the average, to maintain desirable weight, men need about 2,000 to 2,500 calories per day, and women need about 1,500 to 2,000. It is completely understood why some people can eat much more than others and still maintain a desirable weight. Research is still testing factors that determine metabolism, but one's lean body mass (skeleton, organs, and muscle) is believed to be the main determinant (more on this in Chapter 6). One point is absolutely certain: to lose weight, you must take in fewer calories than you burn. This means that choose foods with fewer calories or increase your physical activity (or preferably both). (See Chapter 6 for safe ways to reduce calories and lose weight, as necessary).

While obsessive calorie countingisn't necessary, be familiar with label reading. Below is a "nutrition facts" section of a label from a bottle of reduced-calorie ranch salad dressing:

NUTRITION FACTS

Serving Size 2 Tbsp. (30g)

Servings per container 36

Calories 80

Calories from fat 60

* *Percent Daily Values (DV) are based on a 2,000 calorie diet*

AMOUNT/SERVING	% DV*
Total Fat 7g	11%
Sat. Fat 1g	5%
Cholest. 9mg	0%
Total Carb. 3g	1%
Sodium 280mg	12%
Sugars 1g	
Protein 1g	
Not a significant source of Fiber, Vitamin A, Vitamin C, Calcium, Iron.	

Look at the calories per serving and note the serving size. For this particular item, a two level tablespoons of salad dressing contains 80 calories. This means that if you pour ¼ cup (or more) of this dressing on a salad, you are consuming 160+ calories in salad dressing alone.

FAT

Research shows that eating too many high-fat foods contributes to elevated blood cholesterol levels and is a major risk factor in the development of cancer, diabetes, coronary heart disease, and stroke. High-fat diets may also contribute to a greater risk for some types of cancer, particularly cancers of the breast, ovary, prostate, and colon. While most Americans get more than 40% of their daily calories from fat, the American Heart Association recommends limiting fat to less than 30% of daily calories, which means restricting the fats consumed to 50-80 grams per day.

CHOLESTEROL

The American Heart Association recommends eating no more than 300 milligrams of cholesterol per day. But don't just look at the cholesterol contained in a food item. A product high in total fat or saturated fat can be an even bigger contributor to elevated blood cholesterol levels. For example, "cholesterol free" potato chips may be high in fat and may contribute to the development of atherosclerosis, heart disease, stroke, etc.

SALT

Everyone needs some sodium in the diet to replace routine losses. The Food and Nutrition Board of the National Academy of Sciences/National Research Council has estimated that an "adequate and safe" intake of sodium for healthy adults is 1,100 to 3,300 milligrams a day, the equivalent of approximately ½ to 1½ teaspoons of salt. Americans, on average, consume at least twice that amount—2,300 to 6,900 milligrams of sodium daily, according to estimates by the Food and Nutrition Board. For some people, consuming high amounts of sodium can be a factor in elevation of blood pressure.

SUGAR

Looking at the fast food tables above, you might be surprised at the grams of sugar listed. Granted, each of these meals carries 40 grams of sugar from the 16-ounce soda alone; by eliminating the soda completely, the meals still average approximately 10 grams of sugar each. When you take into account that there is *no* daily recommended intake for sugar, but rather a "less than" limit imposed, you can see why it is important to watch out for hidden sugars in food. Read labels and avoid unnecessary sugar. Don't let daily food consumption be packed with empty calories that, in turn, contribute to excess weight.

With the above facts in mind, it is obvious how harmful a constant diet of fast food can be. The excessive calorie, fat, cholesterol, sodium, and sugar problems with fast food alone would drive our obesity epidemic; but, let's also factor in the "value marketing" concept—the super-sizing of many fast food options. A study conducted by health organizations nationwide attempted to quantify just how much damage "value marketing" does. Here are some of their results:

- At Cinnabon, when one Minibon (300 calories) was ordered, the clerk said, "It's only 48 cents more for a classic Cinnabon (670 calories)." This resulted in researchers paying 24% more for 123% more calories.

- At 7-Eleven, researchers asked for a "Gulp" of Coke (150 calories) and left the store with a "Double Gulp" (600 calories) for only 37 cents more. That's a 42% increase in price for 400% more calories.

- At movie theaters, researchers asked for a medium popcorn without butter (900 calories) and were told you can get a large (1,160 calories) for only 60 cents more. That's 23% more money for 260 more calories.

- Researchers found a whopping "Big Deal" at McDonald's. There they paid 8 cents less to buy the large value meal (Quarter Pounder with cheese, large fries and large Coke at 1,380 calories) instead of the Quarter Pounder, small fries and small Coke (890 calories). That is, they spent 8 cents less to purchase 490 calories more.

We are "super-sizing" our lives today. The result is a frightening acceleration of the diseases and health challenges associated with modern excessive diets. Type 2 diabetes was known as Adult Onset Diabetes until the 1980s, and was rarely diagnosed before the age of 50. It is caused by obesity in genetically predisposed individuals. Today, we are diagnosing this type of diabetes in obese adolescents. The incidence of Type 2 diabetes increased 1000% in people in their 30's in the 1990s.

Remembering that research links being overweight with increased risk of cancer, it is easy to see how deadly a constant diet of fast food can be. Scientists now believe that excess weight and inactivity account for one-quarter to one-third of all breast, colon, endometrial, kidney, and esophageal cancers.

In addition, in the Summer 2003 American Institute of Cancer Research (AICR) Newsletter, Dr. Homer Black, Professor of Dermatology at Baylor College of Medicine in Houston, Texas, tells about a number of AICR-funded studies he has conducted to find out how what we eat influences the development of skin cancer.

In a two-year clinical trial, Dr. Black studied 115 patients with non-melanoma types of skin cancer to see if cutting the fat in their diet would affect whether they developed additional skin cancers. Half of the participants were randomly assigned to a control group that maintained their usual fat intake of at least 37% of calories. The other group adopted a diet that reduced fat to 20% of calories. This second group ate the same number of calories as the first group.

"Once an individual has a skin cancer, we know that he has 25% risk for developing a second skin cancer within two years after diagnosis," Dr. Black said. "We found out that reducing fat in the diet by nearly half seemed to have a strong impact on how many second cancers developed and how fast."

The results showed that patients on a low-fat diet developed one-third as many additional tumors as the patients on the regular diet. Also, the rate at which these tumors developed was slower. This was especially true after they had followed the low-fat diet for 16 months and were in the final eight months of the study.

"The level of fat in these patients' diets certainly had a strong impact on their rates of cancer occurrence," Dr. Black said. "Although we don't know for certain yet, we suspect that [the effect of fats (especially saturated fats)] on the human immune system may be one possible explanation."

In a previous study that Dr. Black conducted with mice, a high-fat diet suppressed the immune reaction to UV radiation, and did not do so in another group of mice that were fed small amounts of fat. In another mouse study, tumors from mice on high-fat diets were transplanted to others fed low-fat diets. The low-fat group rejected the tumors faster and experienced slower tumor growth than the high-fat group.

"Skin cancer may take 40 or 50 years to develop in a person, so it is very difficult to do a dietary fat study using human subjects who have not had skin cancer," Dr. Black said. "But the studies we have done show a strong possible link between dietary fat and the body's ability to fight development of the disease."

If you also consider that—in addition to diabetes and cancer—heart disease, stroke, and arterial damage have also been linked to what you eat, it is easy to see why scientists say there is a strong link between dietary deficiencies and the onset of disease. Our nutritional deficits and dietary excesses are, without doubt, accelerating the commencement of disease.

Despite the fact that the United States is one of the wealthiest countries in the world and a relatively small percentage of Americans go hungry, too many suffer the effects of malnutrition because of the poor food choices that make up their diet. We have the paradox of malnourished overweight to obese individuals on every street across America. While we are eating an abundance of calories, we are eating diets that are deficient in the right types of proteins, carbohydrates, and fats.

PROTEIN

Protein provides amino acids, which are the building blocks of most hormones and enzymes in the body, as well as the neurotransmitters that control mood, sleep, and thought patterns. While most Americans consume adequate amounts of protein, there are three key areas regarding this essential nutrient where changes need to be made.

1. Replace Animal Protein with Vegetable Protein

Far too much meat and high-fat dairy products are consumed in America. Human beings don't actually digest meat protein as well as vegetable protein, which can lead to kidney dysfunction over time. Focus on eating more soy, beans, and legumes, limiting animal protein to one serving per day.

2. Stop Chronic Dieting

Women who are chronic dieters tend to skip the protein foods, eating more vegetables, fruits, and breads. This leads to a loss of muscle mass over the years and a slowing of the metabolism. Bone mass is often impacted from this dietary deficiency.

3. Increase Protein for Improved Weight Loss

Weight loss can be more easily achieved with adequate protein intake. Protein helps control hunger by signaling the brain of satiety. It also elevates mood, which is helpful because people have a tendency to overeat when depressed. Finally, it increases muscle mass, which speeds up metabolism, which determines how fast your body burns calories.

CARBOHYDRATES

"Carbs" have been given a bad name in the past few years.

"Carb-Free" and "Low Carb" products are everywhere, filling up entire aisles in the grocery store. But, are carbohydrates bad? Absolutely not—if you consume the right kind: complex carbohydrates—fruits, vegetables, and fiber-rich whole grain breads and cereals.

The low-fat craze of the 1980s led to a dramatic rise in the consumption of low-fat/fat-free foods. Often these foods, although reduced in fat, contained large amounts of refined or simple carbohydrates—sugars and starches. These carbohydrates tend to increase hunger and, since these products were touted as "healthy" versions of high-fat favorites, people ate larger quantities of the fat-free cookies or low-fat ice cream. This led to the consumption of more calories in the long run than would have been consumed with a smaller portion of the higher fat cookies or ice cream. The result was that America got fatter on fat-free foods.

The solution to this situation, however, is *not* to go to the extreme of no carbs. Fruits and vegetables (fresh or frozen) are nutrient-rich foods that the body needs. You cannot get fat by eating fruits and vegetables. Favor vegetables which are higher in phytonutrients and lower in calories than fruits; and remember the American Cancer Society recommends five to nine servings of fruits and vegetables daily.

The diet also needs to include moderate amounts of whole grains. Focus on dark, whole grains,and be sure to check labels to ensure adequate fiber content. The best carbohydrate bread choices will have a minimum of two grams of fiber per slice; while the best cereals will contain three to five grams of fiber per serving.

FATS

Monosaturated fat is the type of fat to include in the diet. This type of fat is found in olive oil, fish oil, and other oils with high percentages of omega-3 fatty acids. Our ancestors' diets used to be very high in omega-3 fats from eating nuts and seeds. Today, our diets are no longer rich in omega-3 fats, but rather tend to provide up to a 10:1 ratio of omega-6 fats to omega-3 fats. These omega-6 fats are pro-inflammatory, and many scientists now believe this change in our fat intake may play a role in the many inflammatory conditions that exist today, such as inflammatory bowel disease, autoimmune conditions, and certain types of arthritis. Cholesterol deposits in the artery walls (leading to atherosclerosis and heart disease) begin with inflammatory changes in the arterial wall. Even obesity is now believed to be an inflammatory condition, and there is emerging science showing that supplementing the diet with omega-3 fatty acids (i.e. a fish oil capsule two to three times per day) may decrease the accumulation of fat in intra-abdominal fat cells!

Therefore, the bottom line on fats is:

1. Focus on olive oil- or canola oil-based salad dressings. Use reduced-fat versions if you are trying to lose weight or have elevated cholesterol levels.
2. Avoid saturated fats as much as possible. Limit butter *and* margarine to one to two tablespoons per day *maximum*.
3. Watch for labels listing "transfats" (this labeling is mandated by 2005) and avoid products or foods containing these types of fats entirely.
4. Consume marbled meats less than two times per week.
5. Use nonfat dairy products.

Because many American diets are lacking adequate amounts of the right kinds of proteins, carbohydrates, and fats, they are at risk for the following vitamin and mineral deficiencies:

Vitamin A Deficiency

Vitamin A deficiency causes the eyes to become sensitive to

light, results in night blindness, and roughens the skin. You can get too much of a good thing, however, because excessive dosages of vitamin A can cause headaches, nausea, vomiting and fatigue.

Vitamin D Deficiency

Vitamin D deficiency causes rickets in children and bone abnormalities in adults. The body needs vitamin D to use calcium and phosphorus to build strong bones and teeth.

Vitamin C Deficiency

Vitamin C deficiency can cause scurvy, bleeding gums, bruising, loss of teeth, and anemia. Lack of adequate amounts of vitamin C also results in immune system dysfunction and an increased risk of heart attack.

B Vitamin-thiamine Deficiency

A thiamin deficiency can cause severe problems with the nervous system and fosters heart problems.

B Vitamin-riboflavin Deficiency

A riboflavin deficiency can cause cracked and swollen lips, as well as skin lesions. Without riboflavin, the body can't help cells use oxygen and can't help keep the skin, tongue, and lips normal.

Calcium Deficiency

A deficiency in calcium can cause malformed and weak bones which can lead to osteoporosis. Osteoporosis disease causes the bones to be brittle and porous, causing the bone to break or fracture easily (See chapter 13).

And last, but not least, many of us fail to drink sufficient water every day, which can cause the following problems:

Water Deficiency

A water deficiency can cause dehydration, dryness of the

mouth, weakness, increased pulse rate, flushed skin, fever, and even death. Without water, the body can't adequately perform daily life functions such as digestion, cell growth and maintenance, chemical reactions, lubricating joints and body cells, and regulating body temperature.

As you can see, nutritional deficiencies in the diet can dramatically affect how well the body works.

I started this chapter talking to you about a Porsche owner and the care he took with his expensive car. As I told you, he put only the best gasoline in his car. This is understandable when you realize that cars run only as well as the fuel they are given.

It is important to remember that this also holds true with the human body. If you believe that a car that you only expect to keep for 3 to 7 years needs good gas, how much more does your body, which you will need for a lifetime, require good fuel? To operate in peak condition, your body needs to be fueled daily with a healthy, well-balanced, nutritional diet. You only get one body. Feed it well.

FOLLOW-UP PREVENTIVE PERSCRIPTION

KEEP A FOOD DIARY

Before determining what changes are needed in your diet, determine what you are eating now. Experts suggest keeping a food diary or a food log of what you eat for a week. This will allow you to spot trends in your eating and get an overall picture of your diet. Below is a sample diary page:

MONDAY

Breakfast

2 eggs, scrambled—using zero-calorie vegetable cooking
spray

Cinnamon roll

½ grapefruit

8 oz. glass of milk

Mid-Morning Snack

½ doughnut leftover in the break room

16 oz. fruit juice

Lunch

2 cups of mixed greens–iceberg lettuce, spinach, & romaine lettuce

1 sliced cucumber & 1 sliced tomato

½ cup grated cheese

2-ounce sliced low-fat ham & 2-ounce sliced low-fat turkey

½ cup croutons (plus a handful I ate while making my salad)

Salad dressing (planned on having "light"–but got regular by mistake; didn't measure, just guessed–later looking at bottle, I probably had over ¼ of a cup, which is 375 calories!)

Diet 7-Up

Afternoon Snack

Yogurt with a sliced apple

6 Hershey Kisses out of my bosses' candy dish

1 eight-ounce glass of water

Dinner

6-ounce steak with 4 T. steak sauce

6-ounce baked potato with 2 T. sour cream and
    1 T. margarine

1 cup green beans

Diet Coke

Late Night Snack

1 cereal bowl of vanilla ice cream with only a few squirts of chocolate syrup

Fill out similar detailed pages for Tuesday through Sunday. Next, look back over the seven days of the food diary and examine food choices, serving sizes, fluids consumed, etc. Then ask yourself the following questions:

- Where did I make healthy food choices?
- Where did I get off track nutritionally?
- Are there certain times of the day when I consistently make poor food choices?
- Do I eat 5 to 9 servings of fruits and vegetables each day?
- Are omega-6 fats part of my diet? How healthy are my protein choices?
- Do I drink at least eight eight-ounce glasses of water each day?
- What changes do I need to make to have a more nutritious diet?"

Finally, make a commitment to a healthier, more nutritious diet for a healthier, happier you!

BECOME A LABEL READER

A great aid in making nutritional food choices is the nutritional breakdown that is required on food labels. This allows you to see some important information about the food choices you are making. Below is a sample label off a can of chili con carne with beans. Note how the nutrition facts indicate serving size and spell out the calories and the amount of fat, cholesterol, sodium, carbohydrates, and protein in each serving.

NUTRITION FACTS

Serving Size 1 Cup

Servings Per Container about 2

Calories 260   Calories from Fat 60

Note that the serving size is *one* cup and that there are *two* servings per can

AMOUNT PER SERVING	% DV*
Total Fat 7g	11%
Saturated Fat 3g	15%
Cholesterol 30 mg	10%
Sodium 1140 mg	48%
Total Carbohydrates 32g	11%
Dietary Fiber 10g	40%
Sugars 3g	
Protein 19g	
Vitamin A 25% Vitamin C 0%	
Calcium 8% Iron 20%	

These values all relate to a *one* cup serving

Percent Daily Values are based on a 2,000 calorie diet. Your daily values may be higher or lower depending on your calorie needs:

CALORIES	2,000	2,500
Total Fat	Less Than 65g	80g
Saturated Fat	Less Than 20g	25g
Cholesterol	Less Than 300mg	300mg
Sodium	Less Than 2400mg	2400mg
Total Carbohydrates	300g	375g
Dietary Fiber	25g	30g

Calories per gram   Fat 9   Carbohydrate 4   Protein 4

Become an informed consumer to make more nutritious food selections. Always check out labels before you buy!

CHAPTER 5

THE NUTRIENT CONNECTION
to Disease Prevention

Points to ponder as you read:

- ✓ What is "nutritional insurance?"
- ✓ How can changing your diet decrease the risk of developing certain diseases?
- ✓ Why is soy a good addition to your diet?
- ✓ What is the role of antioxidants and how do I increase them in my diet?
- ✓ Can supplements help my diet and if so, how?
- ✓ How do I create my own Optimal Wellness eating plan?

What would you say to someone who told you that they don't think it is necessary to carry insurance? Their justification being that they feel really lucky, and they're willing to just go along and play the odds that nothing will go wrong. Would you tell them this is a foolish way to live? Would you explain that by paying a small premium on a regular basis, they could have protection against the incredible costs that may be incurred in the future, due to illness or injury? Would you point out the relative cost between a health insurance payment and one hospital visit, the cost of car insurance versus paying out-of-pocket for a car accident, or the price of homeowner's insurance as opposed to paying to replace a home and contents ravaged by fire? If all this seems clear to you, then you understand the principle behind insurance and the peace of mind and financial protection it provides.

Now, what would you say if someone asked you about nutritional insurance? Just as you would invest in insurance to protect a car or home, invest in nutritional insurance to protect your health. This means paying attention to diet, eating those foods that give nutritional protection against future disease, and understand the benefits using nutritional supplements can provide.

While the 20th century saw dramatic advances in our understanding of the relationship between nutrient intake and health, specifically in the area of disease prevention, the connection between health and food is not new. Over 400 years ago, the Greek physician Hippocrates said, "Let medicine be thy food and food be thy medicine." It seems even more surprising that the actual scientific study of nutrition (food) and its role in health preservation and disease prevention just began in the last quarter of the 20th Century!

Even though we may have been slow to pursue scientific validation of the functional aspects of food and the health benefits associated with eating certain foods, it is now an active hotbed of research, rapidly evolving, with plenty of answers still needed. Although far too many research dollars go to fund the development of pharmaceuticals rather than validate the components of foods and herbs that confer various health benefits, research has netted important findings regarding the role of nutrition. We have been able to study the various components of foods to determine what helps keep the body healthy.

For example, it was once believed that vitamin C in an orange fueled the body's immune system; however, new research suggests bioflavenoids (plant chemicals or phytonutrients) in an orange may be even more important. Scientific study has helped us understand that nutrition plays a key role, not only in achieving and maintaining good health, but also in reducing the risk and preventing the onset of disease.

Much of the excitement about the role nutrition plays in disease prevention came initially from population studies and epidemiological evidence. Epidemiology is the study of the incidence, distribution, and control of disease in a particular population, whether it be an ethnic group (such as Eskimos), a region (such as the Mediterranean), or a country (such as Japan). For instance, western medical experts began to examine the connection of soy to various health parameters because of the extremely low incidence of many cancers (especially breast, prostate, and colon) in Japan, where the diet is extremely rich in soy. We now have evidence that it is the isoflavone content of soy, at least in part, that is responsible for these benefits. We also know that soy helps to protect bone mass, especially in women, which is probably why the incidence of osteoporosis is quite low in the Japanese population, despite their low calcium intake. In addition, soy is quite helpful in improving the troubling symptoms of perimenopause and menopause, especially hot flashes, the scourge of 45- to 55-year-old women in the west. Women eating a traditional Japanese diet do not seem to have these hormonal temperature fluctuations, which is probably why there is no word in traditional Japanese for the phrase "hot flash."

The prevention of cancer through dietary changes has been studied for many years. Since population studies in the 1970s pointed to a connection between fruit and vegetable intake and a reduced risk of certain cancers, oncology researchers have been studying foods and food components. The American Institute for Cancer Research estimates that at least one-third of all cancers in the United States could be prevented by improved nutrition. Mitchell Gaynor M.D., head of Medical Oncology at New York's Strang Center of Cancer Prevention, equates the relationship between eating the right foods and lowering the risk of cancer to wearing a seat belt and lowering the risk of having a fatal automobile accident.

The American Cancer Society recommends at least five to

nine servings of fruits and vegetables to reduce the risk of most cancers. It is believed that the antioxidant properties of fruits and vegetables neutralize free radicals, which can otherwise be carcinogenic, or cancer-causing. A daily intake of antioxidants, in the form of healthy food sources and supplements, can protect cells from cancerous transformation. (For a detailed discussion of antioxidants and free radicals, see the "Antioxidants" section below and chapter 18).

Obesity, now considered an inflammatory disease, is another strong dietary factor in the development of cancer. Free radicals are a by-product of the normal metabolizing of food. An obese individual has increased exposure to free radicals due to the body processing more food or, to state it simply, the more calories consumed, the more free radicals that need neutralizing. In addition, there is generally a lack of healthy cancer-fighting nutrients in the diets of most obese individuals.

Having established that nutrition is connected to disease prevention, let's review some general groups of nutrients and food components that have been proven to fight disease. I will single out the most important nutrients, and suggest how to include them in your food choices and use them as supplements.

PHYTONUTRIENTS

Beyond vitamins and minerals, there are other components known as phytochemicals or phytonutrients. These are chemical compounds found in foods that confer health benefits. Scientists are working to link specific phytochemicals to the diseases for which they offer protection. Countless phytonutrients have been identified. A single fruit or vegetable can have a wide assortment of phytochemicals. For instance, an orange contains more than 170 different phytochemical substances.

By eating a variety of plant food on a daily basis, you enhance the chance of consuming sufficient amounts of these compounds to reap their full benefits. One example of this is allium, which is a phytonutrient found in vegetables such as onions, garlic, and leeks. Allium compounds appear to offer protection against stomach and colon cancers. There are studies that show allium may contain antibacterial properties against Helicobacter Pylori, which is the bacteria associated with chronic hyperacidity conditions of the stomach which, in turn, has been associated with an increased risk of stomach cancer. In addition, foods containing allium may help induce the body to produce certain enzymes which help neutralize carcinogens, enhancing the immune system and mildly lowering cholesterol.

PHYTOESTROGENS

Phytoestrogens is a category of nutrients that offers preventive protection to the body by reducing the risk of breast, prostate, and colon cancers. They may also help decrease some of the symptoms of menopause and offer protection from osteoporosis. In addition, this nutrient is thought to lower the risk of cardiovascular disease. Soy is the most common source of phytoestrogens, and the FDA now allows a claim to be put on all foods containing at least 6.25 grams of soy per serving. This claim states, "A diet low in saturated fat and containing a minimum of 25 grams of soy protein per day may reduce your risk of cardiovascular disease as well as help maintain cholesterol levels within the normal range."

Soy has become a popular food source in America. An estimated 27% of all Americans are eating some form of soy every week, including tofu, soy nuts, soy milk, and "power bars" containing soy. One of the great benefits of soy is as a meat substitute. People are replacing diets previously containing higher amounts of saturated fats from red meats and other protein sources with soy protein, which is a complex carbohydrate protein source, containing much less fat than other protein sources.

ANTIOXIDANTS

Dietary antioxidants are nutrients consisting of organic sub-stances, including vitamin C, vitamin E, vitamin A (which is con-verted from beta-carotene), selenium (a mineral), and carotenoids, that help protect cells from free radicals. For years, researchers have sought to understand the role of these antioxidants in re-ducing the risk of chronic diseases such as cancer, cardiovascular disease, eye diseases, and neurodegenerative diseases, which in-clude Alzheimer's and Parkinson's. Although we don't have all the answers yet, we do know that dietary antioxidants can, in some cases, prevent or counteract cell damage that stems from exposure to free radicals.

To help you visualize the relationship between free radicals and antioxidants, think in terms of an old western. Free radicals are the bad guys in black hats. If allowed to go unchecked, these free radicals can cause damage to cell walls, certain cell structures, and genetic material within the cells. In the worst case scenario and over a long time period, such damage can become irrevers-ible and lead to impairment of the immune system, infections, and various degenerative diseases, such as heart disease and cancer. There are a number of known free radicals appearing in our body, the most common one is oxygen-derived, which is where the term "anti-oxidants" comes in.

Free radicals are produced during the metabolism of food. The more a person eats, especially foods high in saturated fats, the greater the risk of free radicals being generated. They may also be formed by radiation exposure, including exposure to sun rays, toxic chemicals, polluted air, and industrial and household chemicals. If one takes care to keep the body healthy in general by eating correctly and limiting exposure to the free radical's best friend—junk food—by exercising and avoiding poisons such as tobacco, alcohol, etc., it will be in much better shape to overcome the free radical scourge.

Riding to the rescue, helping the body fight against these free radicals, is where antioxidants, the guys in white hats, come into play. At the molecular and cellular levels, antioxidants serve to deactivate and round up the free radicals, running them out of town before they can damage the body. That is why a healthy diet with five to nine servings of fruits and vegetables per day, as well as nutritional supplementation, is key in neutralizing these DNA-ruining molecules.

FLAVENOIDS

Flavenoids are found throughout fruits and vegetables, but are especially prevalent in citrus fruits, garlic, onions, and leafy greens. They are a subcomponent of a larger category called phenols, which are found in most fruits, vegetables, herbs, and nuts. Flavenoids perform a variety of helpful tasks, including blocking growth of cancer cells. They may also help inhibit the formation of blood clots and provide anti-inflammatory and anti-viral activity. Flavenoids may be the most predominant antioxidant consumed.

CAROTENOIDS

Beta-carotene is just one carotenoid that is a well known leader in the fight to protect the body. Foods high in carotenoids include red, orange, deep yellow, and some dark green leafy vegetables, such as tomatoes, carrots, sweet potatoes, and broccoli. Diets rich in carotenoids have been associated with a lowered risk of developing many kinds of cancer. Studies suggest that carotenoids enhance both antimicrobial functions and immunity against tumors by increasing activity of natural killer cells. Current evidence suggests that particular carotenoids have potent antioxidant properties that help maintain the health of specific parts of the body.

Beta-carotene has been shown to reduce the risk of heart disease. In a group of heart-disease-prone men who took beta-

carotene supplements every other day for five years, cardiovascular disease events dropped almost 50%. (Smokers, however, please
note that you should *not* take beta-carotene supplements!) Studies have also shown that beta-carotene may be an effective ally
against prostate cancer. A recent study found that men who had
the lowest levels of beta-carotene in their blood were at the greatest risk of developing this type of cancer. Sweet potatoes, winter
squash, and carrots are all good sources of beta-carotene.

CALCIUM

Calcium is the most abundant mineral in the body, found
primarily in bones and teeth. Calcium plays key biologic roles
in nerves, muscles, and even coagulation of the blood. There is
strong evidence that calcium intake directly affects bone density,
and that a lack of this mineral is a key factor in the development
of osteopenia and osteoporosis. We also know that calcium may
help keep blood pressure in normal range, even during pregnancy.
One of the more recent findings is the connection of calcium to
increased protection from colon cancer through both dairy foods
and calcium supplements. In addition, calcium and magnesium
supplements together have been shown to decrease many of the
symptoms associated with PMS.

Recent NIH guidelines recommend higher calcium intake
than the US RDA.

Calcium Recommendations:

Females

Age 11-24	1200-1500 mg
Age 25-50	1000 mg
Pregnancy/lactation	1200-1500 mg
Post-Menopause	1500 mg

Males

Age 11-24	1200-1500 mg
Age 25-65	1000 mg

Over age 65   1500 mg

Supplement:

As above, depending on dietary sources. Calcium citrate is better absorbed than calcium carbonate, although cancer reduction is associated with intake of calcium carbonate.

Best Dietary Sources:

Nonfat yogurt	400 mg/8 oz
Skim milk	300 mg/8 oz
Tofu	400-500 mg/2 oz
Spinach/collard greens	200 mg/cooked cup

ESSENTIAL FATTY ACIDS

Essential fatty acids (EFAs) are poly- and monounsaturated fats that the body requires in the diet because it cannot manufacture them. Paleolithic evidence shows that our ancestors consumed diets that were much richer in omega-3 than omega-6 fatty acids. Today, the typical U.S. diet consists of 10 times more omega-6 fats than omega-3 fats. This is a health concern because of how the fats operate in the body. One of the functions of omega-3 fats is to prevent inflammatory responses in the body, such as certain types of arthritis, inflammatory bowel disease, and psoriasis. Omega-6 fatty acids tend to increase prostaglandins and cytokines, the modulators of the inflammatory response, while omega-3 fats decrease both of these. There is some evidence that omega-3 fatty acids may also be useful in the treatment of asthma, as this is also an inflammatory disease.

The preferred ratio of these two EFAs is 3:1 to 4:1 (omega-6: omega-3) for overall health promotion. As previously stated, the typical diet of most Americans is up to 10:1 (omega-6:omega-3), which tends to favor inflammation in the body. To correct this out of balance ratio, we need to consume more olive oil and omega-3 rich fish (such as salmon, halibut, and tuna) and eat less corn, safflower, and soybean oils.

There is good evidence that eating fish and supplementing a diet with fish oil may reduce the risk of heart attack and stroke by up to 50%. This is incredibly important information with more than 1.2 million Americans dying each year of heart disease or stroke. Additionally, a diet rich in omega-3 fatty acids may help reduce triglycerides and help to lower blood pressure.

Supplement:

Fish oil	3-10g/day
GLA	1.5-3 g/day

Best Dietary Sources:

Mackerel

Salmon

Tuna

Shrimp

FIBER

Fiber is the indigestible portion of fruits, vegetables and grains. Insoluble fiber is abundant in whole grains and is very important in healthy colon function and may contribute to a reduced colon cancer risk. Soluble fiber is found in fruits, vegetables, legumes (beans, lentils), and oats and helps to lower cholesterol, improve blood sugar control, and adds to the satiety factor of foods, which means you feel full sooner. There is good evidence that fiber supplements can help to provide the same benefits as eating a fiber-rich diet. The average fiber intake of American adults is 8-12 grams per day. The recommended daily intake is 25 grams for women and 35 for men.

Supplements:

3-10 grams per day of **soluble** fiber—sources include guar gum, pectin, and beta glucan.

Best Dietary Sources:

Lentils	16 g/cup
Raspberries/blackberries	8-12 g/cup
Apple	3-4 g/medium size
Whole grain bread	2 g/slice

FOLATE

Folate is the naturally occurring B vitamin. Supplemental forms are known as folic acid and folinate. Folate is essential to cell replication, red blood cell metabolism, and other critical cellular functions. Evidence is conclusive that folate deficiency leads to neural tube defects in pregnancy and contributes to heart disease risk by elevating an amino acid called homocysteine. Americans are felt to be uniformly deficient in folic acid. Many cereals and other foods are now fortified with folate and other B vitamins. Folic acid supplements are better absorbed than the folate in foods, especially in older individuals.

Supplements:

400 micrograms for adults

1000 micrograms (1 mg) during pregnancy.

Best Dietary Sources:

Lentils	350 micrograms
Spinach	250 micrograms
Avocado	120 micrograms
Broccoli	90-100 micrograms

LYCOPENE

Lycopene is a carotenoid found in tomatoes and yellow-orange fruits like apricots, guava, and papaya and, as an antioxidant, is a potent scavenger of free radicals. There is good evidence supporting lycopene as being protective against both prostate and colon cancer and possibly playing a role in cardiovascular protection.

Supplement:

3-4 mg/day (Look for supplements that contain whole to-mato extract, including a small amount of oil that helps release lycopene.)

Best Dietary Sources:

Raw tomatoes	2.9 mg/100 gm
Tomato sauce	6-7 mg/100 gm
Papaya	3 mg/large
Dried apricots	1 mg/10

LUTEIN

Lutein may decrease the risk of developing macular degen-eration, the eye disease that afflicts one in three people over age 75. Foods rich in lutein include broccoli, Brussels sprouts, spinach, kale, and egg yolk. Lutein supplements, especially when combined with vitamins A and C, are a prudent way to assure adequate in-take of eye health-protecting nutrients.

Supplement:

5 mg/day

Best Dietary Sources:

Kale (cooked)	33.8 mg/1 cup
Spinach (cooked)	22.1mg/1 cup
Broccoli (cooked)	3.4 mg/1 cup
Lettuce (Romaine)	1.5 mg/1 cup

VITAMIN B-6

Vitamin B-6, also known as pyridoxine, is essential in protein metabolism, neurotransmitter production, glucose production in the liver, and many other cellular functions. It has been shown to be generally deficient in the typical American diet, largely due to the consumption of highly refined foods. Deficiency in vitamin B-6 also contributes to elevation of homocysteine and increased

risk of heart disease. Since smokers and women using oral contraceptives seem to be highly deficient, supplementation is extremely important in these groups. There is reasonably good evidence
that "mega-dose" levels of B-6 may be helpful with PMS, asthma,
and carpal tunnel syndrome.

Supplement:

Females	1.6 mg
pregnancy/lactation	2.2 mg
Males	2 mg

Best Dietary Sources:

Tuna/salmon	0.8 mg/3 oz
Turkey	0.6 mg/3 oz
Banana	0.7 mg/ medium
Green peppers	0.3 mg/one

VITAMIN C

Vitamin C, also known as ascorbic acid, is essential as a cofactor in myriad metabolic pathways in the body. Severe deficiency
is known as scurvy. This was the earliest proven nutrient connection to disease prevention. Vitamin C was made famous in
the 1950s by two-time Nobel Prize Laureate Linus Pauling. Dr.
Pauling had endured much criticism and skepticism in the 1950s
and 60s with his controversial belief that vitamin C supplementation could significantly reduce the severity of the common cold,
as well as potentially lessen the risk of contracting many respiratory viruses. Of course, today, vitamin C is recognized as a potent
water-soluble antioxidant that may help to reduce your risk of
cancer and heart disease, as well as decrease the risk and severity
of respiratory infections.

Supplement:

500 mg/day (many medical professionals recommend up to
2 g/day)

Red peppers	280 mg/cup
Orange juice, fresh	125 mg/8 oz
Strawberries	85 mg/cup
Broccoli	85 mg/cup

VITAMIN E

Vitamin E is also known as tocopherols and tocotrienols, which are potent fat-soluble antioxidants. Vitamin E plays a role in platelet function, helps support immune function, and is a co-factor in many cellular functions. The main food source of vitamin E is in fats, so people on fat-reduced diets are often deficient. There have been thousands of studies examining the connection of vitamin E supplementation to a reduction in the risk of cardiovascular disease. There is evidence that vitamin E plays a role in the prevention of further cardiac events in people with existing coronary artery disease and helps protect the lining of the arteries. Studies also show that vitamin E reduces cancer risk with supplementation of 400-800 IU/day. The FDA now allows a claim on supplements with at least 400 IU of vitamin E, that consumption of antioxidants may reduce the risk of certain cancers.

Supplement:

400 IU/day

Discuss vitamin E supplementation with your physician if you are using blood-thinning medication, have a bleeding disorder, or are contemplating surgery.

ZINC

Zinc is an essential mineral that is a cofactor in multiple enzyme processes in the body. It is also involved in DNA synthesis, immune function, and collagen synthesis. Zinc has been shown to boost immunity, reduce the severity of respiratory infections, and is very important in fertility in both men and women and sexual performance in men. It is generally believed that the American diet is deficient of zinc. And, while all adults may benefit from zinc supplementation, older adults should definitely supplement.

Supplement:

Females	12 mg/day
Males	15 mg/day

Best Dietary Sources:

Oysters	76 mg/6 oz.
Turkey breast	5 mg/4 oz
Lamb	4 mg/3 oz
White beans	2.3 mg/cup
Avocado	1 mg/half

Now that you are conversant with the nutrients needed to protect the body from disease, I want to introduce you to the six steps to Optimal Nutritional Wellness—a newer, healthier version of the Food Pyramid. It is time for us to re-visit how we eat!

*   Aim to consume more vegetables than fruit each day. Avoid fruit juice, unless made in a juicing machine. Commercial fruit juice is high in sugar (even if it says "natural" on the label). Eat fresh or frozen whole fruit instead.

**   Dairy can include calcium-fortified soymilk instead of, or in addition to regular dairy. Be sure to use nonfat versions primarily, containing no more than 1% fat.

***   The tiny top block of the steps to wellness actually represents the greatest volume of food consumed each day by most Americans! This has to change if we are to be a healthier nation and world. The empty calories from doughnuts, fries, chips, cookies, and pastries just have to go! If you eat meals and snacks with everything found in the bottom five steps and have something from that tiny top tier only once or twice per week (and gradually once or twice per month), you will be providing the body with what it needs on a daily basis to protect your health.

By paying attention to diet, improving the level of nutrition, incorporating healthy food selections into daily meals, and utilizing food supplements, you can have the advantage of nutritional insurance to safeguard your health. Think about it. If nutrients consumed today could stop you from having to suffer from cancer, a stroke, or heart disease, isn't it worth it to choose nutrition?

Herophilies, in 300 BC, said "When health is absent, wisdom cannot reveal itself . . . wealth is useless and reason is powerless." By investing in proper nutrition, you have the power to insure your fitness. There is no greater gift than good health. Protect yours.

FOLLOW-UP PREVENTIVE PERSCRIPTION

STEP UP TO GOOD NUTRITION

For one week, write down everything—and I do mean *everything*—you consume. Check your food diary against my six steps to Optimal Nutritional Wellness. How do you measure up? Get a feel for the changes you need to make in your meal plans to invest in nutritional insurance.

STEPS TO OPTIMAL NUTRITIONAL WELLNESS
Daily Food Suggestions to Promote Health

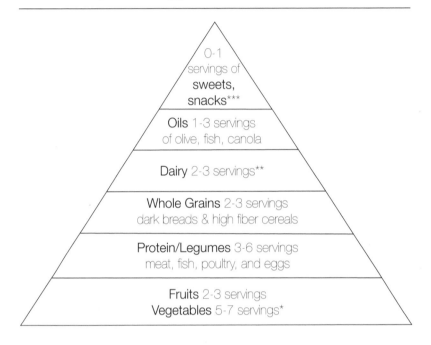

0-1 servings of
sweets,
snacks***

Oils 1-3 servings
of olive, fish, canola

Dairy 2-3 servings**

Whole Grains 2-3 servings
dark breads & high fiber cereals

Protein/Legumes 3-6 servings
meat, fish, poultry, and eggs

Fruits 2-3 servings
Vegetables 5-7 servings*

Below I have included a sample "Diet Diary," representing a typical day's food intake for me. Follow the sample meals for a few days, and you will become familiar with healthful, body-protective eating.

Breakfast

1 ½ cups high fiber whole grain cereal

2 tbsp. soy/whey protein powder

½ cup fresh berries

1 cup plain soymilk

Lunch

8 oz carton fruit-flavored yogurt with 2 tbsp. soy protein vitamin enriched powder mixed in

½ whole grain bagel—toasted

1 tbsp. light cream cheese

Mixed green salad or carrot and celery sticks

Afternoon Snack

Protein bar (I enjoy several varieties)—shoot for 12-15 grams of protein and 150-180 calories

Hot green tea

Dinner

Large mixed green salad with romaine lettuce, spinach, red bell pepper, broccoli, tomatoes, mushrooms, and shredded carrot topped with balsamic vinaigrette dressing and a few croutons

Select from the following protein choices to add to the salad:

1 cup cubed tofu and ½ sliced hard boiled egg; or

3 oz baked salmon; or

¾ cup black beans and shredded mozzarella cheese.

(The above protein choices are all different, healthy and enjoyable. Two are vegetarian choices, which is where I gravitate. I try to include fish, especially omega-3 rich choices like wild salmon at least 2 or 3 times per week. The remainder of the time I am primarily vegetarian.)

A whole grain roll or a baguette—toasted and topped with a sprinkling of minced garlic and parmesan cheese and briefly broiled to melt the cheese

Evening snack

4-ounce red wine with a 1-ounce soy "ice cream" bar; or

eight-ounce sparkling water and air popped popcorn; or

1-2 sliced kiwi topped with 1/4 cup cottage cheese.

My breakfasts and lunches are quite static when I am at home, but I enjoy great variety with my snacks and evening meals. If I eat lunch out, I usually order a vegetarian wrap sandwich. A typical dinner out for me will include a fresh fish dish, a salad, some bread (fresh, warm bread is my weakness!) and steamed vegetables (yes, I request that they be steamed). As an alternative, I may order linguini or angel hair pasta with some sort of spicy red sauce and seafood. (Red sauces are lower in fat and much lighter than creamy sauces.) I focus on enjoying conversation, eating slowly, and savoring every bite.

CHAPTER 6

WEIGHT
Control It or It Will Control You

Points to ponder as you read:

- ✓ How does being overweight or obese control you?
- ✓ Why should you be worried about being above your ideal body weight?
- ✓ How can you determine a healthy weight for you?
- ✓ There are so many diets out there—how can you lose weight safely?
- ✓ Is it possible to keep your excess weight off forever and still enjoy eating?

A friend of mine commented recently that she was tired of the "battle of the bulge" and had resigned herself to being overweight. She was tired of trying to stay in control. She just wanted to eat what she wanted, when she wanted. She asserted, "I am not going to let my weight control me!" And, yet, that was exactly what she was doing. Because she was so overweight, her life was limited in many ways. She often chose not to participate in family outings or activities because she was embarrassed to be seen in shorts or a swimsuit. She became out of breath from walking uphill or playing with her young children at the park. She was reluctant to go to movie theaters or sports stadiums because, due to her size, the seats were uncomfortable. She often shared with me that her lower back always hurt, that she was noticing "some arthritis pains" in her knees, and that she had frequent heel pain—"probably from my shoes." Since her husband didn't have weight problems and didn't seem to understand her slow metabolism, she was afraid her marriage was suffering. Many days she just didn't have the energy needed to manage her children's activities, plan her family's meals, keep up with her housework, and maintain her part-time job. She was now on Prozac for depression, Maxzide for mild hypertension (which would probably normalize with weight loss) and Celebrex for knee and heel pain (which would probably cease with less weight stress on the joints). So, tell me, was she in control of her weight or was her weight controlling her?

Despite the interest in fitness and the explosion of new ways to stay fit (The Total Gym, TaeBo, Pilates, etc.), as a nation we are fatter and less fit than we were 20 years ago. Our meals are rushed and largely eaten away from home. The fast food industry has a drive thru on every corner. We are eating foods that are highly refined, full of hidden fat and sugar, creating "the 21st Century Paradox"—malnourished, obese people by the tens of thousands. As a nation, we are eating 25% more than in 1960, and yet our activity level has decreased by 25%.

Our inactivity is attributable to several lifestyle factors. We are watching more television than ever before, with the average American family tuned in for approximately five hours per day! This is problematic because obesity, especially in children, is directly related to the amount of TV watched. In addition, children spend another two to three hours in front of computers or playing video games. Is it any great surprise that we are seeing rapidly increasing numbers of overweight adults and children? As a physician (and mother) I am horrified. In 1980, 37% of Americans were overweight to obese. In 2001, that number had increased to a staggering 62% of Americans. The number of overweight children and teens has doubled in the past 10 years.

USA Today recently printed an article about, "The Freshman 15," which refers to the 15 pounds the average college freshman girl gained in her first year of college back in the 1960s and 1970s. Well, guess what? Today, that 15 pounds has become 25 pounds, with statistics showing that weight gained as a young adult is unlikely to ever be lost. That means that our college freshmen girls are starting on the pathway to becoming just like my overweight friend, controlled by their weight, and at risk for diabetes, pregnancy complications, cancer, and heart disease.

Unfortunately, obesity has no specific symptoms. Eating an unhealthy diet does not give you "instant feedback" as to what that diet is doing to your body. If you developed chest pain every time you ate a hamburger, you would better understand the connection between living on fast food and developing heart disease. If you developed "instant diabetes" with the pain of diabetic neuropathy every time you ate chocolate chip cookies or ice cream, you would probably think twice about having dessert every night.

Even without immediate consequences, the body *is* being affected by what you overeat. Obesity increases your risk of developing two of the main triggers for heart disease: high cholesterol and high blood pressure. If one out of three Americans will die of heart disease, it becomes apparent that you are far more likely to die prematurely from obesity than either smoking or drinking.

Heart disease is not the only life-threatening condition tied to obesity, however. Those experiencing weight problems have a far greater risk of developing Type 2 diabetes, osteoarthritis, cancer, and gallbladder disease, as well as suffering from a stroke. It was estimated in the year 2000 that there were approximately 300,000 unnecessary, premature deaths, all attributable to complications stemming from obesity. If you also calculate in the thousands of obese individuals who have excessive medical bills, side effects from medications, and an overall decreased quality of life from being chronically ill and/or lacking the energy to meet the demands of life, you begin to understand the extent of this problem.

CAUSES OF OBESITY

Conditioned/Programmed Overeating

Beginning in our childhood, we are taught to associate food with rewards, with habits, and even with guilt. In times past, the traditional after-school snack was milk and cookies or some other dessert. Experts believe that the "mid-afternoon sweets craving" that many adults have harks back to these high-sugar, after-school snacks of our childhood.

In addition, many of today's adults were conditioned to over-eat as children by parents or grandparents who lived through the Great Depression. Children were programmed that it was wrong to waste food and were chided at dinner for not cleaning their plate. If you were like me, your parents connected food left on your plate with the starving children in India or Africa. Feeling the guilt, whether hungry or not, you probably cleaned your plate. As a reward for eating all your dinner, you were given a bowl of ice cream, a slice of cake, or several cookies, and you cleaned your dessert plate, too—again whether you were hungry or not.

The reality is that children who are conditioned to overeat continue this habit into adulthood. As an adult, no longer growing, with reduced activity, the conditioned eater begins piling on the pounds.

Modern Lifestyle Overeating—Super-sizing America

Frantic schedules and busy lifestyles have led to higher calorie, higher fat, and higher sugar meals. With more than two-thirds of meals eaten away from home, it is all too easy to take in far more calories than are expended.

Who has time to sit down with their family for a nice hot breakfast, or any kind of breakfast, for that matter, in the morning? Teenagers grab a high-sugar granola bar as they rush out the door in the morning, then gulp down a high sugar soda from a vending machine at 10 a.m. when they are feeling tired and unable to concentrate. Adults breakfast on a Starbuck's Vanilla Latte or Caramel Frappucino, having just one or two of the doughnuts in the break room mid-morning when they're dragging.

The family dinner hour is also a thing of the past. The majority of teenagers in America today have few to no dinners with their families. Studies have shown that young people who do not sit down to dinner with their families have a significantly higher likelihood of not only becoming overweight to obese, but also of suffering from depression and drug use, as well.

Hectic lifestyles have also led to late night eating when the metabolism is at its slowest. Does this scenario sound at all familiar? You work late at the office and come home for dinner about 7:30 or 8:00, absolutely famished. You grab some quick food (which usually means high-calorie and high-fat) and top it off with a dessert containing a day and a half's worth of calories. A little later, you microwave a bag of extra buttery popcorn to enjoy while you relax on the couch and watch your favorite television show(s). Finally, at 11 p.m. you drag yourself off the couch and head to bed, after having ingested 75% of your calories in the evening hours, which encourages the storage of *fat!*

When the "super-size" phenomenon is added to the busy lifestyle of today, it becomes even clearer why America has an overweight epidemic. As previously stated, two-thirds of meals are eaten away from home. Many of those meals are picked up as you are logging miles through the fast food drive-thru. For just an extra 50 cents, you can increase those portions that are already *bursting* with extra sugar, fat, and calories. You end up with a super-sized meal, which gives a totally skewed idea of a healthy portion or serving size.

Emotional Eating

Other weight problems come into play when food becomes tied up with emotions. Many people turn to food when they are stressed or upset. I saw a commercial the other day where a little boy was having a really bad time at a family dinner. He had been shipped off to eat (and suffer) at the children's table, barely on the edge of civilization, where he could just get a glimpse of the exciting time being had by all of those seated at the adult dining room table. This boy was miserable, but said, "Mom had a way of making it up to me." Then the scene shifts to the boy seated at the kitchen table with a huge bowl of ice cream in front of him. This bowl, which has enough ice cream in it to feed the adult table, the children's table, and half the neighborhood, is the boy's solace for suffering through dinner at the "little kids table." The message presented here is "food makes you feel better."

It is interesting to note that the emotional connection we feel with food is never low calorie. I have yet to meet someone who says, "When I feel down, I get a craving for carrots—raw, crisp, and cut on the diagonal." I don't believe I've ever heard anyone comment that "I have a longing for sliced cucumbers with a drizzle of low-fat vinaigrette dressing just like Mama used to make." The emotional tie to food, which has led to phrases such as "stress eating" and "comfort food," is almost without exception, related to the consumption of high-fat, high-sugar, and high-calorie foods.

A long-time favorite "comfort food" for many women is chocolate. Research now tells us that chocolate is a natural antidepressant, especially for women. It actually triggers a release of serotonin, a neurotransmitter in our brains that affects our mood. This physiologic basis reinforces our emotional response to chocolate. (Before you get too excited about the medicinal properties of chocolate, however, remember that another natural anti-depressant is exercise, which contains *no* sugar, fat, or calories!)

Unconscious Eating

If the above phrase gives you a mental picture of force feeding a person in a coma, you are actually not far off. You could rename this "unaware" eating, and perhaps get a better idea of this incredibly common problem in today's world. Have you ever been watching a TV show or movie while snacking on a bag of popcorn or chips, and, suddenly find the bag empty? You have no conscious recollection of eating the *whole* thing, but nevertheless, there is nothing left in the package.

As previously stated, eating dinner together as a family, sitting down at the table, and actually conversing has, unfortunately, become a thing of the past. Today, many eat meals in front of the television or the computer screen. Some gobble meals at their desk, while others gulp down a sandwich in the car between appointments. The problem with this type of eating is that it becomes automatic—eating without being aware of what you are eating.

Unconscious eating can lead to weight problems for two reasons. If you are involved in watching TV or playing a computer game, unaware of what you are eating, you will consume much more food and many more calories than if you sat down with a single serving and paid attention to what you were eating. In addition, experts tell us that it takes 20 minutes after eating to achieve a feeling of satiation. This means that if you gulp down your lunch in 10 minutes without paying attention, chances are you will still feel hungry. In this circumstance, many will grab a candy bar, bag of chips, or other high calorie snack to fill up on.

Chronic Dieting

This has become the most common, and probably the least publicized, reason for being overweight. Women began dieting in the 1960s in response to the increasing numbers of women's magazines available—all with a very thin supermodel on the cover. Diets of all sorts were written about, talked about, and connected to this or that celebrity. Over the years, many, many diets have come and gone. All such diets, the grapefruit diet, the popcorn diet, the cabbage soup diet, the Twiggy diet, the Cambridge diet, etc. have one thing in common. Each of these diets is too low in overall calories and contains inadequate amounts of protein and other nutrients, which can trigger a vicious cycle of dieting.

You begin one of these diets, lose 10 pounds in 3 weeks, and are soooo excited. However, eventually, the body begins to tell you that you're tired, you're nauseous and/or constipated. The body can only handle this kind of treatment for so long. Eventually, you give up and return to old eating habits. Because the protein content of most diets is too low, the 10 pounds you lost was fat *and* muscle. However, the 10 pounds that is gained back over the next three to four weeks, when old eating habits return, will be all fat, because that is how the body stores extra calories. Consequently, with repeated cycles of dieting, lean muscle mass declines and body fat increases. Metabolism—the number of calories the body burns each day, is completely determined by body mass. The lower the lean body mass and the higher the body fat, the less calories the body burns each day. This makes it successively harder to lose weight and easier to gain it.

For instance, let's look at Mary, a chronic dieter since age 15. She is now 45 years old, 5'6" tall, weighing 190 pounds. Her body fat is 34% and her LBM (lean body mass), which consists of her muscles, skeleton, and organs, is 142 pounds. Mary's RMR (resting metabolic rate or the number of calories burned at rest) is 1,538. In order to lose one pound a week, one ideally needs to reduce his or her caloric intake to 500 calories less than the body uses. That means for Mary to lose one pound per week, she would have to eat no more than 1,038 calories a day—unless she adds activity. I do not recommend eating less than 1,200 calories per day; because the caloric intake drops to less than that as weight is lost, muscle mass is lost along with fat. For Mary to lose weight then, by eating 1,200 calories a day to avoid muscle loss, she will need to walk 30 to 45 minutes every day, along with consuming 100 to 125 grams of protein daily. By looking at Mary's weight loss challenge, it is easy to see how chronic dieting leads to the problem of being overweight and/or obese.

Let's break out of the obesity trap. Realize that you can take control of your future health by learning how to control your weight forever. Take the steps today to be in control of your weight, your health, your vitality, and your enjoyment of life. Here is a plan to put into action—a plan that is easy, enjoyable, and rewarding.

DR. JAMIE'S STEP-BY-STEP PLAN TO ACHIEVING A HEALTHY WEIGHT— FOREVER

Step One—Determine Your Healthy Weight

First, determine your ideal body weight. Ideally, using a bio-impedence machine, one that measures lean muscle mass and body fat with excellent accuracy, is the best way to determine your ideal weight. (Bioanalogics is the most scientifically validated bioimpedence machine. Visit bioanalogics.com.) If that is not available to you, the following BMI (body mass index) chart is a good starting point. Find yourself on the chart, but remember if you are a highly-muscled person, your BMI may put you into an overweight category, even when you are not overweight. I firmly counsel my patients to not focus on a particular number, but rather a dress size (for women) or a waist size (for men). This is a more accurate measure of body fat.

To use this table, find your height in the left-hand column. Move across the row to your weight.

The number at the top of the column is your BMI.

BMI (KG/M^2)

Height (inches)	19	20	21	22	23	24	25	26	27	28	29	30	35	40
							Body Weight (Pounds)							
58	91	96	100	105	110	115	119	124	129	134	138	143	167	191
59	94	99	104	109	114	119	124	128	133	138	143	148	173	198
60	97	102	107	112	118	123	128	133	138	143	148	153	179	204
61	100	106	111	116	122	127	132	137	143	148	153	158	185	211
62	104	109	115	120	126	131	136	142	147	153	158	164	191	218
63	107	113	118	124	130	135	141	146	152	158	163	169	197	225
64	110	116	122	128	134	140	145	151	157	163	169	174	204	232
65	114	120	126	132	138	144	150	156	162	168	174	180	210	240
66	118	124	130	136	142	148	155	161	167	173	179	186	216	247
67	121	127	134	140	146	153	159	166	172	178	185	191	223	255
68	125	131	138	144	151	158	164	171	177	184	190	197	230	262
69	128	135	142	149	155	162	169	176	182	189	196	203	236	270
70	132	139	146	153	160	167	174	181	188	195	202	207	243	278
71	136	143	150	157	165	172	179	186	193	200	208	215	250	286
72	140	147	154	162	169	177	184	191	199	206	213	221	258	294
73	144	151	159	166	174	182	189	197	204	212	219	227	265	302
74	148	155	163	171	179	186	194	202	210	218	225	233	272	311
75	152	160	168	176	184	192	200	208	216	224	232	240	279	319
76	153	164	172	180	189	197	205	213	221	230	238	246	287	328

Chart adapted from Bray, G.A., Gray, D.S., *Obesity, Part I, Pathogenesis, West J. Med. 1988: 149: 429–41.*

Step Two — Set Realistic Goals

You did not gain weight overnight, and you won't lose it overnight. Losing weight, while enhancing your health, is a gradual process. Women tend to lose weight slower than men, because they are smaller and, generally have less to lose as a percentage of their total weight. Women usually have a lower metabolic rate because they have a lower lean muscle mass. Remember that the metabolism is almost entirely determined by the muscle mass, along with a small genetic contribution. The total number of calories burned is determined by the metabolic rate plus the activity level. There is no magic formula! This is straight physiology.

Women should plan to lose 1-2 pounds per week, while men should plan to lose 2-3 pounds per week. So, if you have 30 pounds to lose to reach the ideal weight determined in Step One, plan on approximately 20 weeks if you are female and 12 weeks if you are male (30 pounds divided by 1.5 pounds per week for women and 2.5 for men). That means if your 20-year reunion is coming up in 6 months, you had better get started!

Step Three — Make Yourself Accountable

Be honest with yourself. I recommend not only weighing yourself, but also measuring. For women, the following measurements can be especially helpful. You will definitely lose inches faster than pounds on my program, which is the true measure of decreased body fat. Lose fat and build muscle. Muscle weighs more than fat, but is denser, so takes up less space—hence the "magical" dropping of dress and pants sizes. Men should follow their waist measurement as they tend to carry most of their excess fat around the middle. Women should measure waist, hip (about 4-5 inches below the natural waistline), thighs, and upper arms.

Weigh and measure only once a week, preferably at the same time of the day. If you are losing weight more slowly than we discussed in Step Two, then I recommend a Food Diary. Write down every morsel eaten (yes, even the last few bites you ate of your family's casserole as you did the dishes!) and the portion size. Do a rough determination of calories. You may be shocked at the hidden calories (check the labels), the forgotten calories (oh yes, I *did* have two glasses of wine at dinner), and the calories assigned to "the entertainment package"—popcorn and Coke at the movies.

Step 4—Develop a Healthy Weight Loss Plan

Below is my "Optimal Eating Guide for Weight Control," followed by suggested servings:

0-1 servings of
sweets, snacks***

Oils 1-3 servings
of olive, fish, canola

Dairy 2-3 servings**

Whole Grains 2-3 servings
dark breads & high fiber cereals

Protein/Legumes 3-6 servings
meat, fish, poultry, and eggs

Fruits 2-3 servings
Vegetables 5-7 servings*

DAIRY PRODUCTS GROUP

- 1 cup (8 oz.) nonfat milk, yogurt
- 2 slices cheese, 1/8" thick (1 oz. each)
- ¾ cup low-fat cottage cheese
- ¾ cup low-fat frozen yogurt or ice milk

WHOLE GRAINS GROUP

- 1 slice whole wheat bread
- ½ bagel or English muffin
- 4 small crackers
- 1 whole wheat tortilla
- 1 cup high fiber cereal

- ½ cup cooked cereal, preferably oatmeal
- ½ cup brown rice
- ½ cup whole wheat pasta

PROTEIN GROUP

- 3-4 oz. (size of a deck of cards) cooked lean meat, poultry, or fish
- 2 eggs or 4 egg whites
- 4 oz. tofu
- ¾ cup cooked legumes (dried beans or peas)
- 2 tablespoons peanut butter, preferably natural style
- ½ cup almonds, walnuts, or cashews

FRUIT GROUP

- 1 whole medium fruit (about 1 cup)
- ¼ cup dried fruit
- 1 cup fresh frozen fruit (I think berries are the best!)

VEGETABLE GROUP

- 1 cup cooked vegetables
- ½ cup raw, chopped vegetables
- 1 cup raw leafy vegetables
- ½ to ¾ cup vegetable juice

The major food groups are all shown on my eating plan. Each of these food groups provides some, but not all, of the nutrients you need daily. Your Healthy Eating Plan will include servings from all of the food groups, but remember to focus food choices on the foods at the *base* of the Optimal Eating Guide for Weight Control. This plan shows a range of servings for each of the major food groups. The number of servings needed from each group depends on how many calories are needed to lose weight. Women should use the lower number, men the higher. Make healthy choices in each food group. For instance, choose nonfat or 1% milk instead of 2% or whole milk; eat lean meat, such as chicken breast, turkey, or fish, rather than more fatty cuts of meat. Minimize beef, because the fat is marbled throughout and cannot be removed. Choose breads and cereal that contain at least 2-3 grams of fiber per serving and do not contain added sugar.

Step 5 — Work "DR. JAMIE'S PLAN" for Healthy Weight Loss and Maintenance

Replace two meals per day with soy protein-based shakes. These shakes should be vitamin-mineral enriched to be healthy meal replacements. If you are only 10 pounds overweight or so, you could just replace one meal per day with these shakes. These shakes should have 20-25 grams protein (including the nonfat milk or soymilk used) and 200-250 calories. Fresh or frozen fruit can be used for flavoring.

Eat 4 to 5 times per day. Snacks should contain some protein, focusing on portion control. I recommend a 1 oz. bag of soy nuts, a protein bar (at least 12 grams of protein per serving), a piece of fresh fruit, or cut-up raw veggies with low-fat dressing/dip for an occasional treat. Over time, learn to like raw veggies plain. They are another key to long-term success in weight loss as well as good health.

Your main meal should consist of the following:

- 3-6 oz lean meat, poultry, or fish—broiled or baked
- Large green salad, with plenty of colorful additions—red pepper, shredded carrot, sliced zucchini, broccoli florets, mushrooms, green onion, sliced oranges, tomatoes, etc.
- 1 cup steamed veggies—asparagus, green beans, broccoli, red onion, etc.
- Small whole grain roll (plain) or 1/3 cup brown rice
(*Choose foods from my Optimal Eating Guide in this chapter.*)

Never skip breakfast. It is essential to revving up your metabolism each morning and should ideally consist of some protein and fruit. A high-fat or high sugar breakfast will *not* help the metabolism and will make you feel sluggish, rather than energized. Breakfast should be "breaking the fast" of overnight—not a feast!

Drink five to six eight-ounce glasses of fresh (or bottled) water daily. This is essential for optimum kidney function, healthy skin, and appetite control. Sometimes it feels like huger when it's really thirst!

Step 6—Wisely Select from the Best Commercial Plans/Popular Diet Plans to Assist You

I will not provide an exhaustive discussion of the hundreds of diets flooding the market today, but will comment on a few and, hopefully, guide you to a safe and long-term solution. There is a "diet book" for almost every celebrity. Many diets are fads with just a minor change or addition from the last big diet. The main categories in the popular diet plans are "high complex carbohydrate, low-fat" (a la Dr. Dean Ornish) and "high protein, low carbohydrate" (a la Dr. Atkins). Dr. Barry Sears, author of *The Zone Diet*, has a more balanced diet plan, suggesting moderate amounts of protein, fat, and carbohydrates. Most of the celebrity-endorsed diets are versions of one of these three.

The "Ornish approach" has the backing of the American Heart Association, the American Dietetics Association, and the American Diabetes Association. It is also probably the most difficult plan to follow. Many people have trouble in eliminating meat and other fat sources (butter, margarine, etc.), which is necessary in this type of plan. Dr. Ornish has had a great deal of success with actually reversing atherosclerosis in those individuals who embrace his way of eating. He focuses on an almost vegetarian approach, with the elimination of most animal-based products, but includes fish. He focuses heavily on fruits and vegetables, small amounts of healthy oils, and whole grains. This is essentially how I eat personally. I realize, however, that this plan is a hard one to comply with for meat eaters and those who don't have time to prepare fresh foods with plenty of fresh produce.

The Atkins approach has received much publicity—generally

negative—from the medical community and positive from everyone else. Why? People are embracing this approach because 1) it is
easy, 2) you are told you can eat unlimited amounts of meats and
fats, and 3) many people lose weight very quickly. This is exactly
why I do *not* support this approach. It tends to be extremely low
in fiber and micronutrients (found in carbohydrate foods—fruits,
whole grains, veggies), it encourages people to eat high amounts
of saturated fats (proven to raise cholesterol, which is associated
with an increased risk of heart disease and certain cancers), and
it is extremely difficult to stick with (which results in a higher
likelihood of yo-yo dieting).

The Zone approach is more moderate and balanced, as well
as being a scientifically-sound plan that incorporates more grains
and fruit than allowed in the Atkins approach. Dr. Barry Sears has
put his name behind foods that can be used as part of his healthy
eating plan.

The South Beach Diet, a top bestseller in 2003, is another
version of a high protein, low carbohydrate method of weight
loss. Written by Arthur Agatston, a Miami cardiologist, this diet
is a sound one, offering a comprehensive approach that includes
exercise. Its biggest drawback is that it is complicated to follow,
which would be a "deal breaker" for the marginally-motivated
person.

The commercial plans, such as Weight Watchers, LA Physicians Diet Centers, and Jenny Craig, offer the real benefit of
a support structure. You have regular weigh-ins, group support
meetings, healthy eating seminars, and counselors to help you stay
on track. They provide a variety of foods, shakes, and supplements,
and have proven very successful for many.

There are also direct-selling companies, such as Herbalife International, Pharmanex, and Usana that offer a variety of weight
control products. These companies provide an array of meal replacements, healthy snacks, and herbal accelerators. The distribu-

tors with these companies can provide the support needed to help you believe in yourself—to give you the confidence needed to change eating habits and lose weight. These distributors can serve as an outside "conscience," while still allowing the dieter to lose weight "on her own," without having to be weighed by someone else.

I can't emphasize strongly enough that being overweight or obese carries significant health risks. The good news, however, is that you can be in control of your weight. You don't have to live with the challenges and health risks of obesity. Improve your nutrition, develop healthy eating habits, and become a thinner, healthier *you*.

FOLLOW-UP PREVENTIVE PERSCRIPTION

HOW TO PUT YOU IN CONTROL OF YOUR WEIGHT

Go through the following steps to put you in control of your weight for good. Develop your own *Personal Plan for Weidght Reduction!*

First — GATHER THE FACTS

Are you overweight? Check the BMI Chart found earlier in this chapter. If your BMI is 25 or greater, you should lose weight, lose body fat, and look at your health history.

Do you have health problems from being overweight, or are there obesity-related diseases in your family, such as heart disease, high blood pressure, diabetes, stroke, or cancer? If so, consider weight loss goals to be essential to your health! Being overweight, you are a walking time bomb.

Is your BMI 30 or higher? If it is, it's urgent that you lose weight and find a way to keep it off. I guarantee that if you embrace the plan below, permanently adopting necessary changes, you will lose weight *and* keep it off for life.

Are you extremely motivated and highly disciplined? If so, you can probably read the plan below and incorporate needed changes into your lifestyle without any other assistance. The great majority of folks, however, will benefit from enlisting the help of a spouse, significant other, or parents, if still living at home. If you have more than 30 pounds to lose, I really suggest finding an additional support system. Either sign on with a competent trainer at the health club or get involved in a meeting-based system, such as Weight Watchers, Herbalife, etc. You might also join forces with others at work that want or need to lose weight. The important thing is to set up a support system that will motivate and inspire you to find and retain weight loss success.

Second — CREATE A PLAN OF ACTION

Specific suggestions for losing weight and regaining health:

1. Use soy protein-based meal replacement shakes for 1-2 meals per day.
2. Eat 4-5 times per day: ideally breakfast and lunch as shakes, one meal, and one snack.
3. *Do not skip breakfast*—it is essential to revving up your metabolism each day.
4. Take a multivitamin-mineral and a combination antioxidant to assure no nutritional deficiencies.
5. Choose foods from each step on the Optimal Eating Guide.
6. Drink at least 6-8 glasses of fluids per day. Fluids can include green tea, which I recommend for energy and weight loss support, as well as for its immunity properties.
7. Add *movement* to your daily routine, which is critical for weight control. (See Chapter 7 for full discussion/ suggestions).

8. Use safe, science-based herbal supplements as needed.

- **A multi-vitamin & mineral complex.** Should be formulated to be taken 2-3 times per day. Taking a multi-vitamin & mineral complex is important to assure that no nutritional deficiencies occur while reducing calories to lose weight.
- **A green tea supplement.** This can be either liquid tea or a capsule. Look for ECGC content to be specified on the label. ECGC (catechins) can support metabolism and immune function.
- **Omega-3 supplement.** This is important to decrease the inflammation effects of obesity, improve circulation, and reduce risk of heart disease. Overall, our diets are extremely deficient in omega-3, which is believed to be a factor in many chronic diseases.
- **Fiber supplement.** Look for a blend of soluble and insoluble fibers that can be mixed into your shakes or a glass of water after your evening meal, ideally providing 5 grams of fiber per serving.

Third — MOVE

See Chapter 7 to learn more about the importance of physical activity and exercise in your life. Exercise helps with weight control, increases longevity, improves mood, and is essential to overall good health.

Fourth — STAY WITH THE PLAN

Set goals and adhere to them. If you have a few bad days or even a bad week, don't get derailed from long-range goals. Pick yourself up, get back on track, and keep going.

Keep a food diary for a few days. This can be very helpful in assessing how you are doing. Be honest! Remember the soda you grabbed on the way out the door, the crackers you were munching as you prepared dinner, and the six bites of ice cream you ate standing at the freezer door during commercial breaks last night!

Exercise. Get more movement in your day. Remember to see your physician if you have serious or chronic diseases or have been told to limit your exercise in any way.

Keep asking for the support you need from your family and friends. Those who seem to sabotage your plan may be people you'll want to minimize your contact with.

If you have chronic diseases or are on medications, check with a doctor to let her know you are losing weight the right way. Ask her when you should come in for a check up. Keep in mind, some medications may slow weight loss. Other medications, including those for blood pressure, cholesterol elevation, diabetes, and arthritis or digestive disorders, may need to be adjusted or even eliminated as weight is lost—which, of course, is great news!

Be sure to set reasonable expectations. Keep in mind that you didn't gain the weight overnight; and don't expect to lose it quickly, especially if you have a significant amount to lose. I recommend aiming for a weight loss of 1-2 pounds per week. You may lose significantly more in the first week or two, especially if you weigh over 250 pounds. A pound or two may not sound like much, but it can really add up. If you lose 2 pounds per week, that's 52 pounds in 6 months and 104 pounds in a year! Remember to exercise patience. This whole process is not just about losing weight. It's about "resetting your life."

CHAPTER 7

EXERCISE
a Deterrent to Disease

Points to ponder as you read:

- ✓ Why is a sedentary lifestyle a threat to your health?
- ✓ Besides weight control, what other ways does exercise benefit you?
- ✓ How much exercise do you need to be healthy?
- ✓ What are some tips for making exercise a part of your daily life?

Most Americans think of exercise as a four-letter word masquerading in eight letters. While we all find nicely-muscled men and slender, shapely women attractive, we don't always acknowledge that to be in great shape takes consistent attention to physical activity and exercise. Many people will give up before they try, feeling they could never have a great body. But, leading an active lifestyle confers far more benefits than just a fit body. People who exercise regularly increase their chances of living longer, healthier, and more independent lives. Exercise is positively correlated with a reduction in the risk of *many* diseases, including heart disease, breast and prostate cancer, hypertension, Type 2 diabetes, osteoporosis, osteoarthritis—and the list goes on.

According to the surgeon general of the United States, 60% of adults do not engage in the recommended amount of exercise, and another 25% engage in NO physical exercise at all! These statistics confirm the fact that more people die from leading a sedentary lifestyle than from smoking cigarettes! And consider this staggering statistic: approximately 130 million Americans (over ⅓ of the population) suffer from illnesses that could be prevented, at least in part, by regular exercise. Just imagine, by exercising 45 minutes just 4 times per week, you might avoid heart disease, diabetes, breast and colon cancer, hip fractures, and arthritis.

Take a look at the lists of benefits that are possible when you commit to make exercise and physical activity a regular part of your life.

BENEFITS OF REGULAR PHYSICAL EXERCISE

Health Benefits/Disease Prevention
The following are health and disease prevention benefits from being active.

Exercise
1. Helps with weight loss (especially body fat) and maintaining a healthy weight. A study published in the Journal of the American Medical Association in January 2003 showed that regular brisk walking (45 minutes, 5 days a week) resulted in a 4.2% reduction in body weight and a 7% reduction in intra-abdominal fat in overweight and obese postmenopausal women. This is a very important finding as this intra-abdominal fat is directly linked to diabetes and heart disease.
2. Lowers the resting heart rate by allowing the heart to pump more blood per beat, which takes extra stress off the heart when you are at rest.
3. May lower blood pressure, both systolic and diastolic.
4. May reduce total cholesterol and increase HDL, the good type of cholesterol that protects you from developing atherosclerosis. In fact, exercise is the only intervention

which consistently raises HDL.

5. Reduces circulating levels of triglycerides, another risk factor for heart disease.

6. Improves the function of the immune system so it can better defend you from everything from the common cold to cancer.

7. Reduces the risk of developing coronary artery disease, in addition to the lipid-reducing effects.

8. Increases insulin sensitivity of cells to help reduce risk of Type 2 diabetes (adult onset diabetes). Insulin resistance is part of a metabolic syndrome known as Syndrome X, consisting of abnormal blood lipids, insulin resistance, and a high likelihood of heart disease and diabetes. Exercise can improve all of the components of this syndrome, although weight loss is essential as well.

9. Reduces the risk of developing both breast and colon cancer. In fact, the American Cancer Society states that along with healthy dietary choices, exercise is the highest determinant of cancer risk.

10. May reduce the frequency and severity of migraine and tension headaches.

11. May reduce the risk of having a stroke.

Improved Functional Capacity

Another benefit of exercise is improved functional capacity.

Exercise:

1. Increases muscular strength and overall stamina—whether your interest is gardening, dancing up a storm on Friday night, or hiking Saturday afternoon.

2. Improves the body's ability to maximally uptake oxygen (Vo2max) and deliver oxygen to working muscles or, in layman's terms, makes you more physically fit.

3. Protects bone density and decreases the risk of osteoporosis.

4. Helps maintain and improve the resting metabolic rate (RMR). This allows more effective weight loss and prevents gaining it back.

Isometric (weight-lifting) exercise helps provide protection against injury and also helps to maintain joint health. As you age, regular exercise, both cardio and weight-lifting, helps maintain balance and coordination. This can greatly increase your ability to live independently, well into your 90's.

Stress Management and Emotional Well-Being

Regular physical exercise can:

1. Reduce the level of anxiety and help you manage stress more effectively.
2. Improves self-esteem and feelings of confidence.
3. Lessens irritability and moodiness; heightens overall psychological well-being.
4. Allow you to focus on goal-setting, providing an opportunity to achieve goals through consistency and dedication.
5. Assists many to quit smoking without weight gain.
6. Help you fall asleep more quickly and achieve more restful sleep.
7. Boosts energy and improve concentration and job performance.

Weight Management

One huge plus of exercise is that it helps achieve increased muscle mass and loss of body fat. Why is that important? For every one kilogram (about 2.2 pound) of muscle built, an extra 110 calories per day is needed to maintain it. This means that the more muscle, the more you can eat and not gain weight (now is that good news or what)!

Specifically, exercise helps the body with weight loss, and then makes maintaining an ideal weight easier by:

- **Regulating appetite.** Regular moderate exercise actually regulates the appetite, helping you to truly eat fewer calories.

- **Increasing metabolism.** Even moderate exercise creates up to an eight-fold increase in the metabolic rate (calorie burning) for hours after the exercise. This means that the body continues to burn calories at a higher rate for several hours after moderate exercise. This residual effect, not the exercise itself, is its greatest contribution to weight control.

- **Maintaining and building muscle.** The movement involved with exercise requires you to use your muscles, which causes the necessary physiological changes for muscle to maintain (or even increase) its size and strength. Since every pound of muscle requires 50 to 100 calories per day to sustain itself and since fat is burned almost exclusively in the muscle, maintaining your muscle is crucial to losing body fat. Without exercise, you'll tend to lose muscle, which reduces your body's ability to burn fat and maintain a healthy weight. So you either "use it or lose it."

- **Increasing fat-burning enzymes.** Muscles have very specific enzymes which burn only fat. Research has shown that people who exercise regularly have far more fat-burning enzymes in their muscles than people who are sedentary. In other words, exercise causes the body to "gear up" its ability to burn fat more efficiently.

- **Changing the body's chemistry**. Exercise positively affects a number of hormones in the body which are related to fat storage such as insulin, adrenaline, and cortisol. Endorphins, small morphine-like chemicals, are secreted in the brain when you exercise briskly. Research has validated that endorphins help to create a feeling of well-being and alleviate stress. In other words, endorphins are the body's natural Prozac and Valium.

BECOMING A "MOVER"

Are you ready to make exercise a routine? How about just committing to *moving* more every day? Here are some tips for becoming a *mover*, while you begin to create an exercise plan.

1. Walk up the escalator or bypass the elevator and take the stairs.
2. Instead of driving around the mall parking lot until you find that spot right in front, pretend the car is a Ferrari and park it as far as you can from the mall entrance.
3. Turn off the television and walk the dog. This will help the pup maintain a healthy weight too. Dogs and cats are at risk for heart disease, osteoarthritis, and cancer if they are overweight, just like humans.
4. Put on lively music (i.e. Shania Twain's "Feel Like a Woman") while you do housework. It will get done faster and you'll have a smile on your face as well!

The real trick is to be active throughout the day. Stand instead of sit, walk instead of drive, etc. Recent research confirms that three 10-minute bouts of moderate exercise can add up to the same benefits, for weight loss and heart health, as one continuous 30-minute session. Dr. Roseann M. Lyle, Purdue professor and Chair of American College of Sports Medicine (ACSM) Strategic Health Initiative on Aging, defines moderate exercise as any dynamic activity equivalent in intensity to three to six times the average resting metabolic rate, units called METs. To achieve improvements in fitness and health, you need to expend three to six METs in 30 minutes, five to seven times per week. Housework, gardening, and leisurely cycling all qualify under Dr. Lyle's plan. Check out the chart below and see how many METs you are currently using each week. Can you be more active than you currently are?

ACTIVITY (1 HOUR)	METs	CALORIES
Aerobic dancing	6.5	455

Aerobic step exercise	8.5	595
Ballroom dancing	4.5	315
Bowling	3.0	210
Calisthenics	8.0	560
Carrying groceries upstairs	7.5	525
Carrying infant (or 15 lbs.)	3.5	245
Circuit training	8.0	560
Cycling (leisurely)	4.0	280
Cycling (moderate)	5.7	399
Golf (walking with clubs)	4.5	315
Gardening	4.4	308
Heavy house cleaning	3.0	210
Hiking hills (no backpack)	6.9	483
Home repairs (light)	3.0	210
House painting	5.0	350
Jogging in place	8.0	560
Miniature golf	3.0	210
Mopping floors	3.5	245
Moving furniture	6.0	420
Mowing lawn (hand mower)	6.0	420
Mowing lawn (power mower)	5.5	385
Raking the yard	4.3	301
Running, walking with pet	4.0	280
Running (5 mph/12 min. Mile)	8.0	560
Scrubbing floors, bathroom	3.8	266
Slimnastics, jazzercise	6.0	420
Sweeping floors	3.3	231
Sweeping sidewalk, garage	4.0	280
Swimming (slow)	4.5	315
Swimming (fast)	7.0	490
Tai chi	4.0	280
Tennis (singles)	7.5	525
Tennis (doubles)	5.0	350
Vacuuming	3.5	245
Walking for pleasure	3.5	245

Walking 3 mph (uphill)	6.0	420
Walking 4 mph (flat surface)	5.0	350
Walking upstairs	8.0	560
Water aerobics	4.0	280

The actual MET value could be higher or lower; 3 METs is equivalent to expending approximately 210 calories. Actual calories expended depends on body weight.

I strongly suggest you begin by creating a weekly chart to keep track of your progress. This not only keeps you accountable, but will also highlight your progress in making *movement* a part of the path to wellness.

Remember the "Personal Pathway to Health and Vitality?" (See Chapter 2) Exercise/movement is a key component. The surgeon general's report also calls for moderate physical exercise. Activities such as biking, dancing, or brisk walking for 30 minutes or playing basketball or tennis for 20 minutes can burn approximately 150 kilocalories of energy per day. Keep in mind that low impact activities, such as walking or water activities, put the least amount of pressure on joints, but weightbearing activities are key to maintaining bone mass and reducing the risk of osteoporosis. (See Chapter 13)

PLANNING AN EXERCISE PROGRAM

When an exercise program is planned, base it on personal goals, as well as your capabilities. Many of us make the mistake of trying to do too much too soon, burning out on exercise before we really get started. Read the following "Joy of Exercise" and see if you can relate.

THE JOY OF EXERCISE

Dear Diary . . . For my birthday present this year, my husband (the dear) purchased a week of personal training at the local health club for me. Although I am still in great shape since playing on my high school softball team (let's say over 30 years ago and leave it at that), I decided it would be a good idea to go ahead and give it a try. I called the club and made my reservation with a personal trainer I'll call Bob, who identified himself as a 56-year-old aerobics instructor and model for athletic clothing and swimwear. My husband seemed pleased with my enthusiasm to get started. The club encouraged me to keep a diary to chart my progress.

Monday:

Started my day at 6 a.m. Tough to get out of bed, but found it was well worth it when I arrived at the health club to find Bob waiting for me. He is something of a Greek god, with whitish-gray hair, dancing dark eyes, and a dazzling white smile. Woo Hoo!! Bob gave me a tour and showed me the machines. He took my pulse after five minutes on the treadmill. He was alarmed that my pulse was so fast, but I attributed it to standing next to him in his Lycra aerobic outfit. I enjoyed watching the skillful way in which he conducted his aerobics class after my workout today. Very inspiring. Bob was encouraging as I did my sit-ups, although my stomach was already aching from holding it in the whole time he was around. This is going to be a *fantastic* week!

Tuesday:

I drank a whole pot of herbal tea, but I finally made it out the door. Bob made me lie on my back and push a heavy iron bar into the air—then he put weights on it! My legs were a little wobbly on the treadmill, but I made the full mile. Bob's rewarding smile made it all worthwhile. I feel *great*!! This is a whole new way of life for me.

Wednesday:

The only way I can brush my teeth is by laying the toothbrush on the counter and moving my mouth back and forth over it. I believe I have a hernia in both pectorals. Driving was *ok* as long as I didn't try to steer or stop. I parked on top of a Geo in the club parking lot. Bob was impatient with me, insisting that my screams bothered other club members. His voice is a little too perky early in the morning and, when he scolds, he gets this nasally whine that is *very* annoying. My chest hurt when I got on the treadmill, so Bob put me on the stair monster. *Why* would anyone invent a machine to simulate an activity rendered obsolete by elevators? Bob told me it would help me get in shape and enjoy life. He said some other [deleted] things too.

Thursday:

Bob was waiting for me with his vampire-like teeth exposed and thin, cruel lips pulled back in a snarl. I couldn't help being a half an hour late; it took me that long to tie my shoes. Bob took me to work out with dumbbells. When he was not looking, I ran and hid in the men's room. He sent Lars to find me. Then, as a punishment, he put me on the rowing machine which I promptly sank.

Friday:

I hate Bob more than any human being has ever hated any other human being in the history of the world. Stupid, skinny, anemic little cheerleader! If there was a part of my body I could move without unbearable pain, I would beat him with it. Bob wanted me to work on my triceps. I don't have any triceps! And if you don't want dents in the floor, don't hand me the *@*#$ barbells or anything that weighs more than a sandwich (which I am sure you learned in the sadist school you attended and graduated from suma cum laude). The treadmill flung me off, and I landed on a health and nutrition teacher. Why couldn't it have been someone softer, like the drama coach or the choir director?

Saturday:

Bob left a message on my answering machine in his grating, shrill voice, wondering why I did not show up today. Just hearing his voice made me want to smash the machine with my planner.

However, as I lacked the strength to even use the TV remote, I ended up catching eleven straight hours of the Weather Channel.

Sunday:

I'm having the Church van pick me up for services today so I can go and thank God that this week is over. I will also pray that next year my husband will choose a gift for me that is more fun—like a root canal.

Our diary-writing exerciser from above would have benefited from the following guidelines:

CONSULT A PHYSICIAN. Before starting any exercise plan, check with your primary care physician, especially if there are chronic health conditions. If you have had a heart attack or have significant coronary heart disease, ask your physician for specific guidelines. It is usually safe for just about everyone to begin with a walking program, but, if you are under the regular care of a physician, check with him or her first.

BE REALISTIC. Fitness advertising often promotes unrealistic expectations about what you can achieve with exercise. Losing weight is a goal shared by many but it takes time and commitment for it to be safe and effective. Regular moderate exercise will speed your weight loss, but still plan on losing about two pounds per week. Set short-term goals that highlight achievements other than just pounds lost. For instance, focus on inches lost or improved energy level. Go back to the lists of benefits from regular exercise found earlier in this chapter and pick out a few that mean something for you, such as sleeping better or increased concentration at work.

FOCUS ON THE SHORT-TERM. Long-term goals are important, but a successful exercise program relies on short-term goals based on tangible results or, in other words, outcomes you can appreciate right away. Think about increasing the number of repetitions, the amount of weight being lifted, the distance you are running, or the amount of time spent on the stationary bike. Remember that a successful exercise program calls for continuous goal setting. Map out what you want to accomplish during tomorrow's workout or over the next two weeks. Even the smallest goal is useful. For some, the act of showing up at the gym is a goal in itself. I have found great benefit recently from working with a trainer. He has pushed me to higher weights and more challenging exercises than I have ever done. Years of running as my chief form of exercise has left me with recurrent low back pain and pretty weak arms and shoulders. In just two months of working with my trainer for only two hours per week, I have *far* less back pain and can see better tone in my triceps and in my thighs (I didn't expect that after 25 years of running).

WRITE IT DOWN. Some people find it reassuring and inspiring to record their fitness goals. Use an exercise logbook or journal to write down objectives. Or, sign a "workout contract" outlining goals with a personal trainer or a workout partner. If walking is the choice of activity, find a friend with the same free time and keep each other accountable. Women often find this system keeps them more active and allows for the development of a deeper friendship with a previously casual friend.

CHOOSE ACTIVITIES THAT YOU ENJOY. If you hate running, it's unlikely that you will enjoy going out in the cold, the rain, the heat, etc. to pound the pavement! If you are embarrassed to be seen in workout clothes, then joining a gym probably won't be the best way for you to get fit. Find something you like to do. For instance, if you like sports, find a local adult league or club in which to participate. If you prefer solo exercising, try a video tape at home or go for a long bicycle ride. Do what you can to make exercising fun and not a chore.

START SLOWLY AND DON'T OVERDO IT. Studies show that the most common cause of injury is exercising too aggressively—the "too much, too soon" syndrome. To avoid soreness or injury, start out slowly and gradually build up. Even if you consider yourself to be in good shape, start any new exercise at a relatively low intensity and gradually increase the time, reps, weights, etc. over a number of weeks.

"NO PAIN, NO GAIN" IS A MYTH. Exercise should require some effort, but discomfort isn't necessary and can lead to overuse injuries. If you are in an exercise class, beware of any instructor who says that exercise must hurt (or burn) to do any good. Pain is a warning sign, do not ignore it. If you have pain during an exercise, stop doing it and ask a trainer or instructor for help in doing the exercise properly. General muscle soreness that comes after beginning an exercise program is to be expected. It should be fairly mild and last only a day. If you stretch both before exercising (except when walking) and as part of a cool down routine, there will be less muscle soreness, as well as lessening the possibility of injury.

DO WHAT YOU CAN WHEN YOU CAN. The overall goal is to participate in some activity, ideally both an aerobic activity and a weight-training activity, three to four times per week for 30 to 45 minutes. However, if you just don't have 30 or 45 minutes to set aside, it's okay to divide the activity into smaller sessions, which will still net similar results.

WEAR APPROPRIATE AND WELL-FITTING FOOT-WEAR. Wearing improper or worn out shoes can put unnecessary stress on hips, knees, ankles, and feet. This is important because these are the areas of the body where 90% of all sports injuries occur. It is worth the cost and effort to go to a higher end sporting goods store and ask for a salesperson that is knowledgeable about shoe fitting. Tell him or her what activity you are involved in. Shoes for walking are quite different than running shoes or court shoes (and different ones are needed for tennis as compared to basketball). Your feet, lower back, and hips will thank you for providing them with the proper support.

WATCH YOUR FORM AND POSTURE. In most activities,

stress can result from poor form whether it's landing on the balls of your feet (instead of on your heels) when running or constantly cycling in the highest gears. Keep the back in alignment by following these pointers: keep abdominal muscles contracted (yes, that means suck it in), buttocks tucked in, and check to be sure the patella (knee cap) is aligned over the feet between the big and second toe. This is very important with floor exercises, running, and even brisk walking.

If there is discomfort while using certain weight machines or if you are unable to increase repetitions or weights, ask a trainer for advice. Even if you cannot afford the extra cost of a one-on-one trainer, you can get advice on proper technique and form free of charge. Be sure to alternate your specific exercises. Rotate exercises every other day that focus on the arms and chest with exercises that focus on the legs and back.

WARM UP AND COOL DOWN AND DON'T BOUNCE WHILE STRETCHING. Stretching to your limit and performing quick, pulsing movements, actually shortens muscles and increases the chance of muscle tears and soreness. Instead do "static" stretches, which call for gradually stretching a particular muscle group until you feel resistance. Slow, steady motion is the best. Remember the alignment discussion above.

AVOID HIGH-IMPACT AEROBICS. Surveys have found that most aerobics instructors and many of their students suffer from injuries to their shins, calves, lower back, ankles, and knees because of the repetitive, jarring movements of some aerobics routines. A low impact aerobic routine can easily raise the heart rate enough to provide cardiovascular benefits without the risk of injury. Many studies have shown a greater improvement in fitness and more significant weight loss with low impact aerobics. Water aerobics can be fun and sometimes less intimidating. This exercise is essentially non-weight-bearing, so does not put stress on joints. Note: Water aerobics and swimming do *not* protect bone mass, so menopausal women should be doing walking or some other weight-bearing activity in addition to the water activities.

TRY WALKING. A brisk walk can burn up to 100 calories per mile or 300 calories per hour, and can improve cardiovascular fitness by improving circulation to the heart and lungs and increasing their efficiency. A regular walking program may lower blood pressure in people with hypertension. Many studies have demonstrated the potential for weight loss with brisk walking programs. For instance, a study of 100 postmenopausal women showed an average weight loss of 25 pounds over a year of brisk walking 30 minutes five days a week—without changing diet. Imagine what you can do if you "clean up" your eating habits and begin walking regularly!

TRY YOGA. Yoga and Pilates have become extremely popular recently. They both provide excellent low impact workouts that can lead to great improvements in fitness, strength, flexibility, and calorie burning (weight and fat loss). I recommend joining a class if you are new to either of these disciplines. There are excellent videos, though, if working out at home fits your lifestyle better.

HYDRATE. Always drink a full eight-ounce glass of water before exercising, especially if exercising in warm temperatures. Water hydrates the body and replaces necessary fluids lost when sweating. Unless you are sweating profusely, water is perfectly adequate to rehydrate after exercise. If working out strenuously or for several hours, especially outdoors in warm weather, consider an isotonic sports beverage. But, for most people who are working out moderately for under an hour, these drinks are unnecessary and provide unneeded calories.

MAKE MOVEMENT AND BEING ACTIVE A GOAL FOR LIFE. With all the health benefits that come from exercise, can you really afford to do without it?

FOLLOW-UP PREVENTIVE PERSCRIPTION

MAKE A COMMITMENT TO YOUR HEALTH BY SCHEDULING REGULAR PHYSICAL ACTIVITY.

Keep these helpful hints in mind:

- Start slowly if exercise is new.
- Check with a doctor if there are chronic health problems.
- Set goals and rewards—for instance, treat yourself to a massage at the local day spa for walking four days per week for two weeks.
- Choose an activity you like. Be creative. Join a softball team, find a walking partner, go biking on the local trail, etc.
- Try a pedometer to chart progress. This tiny device clips to the waistband and counts the steps taken. Challenge office-mates to achieve the most steps per month with a small money pool for the winner. The SW-200-024 Digi-walker from New Lifestyles is a reliable and easy-to-use pedometer and costs just $27. (Call 888-748-5377 or visit www.digiwalker.com)
- Remember to eat right. If you are feeling too tired to exercise, make yourself a protein smoothie with soy protein powder mixed in soymilk with a half cup of frozen berries and two ice cubes—blend and drink. You will sail through the workout!
- Try a race or walkathon. There is an abundance of races and walkathons for excellent causes, everything from supporting breast cancer research and childhood leukemia research to promoting AIDS awareness and raising funds for the American Heart Association. Involvement in one of these races provides a goal and raises money for the cause of choice. To find out what events are in your area, go to www.racewalk.com.
- Chart results—weight loss, inch loss, and even body

fat loss. For best accuracy, measure in the morning before having anything to eat or drink.

- Warm up and cool down (see the stretching routine earlier in this chapter). Warming up before and stretching after exercise will prevent soreness and lessen the possibility of injury.
- Breathe! Deep breathing improves oxygenation of tissues, increases energy, and can actually help with form.
- Wear the right shoes for the activity—be sure they fit well. When shopping for shoes, walk around the store, go up on your toes, and mimic the activity you will do in the shoes before you purchase them.
- Supplements may help. Try glucosamine and MSM for joints and ligament flexibility, L-arginine and vitamin E for improved performance and less post-exercise soreness, green tea and protein smoothies for a natural energy boost, and calcium and vitamin D to protect bone mass.

CHAPTER 8

STRESSES AND STRAINS OF THE 21ST CENTURY
Could It Be Anxiety or Depression?

Points to ponder as you read:

- ✓ What are the signs of stress?
- ✓ What are the harmful effects of stress?
- ✓ How do you learn to manage stress?
- ✓ What is the difference between stress, depression, and anxiety?
- ✓ Is medication required to handle stress-related difficulties, depression, or anxiety?

If I were to ask if you could identify stress, you would probably answer with a resounding "YES" and be able to give me examples like the following.

- Stress is getting a phone call from a doctor after having a series of tests run, having her reassure you there is absolutely nothing to worry about, and then insisting on seeing you in her office first thing tomorrow morning.

- Stress is having a heated argument on the telephone with your spouse three minutes before a meeting where you are making the most important presentation of your career.

- Stress is hurrying home after a 12-hour day at the office and, just as you realize you are driving 50 mph in a 25 mph zone, seeing flashing lights in the rearview mirror.

- Stress is teaching your teenage son, a Mario Andretti wannabe, how to drive.

- Stress is sitting down to pay bills and realizing that you have more month than you do money.

Drawing on your experiences with stress, look at the list below and identify which of the following are stressors:

- You receive a promotion at work.
- Your car has a flat tire.
- You go to a great party that lasts till 2:00 a.m.
- Your two-year-old has an ear infection.
- Your new bedroom set is being delivered.
- Your best friend from college and his new wife come to stay at your house for a week.
- Your allergies are acting up.

If you believe that "all of the above" are stressors, you'd be correct. To most people, stress is synonymous with a negative event or interaction. Our bodies, however, potentially perceive any change, positive or negative, as stressful. Anything that causes a change in your life may result in a sense of stress in your body. Even imagined change fosters stress. For instance, if you fear you will not have enough money to pay your rent or worry about being laid off, your body perceives these experiences as stress.

In the early part of the 20th Century, a scientist named Walter Cannon coined the term "fight or flight response" to describe the body's response to stress. From an evolutionary perspective, this response allowed early humans to "jump into high gear" to avoid a saber-toothed tiger or wooly mastodon. Today, if the body is responding to stressors, it will go through the same physical changes our early ancestors experienced. Pupils widen to let in more light. There is an increase in alertness because of more neurotransmitters in the brain. Adrenal glands begin to pump more adrenaline and other hormones into the bloodstream. The heart races, the blood pressure rises, and muscles tense. The liver starts converting starches to sugars for energy, and digestion slows. Sweat production increases, and the hair on your body may feel prickly and actually stand on end. Experts have even determined that the blood's clotting powers will be enhanced during stressful situations.

While all these physical reactions in ancient times may have helped save our predecessors' lives by readying their bodies to defend themselves, they are no longer useful in modern life. In fact, they can actually be harmful if you keep yourself in an alert state for too many hours each day. Not surprisingly, a daily regimen of faster heartbeat and blood flow than necessary, chronically tense muscles, dysfunctional digestion, and elevated levels of various hormones, including insulin and cortisol, can take its toll. These responses, day in and day out, increase blood pressure, which can lead to heart disease and stroke; instigate inflammatory responses in the lining of arteries, which can set up atherosclerosis; and wreak havoc with insulin, which contributes to the development of insulin resistance and Type 2 diabetes.

In addition, stress depresses the functioning of the immune system and actually depletes many nutrients from the body, including most B vitamins and antioxidants, as well as zinc and other minerals. A weakened immune system, in turn, produces susceptiblity to colds, coughs, and infections. Stress also increases acid production in the stomach, which can lead to peptic ulcer disease and esophageal reflux problems, especially if you are overweight. Finally, stress can also cause imbalances in the normal flora of the digestive tract and other changes that ultimately lead to irritable bowel syndrome.

It is easy to understand the importance of stress management when you realize that in today's hectic pace of life, many are chronically stressed by job, marriage, financial worries, traffic jams, etc. As a result, their bodies are in a constant low-grade state of "fight or flight." This has long-term possible physiologic results of hypertension and heart disease, cancer, autoimmune disorders, and, of course, chronic anxiety and depression. What begins as a hectic life can result in *real disease*. Therefore, it is imperative that everyone of us examine our lives for signs of stress to determine what can be changed to reduce the likelihood of developing one of the myriad diseases and illnesses associated with chronic stress.

It's important to note that women are particularly vulnerable to the effects of stress. Part of this is societal and part can be attributed to genetics. Women today are juggling more than ever before. Over 70% of American women with young children are in the work force. Although men today participate in running the household and helping with children far more than ever before, the majority of tasks still falls in the woman's lap because women are, by nature, caretakers and nurturers. When men have a stressful day at work, they are usually able to go home and relax. Women tend to be in charge of coming up with an idea for dinner (then preparing it), helping their sixth grader understand the complexities of algebra (then moving on to English), scheduling an appointment to take the family dog to the vet for his shots, (then taking him), getting the stain out of a teenage daughter's brand new skirt, (and dealing with her trauma over "my favorite outfit is ruined and what will I wear tomorrow!"), etc.

It is standard for women to grocery shop on the way home from work, prepare dinner, and then supervise homework, baths, and bedtime, before collapsing in exhaustion. They then get up the next day and do it all over again! Women have a hard time slowing down because (1) they feel guilty if they are not the "24-hour woman" and (2) they often deal with feelings of selfishness if they take time out for themselves. When women become angry about too much to do in too little time, it just adds to their stress load. The result is the development of anxiety, depression, chronic headaches, autoimmune disease, or numerous other conditions associated with chronic stress.

Men, of course, are subject to stress as well. They tend to carry the financial worries of the family, which can exacerbate on-the-job stresses to compete and achieve promotions and recognition, as well as planning for the future. In addition, today more men are single parents than ever before, which means these men have to deal with the same issues as women, discussed above.

Now that you realize how harmful stress can be to the body, take a look at the Social Readjustment Rating Scale below. This scale covers changes that may have taken place in your life over the last 12 months. Read through the 43 stressors below and add up the event values that apply to you to determine your total score.

STRESS	EVENT VALUES
1. Death of spouse	100
2. Divorce	60
3. Menopause	60
4. Separation from living partner	60
5. Jail term or probation	60
6. Death of close family member other than spouse	60
7. Serious personal injury or illness	45
8. Marriage or establishing life partnership	45
9. Fired from job	45
10. Marital or relationship reconciliation	40
11. Retirement	40
12. Change in health of immediate family member	40
13. Work more than 40 hours per week	35
14. Pregnancy or causing pregnancy	35
15. Sex difficulties	35
16. Gain of new family member	35
STRESS	EVENT VALUES
17. Business or work role change	35
18. Change in financial state	35
19. Death of a close friend (not a family member)	30

20. Change in number of arguments with spouse or
    Life partner   30
21. Mortgage or loan for a major purpose   25
22. Foreclosure of mortgage or loan   25
23. Sleep less than eight hours per night   25
24. Change in responsibilities at work   25
25. Trouble with in-laws or with children   25
26. Outstanding personal achievement   25
27. Spouse begins or stops work   20
28. Begin or end school   20
29. Change in living conditions
    (Visitors, changing roommates, remodeling house)   20
30. Change in personal habits (diet, exercise, smoking, etc.) 20
31. Chronic allergies   20
32. Trouble with boss   20
33. Change in work hours or conditions   15
34. Moving to new residence   15
35. Presently in pre-menstrual period   15
36. Change in schools   15
37. Change in religious activities   15
38. Change in social activities (more or less than before) 15
39. Minor financial loan   10
40. Change in frequency of family get-togethers   10
41. Vacation   10
42. Presently in winter holiday season   10
43. Minor violation of the law   5

(Adapted from the "Social Readjustment Rating Scale" by Thomas Holmes and Richard Rahe. This scale was first published in the "Journal of Psychosomatic Research.")

TOTAL SCORE:_____

Your score may surprise you. It is crucial to understand, however, that a major change in life has effects that last for long periods of time. It is like dropping a rock into a pond. After the initial splash, ripples of stress, which may continue in your life for at least a year. If you have experienced total stress within the last 12 months of 250 or greater, even if you have normal stress tolerance, you may be overstressed. Persons with low stress tolerance may be overstressed at levels as low as 150.

Keep in mind that being overstressed will make you sick. Carrying too heavy a stress load is like running your car engine past the red line; or leaving your toaster stuck in the "on" position; or running a nuclear reactor past maximum permissible power. Sooner or later, something will break, burn up, or melt down.

As another measure of your stress load, ask yourself the following questions to see if you are currently suffering from too much stress:

- Do you often feel nervous or anxious?
- Do you feel depressed or sad?
- Are you irritable or moody?
- Are you forgetful or have trouble thinking clearly?
- Can you make decisions without agonizing?
- Is it difficult to learn new information?
- Do you have insomnia?
- Are you plagued by negative thoughts?
- Are you accident-prone?
- Do you bite your fingernails?
- Do you have any of the following physical symptoms:

Back pain	Muscle tension
Headaches	Shaking hands
Diarrhea	Constipation
Pounding heart	Chest pain
Sweaty, cold hands	Shortness of breath
Indigestion/gas pains	Burping
Pain in your stomach	Feeling faint or dizzy
Lingering headache	Ringing in the ears
Grinding your teeth	Loss of appetite
Hives or skin rashes	Nausea, vomiting

These physical symptoms *can* be signs of serious medical problems. If you are having one or more of these symptoms and they are new, call your doctor or, if the symptoms are severe, go to an emergency room. If you have had these symptoms or feelings for months or years, however, they are more likely due to chronic stress (see discussion of anxiety below).

After understanding what stress is and how it can harm you, the next step is learning how to manage it.

Hans Selye said, "Without stress, there would be no life." Stress cannot and should not be avoided completely. Selye further pointed out, "Stress is not always necessarily harmful . . . Increased stress results in increased productivity—up to a point. However, this level differs for each [person]. It's very much like the stress on a violin string. Not enough produces a dull, raspy sound. Too much tension makes a shrill, annoying noise or snaps the string. However, just the right degree can create a magnificent tone. Similarly . . . all need to find the proper level of stress that allows [optimal performance]."

One of the ways to manage stress to create a "magnificent tone" in your life is to follow the Triple "A" Map:

- Alter
- Avoid
- Accept

There are three major ways to deal with stress: alter it, avoid it, or accept it by building our resistance or changing our perception. Herbert G. Lingren, Ph.D,. an Extension Family Life Specialist states, "...choosing a low-stress response to life's bumps and bruises will not only preserve your sanity but also your physical health." Try the following to deal with the stresses in your life.

- ALTER YOUR LIFE BY REMOVING THE SOURCE OF THE STRESS. Be more organized in personal and family life, and becoming more efficient in the use of time. Try to have backup plans for any emergency.

- AVOID STRESS BY REMOVING YOURSELF FROM THE STRESSFUL SITUATION, OR FIGURING OUT HOW NOT TO GET THERE IN THE FIRST PLACE. Sometimes it's okay to walk away, to let go, to say "no," to withdraw, to know your limits so you can "live to fight another day."

- ACCEPT THE SITUATION BY EQUIPPING YOURSELF PHYSICALLY AND MENTALLY FOR STRESS. Nutritional choices can help you deal with stress. Eat a balanced diet that emphasizes whole foods, such as lean protein, fresh fruits and vegetables, and whole grains; avoid processed foods, as well as white sugar, flour, and fried foods. Restrict caffeine and alcohol intake to moderate levels to enable the body to deal better physically with stress. Performing regular exercise and have regular health checkups. A body that is physically stressed because of sedentary living and poor eating habits is more likely to buckle under the additional weight of mental stress. Mental health is bolstered by 1) taking a few minutes a day for yourself to recharge your batteries; 2) getting clear about your own goals and priorities in life; and 3) becoming the best person you can be.

Here are some other approaches to dealing with everyday stress that may be helpful:

- TAKE A PROBLEM-SOLVING APPROACH TO A POTENTIALLY STRESSFUL SITUATION. Has this happened before? If so, what did you learn from it? Decide the worst that could happen, and consider your options. Ask yourself: "Will I even remember this incident five years from now?"

- TAKE STOCK OF YOUR WORRIES AND FEARS. Look back over the last year and see how many things worried about came true and how many never happened. Listen to the way you talk to yourself and to others. Do you create unnecessary stress by over-dramatizing situations and making things seem worse than they are? Do you agonize about falling short of perfection?

- TUNE UP YOUR ATTITUDE. Do you dwell on criticism? Jump to conclusions? Expect the worst? Worry about how you appear to other people? Beware of negative thinking. Negative thinking causes stress because it undermines self confidence, causing you to doubt whether or not you are equal to the task you face. You are thinking negatively when you put yourself down, criticize yourself for errors, doubt your abilities, expect failure, etc.

- TALK TO YOURSELF IN A POSITIVE WAY. Say whatever helps you to calm down. "Some day I'll laugh about this," "things could be worse," or "this is a character-building experience."

- PREPARE FOR STRESS. By anticipating stress will be can prepared for it and control it when it happens. For instance, prepare for giving a speech by practicing it several times in advance, polishing your performance and building confidence. Top-level athletes use this technique to ensure that they respond effectively to the stresses of competition.

- USE LAUGHTER TO DIFFUSE STRESS. Proverbs says, "A cheerful heart is a good medicine, but a downcast spirit dries up the bones." We've known for a long time that laughter is helpful to those coping with major illnesses and the stresses of life's problems. Now scientists are saying that laughter can do a lot more. According to research studies, a good laugh increases blood circulation, works abdominal muscles, raises heart rate, and gets the stale air out of your lungs. But, that's not all. An entire hour spent laughing lowers levels of the stress hormones cortisol and epinephrine. It strengthens the immune systems as well, with the body's T-cells, antibodies, and natural killer cells all showing signs of increased activity.

Studies with cancer patients have demonstrated that those who watched funny movies and used laughter had better survival rates. Laughter also releases endorphins that improve mental health, get creative juices flowing, help in problem-solving, and smooth the way during difficult times.

There are also methods to turn off physical responses to stress. Try one of the following methods the next time you feel yourself being physically engulfed by stress.

- BREATHE DEEPLY. Breathing is critical to dealing with stress effectively. A lack of oxygen restricts blood flow and causes muscles to tense. When panicked, you tend to take short, shallow gasps of air, hardly using the diaphragm at all. Your chest muscles and the accessory breathing muscles in your shoulders are overloaded and do all the work of respiration. The next time you are in a stressful situation, (1) sit up straight, (2) inhale through your nose with your mouth closed, (3) exhale through your mouth with your lips pursed (as if you were whistling), (4) make your exhalation twice as long as your inhalation (inhale for two seconds, exhale for four). Use your abdomen when breathing out, consciously pushing the belly out. Try putting one hand over the stomach to see how it rises and falls. You are allowing more air to enter the body, and in the process you will slow down the heart rate, lower blood pressure, and eventually break the stress cycle.

- PRACTICE PROGRESSIVE RELAXATION TECHNIQUES. Two of my favorite ways to deal with stress to lessen its effects upon health and longevity, are exercise and relaxation techniques. Earlier I wrote about the "fight or flight response." Nobel Prize winning physiologist Walter Hess described the opposite response, called—"the relaxation response." By stimulating other parts of the brain, muscle tone relaxes, pulse decreases and breathing and plasma cortisol declines, another hormone secreted by the adrenal glands in response to stress.

There are a variety of relaxation techniques to trigger "the relaxation response," but remember that the optimum approach to dealing with any stress must include exploring the root problem and making changes.

Try this exercise. Sit in a quiet spot and take off your shoes or any uncomfortable clothing, including eyeglasses. Close your eyes, uncross your legs, place your hands in your lap palms up, and let your head rest easily (you can also lie down). Tightening the muscles in your feet and toes and then relax them. Gradually work this tightening and relaxing pattern up through your legs, back, chest, and head, including your face. Clench your jaws, hold the tension, then relax.

Another relaxation exercise is to picture yourself in a pleasant place. Perhaps it's a calm lake or a mountain view that puts your mind at rest. Visualize this scene in your mind as you slowly let each part of the body go limp. Breathe deeply. Aim for at least 10 minutes or more of progressive relaxation, if possible.

To know if you are truly relaxed, feel the temperature of your hands. Warm hands mean a relaxed body. If your hands are still cool, you know you are still tense (put them on your neck to test the temperature). Continue your relaxation until they warm up.

To get the most benefit from any relaxation technique, you'll have to practice it often. Choose a time of day when you won't be interrupted. Turn off the radio, TV, and stereo. If you learn how to switch into this relaxation mode in private, you'll be better able to do it under stress.

- EXERCISE YOUR SHOULDERS AND NECK MUSCLES. We store stress in the muscles of the upper back, shoulders, and neck. Learn how to release this tension by gently moving that area of the body. The movements don't have to be complicated. To loosen up the tightness:

  - **Shrug your shoulders.** Stand up or sit. Push the shoulders up around your ears and tighten the muscles as much as possible. Let them drop and relax. Repeat.

- **Stretch up and overhead.** While sitting in a chair, bring your arms overhead, holding them straight with fingertips pointing toward the ceiling. Elbows shouldn't be locked. Reach skyward with your right hand and then with your left hand. You should feel the stretch, but nothing should hurt. Breathe comfortably throughout this motion.
- **Swing your arms**. Stand up. Let your arms hang loose at your sides. Lean forward slightly and swing your arms back and forth and from side to side across your chest. Relax. Stop swinging. Lift one arm up over your head, and look over your right shoulder. Hold that position. Relax and breathe deeply.
- **Walk.** Go for a walk, but leave your pocketbook behind; if you carry a bag, you might throw your body off balance. Walk briskly and throw your shoulders back as you move. Don't race. Hurrying may make you slouch forward unconsciously, creating tension in the curve of your shoulders. Throw your shoulders back, expand your chest area, and breathe deeply.

There are literally thousands of studies that have documented positive results and health benefits of using the methods described above to turn off physical responses to stress. Below is a list of conditions that have shown measurable improvement from these methods:

- Anxiety
- Anger management problems
- Asthma
- Depression
- Diabetes, both Type 1 & 2
- Headaches and various pain syndromes
- Heartburn and reflux
- Hypertension

- Irritable bowel syndrome
- Premenstrual syndrome
- Smoking cessation
- TMJ dysfunction (temporal-mandibular joint)

(Some suggestions above were adapted from The American Medical Women's Association Women's Complete Healthbook, edited by Roselyn Payne Epps and Susan Cobb Stewart.)

Finally, here are some additional alternative therapies to try for stress reduction:

Acupressure	Aromatherapy
Arts therapies	Chiropractic
Vitamin & mineral therapy	Music therapy
Pet therapy	Yoga
A warm, hot bath	Massage
Nature walks	

For some, it is difficult to determine if the symptoms experienced are a result of stress, or something potentially more serious—such as an anxiety disorder or depression. If your symptoms are interfering with your life in a significant way, you should definitely consult your primary care physician or a mental health counselor. Statistics from the National Institute of Mental Health indicate that about 20 million Americans are diagnosed with anxiety each year, or approximately 13% of the population. People with anxiety are likely to visit up to 10 health professionals before they are properly diagnosed. Even after diagnosis, people with anxiety are three times more likely to use medical services than those with other diagnoses.

ANXIETY DISORDERS

Anxiety disorders come in different forms—the most common being generalized anxiety disorder (GAD). Others include Obsessive-compulsive disorder (OCD), panic disorder, phobias, and post-traumatic stress disorder (PTSD). Doctors tend to classify people with anxiety disorders as "the worried well" because anxiety makes itself known through a wide variety of physical symptoms, including shortness of breath, chest pain, dizziness, odd or atypical aches and pains, difficulty sleeping, etc. If you have one of these anxiety disorders, it is important to be aware of changes in your health and not just assign every symptom to "my anxiety." If something new is going on in your body, be sure your physician is aware that this is a new problem and you are not sure if it is connected to your anxiety or not.

People with anxiety have a high likelihood of turning to alcohol or drugs to deal with their symptoms, especially if their doctor doesn't provide them with suggestions for relief or refer them for psychological support. People with GAD may also have a depressive disorder. Eating disorders are somewhat common manifestations of both GAD and OCD. Irritable bowel syndrome is seen frequently in people with panic disorder, and chronic sleep disturbance is common to all who suffer from anxiety.

Researchers are trying to determine the cause of anxiety disorders. They know that genetics play a role. They are also studying a part of the brain called the amygdale, a small structure deep in the brain that communicates directly with the autonomic nervous system. The amygdale has a "memory" of stressful experiences and triggers autonomic responses, such as shortness of breath, chest pain, sweatiness, and irrational fear, whenever danger is perceived.

If you have one of these disorders, the good news is that there are several helpful interventions. One of the most effective ways to deal with any type of anxiety is exercise. Almost every study on this subject has demonstrated a decrease in symptoms with regular exercise, especially aerobic activity of moderate duration. The exercise is most effective when it lasts from 40-45 minutes. It also appears that the more regular the exercise, the more long-lasting the benefit between bouts of exercise. Exactly why exercise helps is not known, but it is most likely due to effects on the neurotransmitters in the brain. Both serotonin and norepinephrine play a role in mood. The endorphins that are released with moderate exercise are probably another factor. I call endorphins the "positive" hormones that can compensate for the negative stress-induced hormones.

Nutrition is another important area of intervention. Caffeine or any other stimulant tends to increase anxiety in those who are prone to it. Generally, one to two cups of coffee or tea are tolerated, but not in every one. If you note an increase in your symptoms after you've had a cup of coffee, you should eliminate coffee entirely. In place of coffee, drink herbal tea, ideally decaffeinated green tea. You may believe you cannot give up coffee because you "need the energy!" Keep in mind, however, that you are not lacking energy because you are "deficient in caffeine." Despite what Starbucks and Tullys might have us believe, there is no recommended daily allowance for caffeine.

If you are suffering from anxiety, review the overall diet. Be sure to eat plenty of fresh fruits and vegetables, adequate protein, and take a good multivitamin-mineral product (See Chapter 5—Follow-up Preventive Prescription for specifics).

Be aware that there is strong epidemiologic data, as well as animal studies, indicating that improper ratios of omega-3 and omega-6 fatty acids in the diet may contribute to mood disorders, both anxiety and depression. Today, the typical American diet is quite imbalanced. Our diets are rich in saturated fats and omega-6 oils found in margarines, salad dressings, and many processed foods. The healthiest ratio, for *many* reasons, is about three or four to one. It's important to eat fatty fish, such as mackerel or salmon two to three times per week and/or take fish oil supplements that contain both EPA and DHA (the essential fatty acids humans need).

B vitamins, in particular, are deficient in people with anxiety and other mood disorders. One theory is that B vitamins are over-utilized in people who are highly stressed or anxious. Vitamins B-6 and B-12 are linked with the synthesis of SAMe, which plays a role in neurotransmitter balance. Vitamin B-6 is also a key cofactor in the synthesis of serotonin. Folic acid, another B vitamin, can be helpful, as well. Deficiency of folic acid in the diet may lessen the effectiveness of the class of drugs known as SSRIs (selective serotonin re-uptake inhibitors).

Traditionally, a class of drugs called anxiolytics, has been used for both acute and chronic anxiety. Despite the intense potential for abuse, physicians still prescribe these drugs today. I strongly believe that the only place for anxiolytics is in the setting of acute anxiety or trauma in a person who does not have chronic anxiety. Recently, SSRIs, such as Zoloft and Paxil, have become popular. Because of the serotonin involvement in the etiology of anxiety disorders, there is a place for these drugs. However, if not absolutely necessary, I prefer to try other alternatives with patients, as described below, to avoid the side effect profile of pharmaceuticals.

The main botanicals that have reasonable scientific support in the treatment of anxiety are valerian, lemon balm, and kava. Valerian is a botanical which has been used for sleep disturbance, as well as anxiety. It has been studied with Passionflower and St. John's Wort for anxiety and with melatonin for sleep disturbance. The studies have been small clinical trials, but the results are promising.

For mild to moderate anxiety, I suggest 150 mg of Valerian in the morning and 300–450 mg in the evening. Look for a preparation that contains a standardized extract. Valerian is traditionally combined with lemon balm, hops, passionflower, chamomile, and lavender. Although good studies are lacking, adverse effects appear limited and may include mild impairment of driving ability for up to two to three hours after use, and rarely, headache or nausea.

By far, the most extensive scientific study of botanicals for the treatment of anxiety disorders has been with kava. Kava (Piper Methysticum) grows wild in the South Pacific and has been used traditionally for centuries. There have been seven small clinical trials that have shown kava to be superior to placebo in the symptomatic treatment of generalized anxiety. Many companies in the United States have stopped marketing their kava products because of reports of liver toxicity in Europe. There have been no reports in the U.S. or Canada to date, but people should check with their physicians prior to using kava. While taking kava, also have liver enzymes monitored. The standard dosage is 50-70 mg of purified extract (or 150-250 mg of dried root) two to three times per day.

Relaxation therapies, especially massage, aromatherapy, and hypnosis, have shown significant benefit for anxiety disorders. Massage therapists often combine aromatherapy with massage. There are many oils and fragrances that can relax muscles, sedate, provide pain relief, and reduce stress and depression. A number of studies have validated the benefits of aromatherapy in treating conditions from depression to schizophrenia to migraine headaches. Just breathing in an apple or peach scent can be calming. Experiment to see what works for you. Lavender, rose, cypress, and violet have been found to be especially effective with anxiety.

Psychotherapy, including both behavioral and cognitive-behavior therapy (CBT), has also been shown to be effective in treating anxiety disorders. Behavior therapy focuses on using specific techniques to stop or lessen the anxiety response, while CBT focuses on trying to change thinking or reacting patterns as they relate to anxiety response triggers.

DEPRESSIVE DISORDERS

There are many types of depression, but the three most common are 1) reactive depression, 2) major depressive disorder and 3) bipolar (or manic-depressive) illness. Feeling "down in the dumps" or "blue" is something just about everyone experiences at one time or another. A relationship ends, a teacher yells at you in class, a dear friend is diagnosed with cancer, and you find yourself feeling a bit depressed. Usually this situation is self-limited or the situation improves—your boss apologizes for blaming you for something you had no involvement with, the sun comes out after three weeks of cloudy days, or you just start feeling better!

Clearly, genetic influences play a central role in depressive disorders, just as they do in anxiety and dealing with stress. Reactive depressions can be severe if the situation is intensely emotional, as in the death of a loved one. If you do not have a good support structure during traumatic times, you can feel extremely hopeless and isolated. If these symptoms are persistent, are not related to a trauma in your life, or are very severe (especially if you have thoughts of self-harm), it is extremely important that you see a doctor immediately or call a mental health facility.

Major depressive disorder is characterized by the feelings listed below:

- Loss of interest or pleasure in hobbies and activities that were once enjoyed, including sex
- Feelings of hopelessness and sadness for much of the day, lasting at least two weeks
- Decreased energy and feelings of fatigue
- Difficulty concentrating, remembering, and/or making decisions
- Insomnia or early-morning awakening
- Oversleeping or excessive sleepiness
- Appetite and/or weight change—increased or decreased
- Restlessness, irritability
- Persistent physical symptoms that do not respond to treatment, such as headaches, digestive disorders, and

chronic pain

You might feel you are the only one who has ever felt hopeless and helpless, but this is not true. Clinical depression is an increasingly common disorder in the 21st Century, affecting at some time in their lives, up to 25% of all women and 10-12% of all men. At least 15 million Americans seek treatment each year for this condition, and two of the top five prescribed pharmaceuticals are Prozac and Zoloft (although these drugs may be prescribed for disorders other than depression).

Depression affects people of all ages. Depression and suicide attempts have greatly increased in teenagers and even young children over the past 15 years. We do not yet know all the causes of depression, but there seems to be biological and emotional factors that may increase the likelihood an individual will develop a depressive disorder. Research over the past decade strongly suggests a genetic link to these disorders. Stressful experiences in early life, combined with certain personality types, seem to contribute to an increased risk for developing a depressive illness. Low self-esteem also greatly increases the tendency toward depression.

Bipolar depression is also known as manic-depressive illness. This condition, usually diagnosed in early adulthood, also runs in families and is associated with periods of depression, alternating with periods of mania. Mania is characterized by hyperactivity, as in impulsive behavior or wild buying sprees. People with bipolar disorder vacillate between "highs" and "lows," although they can spend the majority of time in a state of either mild depression or low-grade mania (driven to succeed, mildly impulsive).

As with anxiety disorders, we do not completely understand the cause of depression, but it is clear there are genetic factors. People are born with a certain "wiring" of their brain biochemistry, and life's events may cause a certain set of responses that result in anxiety or depression. Although these neurobiological tendencies may not be entirely in one's control, the good news is that there are *many* different things that can help immensely. It's important to note that both medication and psychotherapy can be effective and sometimes necessary in dealing with moderate, severe, or recurrent depression.

Pharmaceuticals

There are two main classes of drugs used in the treatment of unipolar depression—SSRIs (selective serotonin re-uptake inhibitors) and tricyclic antidepressants. The SSRIs are well-known to most people, with Prozac, Zoloft, Celexa, and Paxil being the most commonly prescribed. These drugs have a better safety and side effect profile than the older tricyclics (such as Elavil). Heterocyclic antidepressants, such as Trazadone and Wellbutrin, can be useful in specific cases. For instance, Trazadone is quite sedating, which can be helpful with sleep disturbance, often associated with depression. For bipolar depression, lithium has been the gold standard of treatment for many years, although Depakote is commonly used today. Because of potential side effects, I strongly suggest trying botanical preparations such as valerian and passionflower before using pharmaceuticals. The most important fact to keep in mind about the use of pharmaceuticals in treating depression is that they are only a part of the treatment. Lifestyle modification, dietary changes, and talk therapy are essential as well.

Nutrition and Lifestyle

Moderate exercise, especially aerobic (cardio), is useful in lessening symptoms of depression, as well as anxiety. This is important to remember because many people have a combination of depression and anxiety, and the use of pharmaceuticals may be complicated and not always successful. Always try to incorporate the safe, health-enhancing improvements to your diet and activity level first.

The nutritional factors in depression are very similar to the ones we have discussed with anxiety. Several trials have shown depression to be associated with high intakes of caffeine (greater than 750 mg/day, which is the equivalent of five to six cups of coffee). Examination of the diets of individuals suffering from depression reveals a significantly higher intake of simple sugar when compared to controls. This may partially be an attempt to feel better, as many people get temporary relief from a high carbohydrate meal. Carbohydrate intake will stimulate serotonin release—thus the scientific data confirming chocolate as "nature's antidepressant." The most effective chocolate is dark chocolate and not much is needed. (*NOTE*: this is not a license to eat fat and calorie-laden chocolate candy all day!)

Population studies again associate depression with high intakes of "the wrong fats," and show improvements when increasing the intake of omega-3 fatty acids "the right fats," in the diet. We know that the omega-3 fatty acids are essential components of brain cellular membranes, although clinical trials are needed to further elucidate these factors. Because of the other health benefits of increasing omega-3 intake and decreasing omega-6 intake (see Chapter 5 for details), people with depression should either eat three servings of salmon, halibut, or mackerel per week or supplement their diets with 1000-3000 mg of high quality fish oil each day.

As with anxiety, the B vitamins play a vital role in the health of neurotransmitters. Deficiencies are relatively commonly because of the highly processed diets Americans eat today. I recommend, at a minimum, a balanced multivitamin-mineral preparation that provides at least 20 mg vitamin B-6, 8 micrograms vitamin B-12, and 400 micrograms of folic acid.

SAMe is needed for neurotransmitter production, and it appears to be deficient in many individuals with depression. The starting dose is 200 mg twice daily. Slowly increase the amount used over two to three weeks until improvement is noted. Doses up to 800 mg per day can be necessary. (*NOTE*: People with bipolar depression should not use SAMe).

5-Hydroxytryptophan (5-HTP) is another supplement to

consider. It is a serotonin precursor that can be helpful with appetite control, insomnia, and depression. 5-HTP is available as a dietary supplement, but be sure to buy from a reputable company to assure it is free from the Peak X contaminants that were associated with tryptophan supplements in the 1990s. 5-HTP can be effective in a range of 200-300 mg per day, divided into three doses taken before meals.

Psychotherapy and Other Mind-Body Techniques

As with anxiety, cognitive therapy can be helpful in determining certain lifestyle, relationship, and behavioral triggers in any given individual. I urge people to shop around a bit to find a therapist or counselor with whom they feel comfortable. Effective therapy requires rapport and trust. Meditation, hypnosis, and even acupuncture have been studied as treatments for depression. Relaxation therapy, including yoga and Tai-chi, has also been shown to be helpful—especially when used as part of a concentrated focus of lifestyle improvement through nutrition and exercise. (*NOTE*: If you have been diagnosed with severe depression and/or have thoughts of harming yourself, I strongly recommend you contact your primary care physician or mental health professional immediately.)

If you, or someone you care about, are dealing with anxiety, depression, or the overwhelming stresses and strains of life, contact professional help. Here are some of the resources available:

- Primary care physicians (Family practitioners, general internists and pediatricians)
- Mental health specialists, such as psychiatrists, psychologists, marriage and family counselors (MFCCs)
- Community mental health centers
- University or medical school-affiliated programs

- State hospital outpatient clinics
- Family service, social agencies, or religious clergy
- Private clinics and facilities
- Employee assistance programs

Don't just endure these kinds of life challenges. There is help out there, and many, many modalities to try. Stress, anxiety, and depression are realities of life—but so is the treatment to deal with them.

FOLLOW-UP PREVENTIVE PERSCRIPTION

STRESS MANAGEMENT

It is imperative that we all admit to the stresses in our lives, make a commitment to our mental health, and implement the necessary changes or adjustments to achieve our own optimum level of mental and emotional health. Stress management is an integral part of your Personal Pathway to Health and Vitality. Follow the recommendations below to "be happy."

Dietary Goals

1. Decrease refined sugars (cookies, candy, white bread— look for sucrose on labels and avoid foods that have more than 10 grams)
2. Limit caffeine and alcohol
3. Eat fatty fish two to three times per week

Supplements

1. Take a balanced multivitamin-mineral containing all the B's, in particular 400 mcg folate, 8 mcg vitamin B-12 and 30 mg vitamin B-6.
2. For Depression: See a mental health professional
3. SAMe may be beneficial for both anxiety and depression. (*NOTE*: See cautions re: usage in bipolar

depression.)

4. Valerian for anxiety and sleep disturbance/insomnia. May be combined with passionflower and/or lemon balm.

5. Kava for anxiety (*NOTE*: See cautions re: liver function.)

Exercise Recommendations

1. Daily aerobic exercise—walking, jogging, bicycling—has been shown to be helpful for people with anxiety, depression, and stress. I strongly encourage *everyone* to commit to at least a cumulative 30 minutes of moderate activity every day. It can be vacuuming to music—Just do it!

2. Weight lifting can be helpful as well, especially with weight loss. People who are overweight can have a tremendous improvement in mood and faster weight loss.

Other

1. Psychotherapy, relaxation techniques, and yoga are among the most commonly used and effective adjunctive therapeutic modalities that can help with anxiety, depression, and stress.

2. Pharmaceuticals have been covered in detail in the anxiety and depression sections above. Do not rely *just* upon pharmaceuticals. These disorders, including every day stress, can be greatly improved by appropriate lifestyle and dietary changes, which are essentially without risk and will bring other benefits to overall health.

3. Smile and laugh frequently every day. Children laugh approximately 80 to 100 times per day; but, by the time we reach adulthood, we laugh only five to six times per day. Research shows that the psychological benefits of humor can be quite amazing, allowing

stored negative emotions, such as anger, sadness, and fear, to be harmlessly released. Laughter is cathartic.

Finally, remember that life is all too short. Live every day to the fullest, and you will be on the path of happiness.

CHAPTER 9

DIABETES
Out of Control Epidemic

Points to ponder as you read:

- ✓ What is the difference between Type 1 and Type 2 diabetes?

- ✓ Are you destined to become a diabetic if it runs in your family?

- ✓ What specific lifestyle changes can slow or prevent the development of diabetes?

- ✓ If you already have diabetes, what can be done to prevent complications?

When you hear the word "epidemic," you probably do *not* think of diabetes, but rather influenza, smallpox, or possibly SARS. Webster defines an epidemic as "a disease that is especially prevalent; an illness affecting many persons at one time." That definition certainly describes the situation we have in the United States and around the world regarding diabetes. The statistics are staggering. We are seeing rapidly increasing numbers of people suffering from diabetes on a global basis, particularly in Africa and India. Most of these cases of diabetes are Type 2, which means they are the result of being overweight and eating a diet high in fat and sugar and low in fiber. These dramatic increases in Type 2 diabetes in countries like Taiwan, India, and mainland China are due to the westernization of their diets over the past 25 years. McDonald's and other fast food restaurants are a common part of the urban landscape all around the world. The increase in the availability of these high-calorie, fat-laden, nutritionally deficient foods directly parallels the increase in cases of Type 2 diabetes. Diabetes is a serious disease with a host of deadly complications, including heart disease, stroke, and kidney failure.

Diabetes, as mentioned above, occurs in two main types (we will not address the very rare diabetes insipidis in this book)—Type 1 and Type 2. If you are over 40, you probably still think of these conditions as Juvenile (or Insulin Dependent) Diabetes and Adult Onset Diabetes, as these were the names used for these diseases until the late 1980s. Diabetes is essentially the inability of the body to maintain the blood glucose (blood sugar) level within the body's normal range. In Type 1 diabetes, the beta cells of the pancreas stop making insulin, due to an inflammatory or autoimmune reaction in the body. People with this type of diabetes require insulin injections for life to maintain the blood sugar within a normal range. Type 2 diabetes occurs, essentially, as a result of a genetically susceptible individual being overweight. Type 2 diabetics are usually treated with oral medications (called hypoglycemics) that help to maintain normal blood glucose, although many eventually need insulin along with the oral medication. When I was a new doctor in practice, in the early days of the 1980s, most of my patients who had Type 2 diabetes managed their diabetes by changes in their diets. The term was "diet-controlled diabetes." In 1980, there were just three oral hypoglycemic medications. Now there are 12! Why the dramatic increase in the number of drugs? The original three, with possibly a couple of new formulations to minimize side effects and increase effectiveness, would surely be able to address the needs of diabetics, whether there are 1 million or 5 million. The reality, however, is that the pharmaceutical industry is busy developing new drugs because it is *big business*, not because we need more oral medications for a disease that could be managed without any drugs at all!

The goal of this chapter is to 1) help those at risk for diabetes change their diet and lifestyle to prevent the development of diabetes, and 2) help those who already have Type 2 diabetes change their diet and lifestyle to either reduce their risk of developing complications, or, ideally, lose weight and make the necessary lifestyle changes so that their diabetes becomes "diet controlled." Do you know what you call "diet controlled diabetes?" *No diabetes.*

Don't let the fact that diabetes is such a common disease fool you into thinking that it is not a serious one. Diabetes is the leading cause of blindness and kidney failure, and one of the main risk factors in the development of heart and vascular disease. One of the most common vascular complications of diabetes is amputation of the lower leg—a truly gruesome, disabling, and preventable complication. Such serious complications occur when blood sugar is *not* maintained within a certain range, when a person goes years having his blood sugar out of the normal range more than in it. I can't say this strongly enough. Diabetics need to take control of their health *and*, people at risk for developing diabetes (anyone who is in the obese weight range and/or overweight with a family history of diabetes) need to take control of their health.

With these facts in mind, let's take an in-depth look at the two main types of diabetes.

TYPE 1 DIABETES

Type 1 diabetes accounts for only 5% to 10% of all diabetics. This percentage has not changed dramatically over the last 40 or 50 years. At one point in time, Type 1 diabetes was thought to be some sort of spontaneous event. However, we now know that this type of diabetes develops because of an autoimmune response in which the body does not recognize some of its own cells and destroys them. In Type 1 diabetes, the cells that produce insulin (beta cells within the islet tissue of the pancreas) are destroyed, an action most likely triggered by a viral infection. This eventually results in insulin not being produced by the body at all, leading to a life-long dependence on insulin injections (or use of pumps and other newer devices). Type 1 diabetes can develop at any age, although it usually develops in children and young adults.

Symptoms of Type 1 diabetes are increased thirst, increased urination, weight loss, fatigue, and blurred vision. Symptoms usually develop quickly, over a few days or weeks. Occasionally, symptoms are first noticed after an illness, such as the flu. The person may think the symptoms of high blood sugar (hyperglycemia) are related to the illness and may not think that medical care is needed. However, without medical attention, blood sugar levels can rise high enough to cause severe problems, such as confusion or even coma.

People at risk for developing Type 1 diabetes are those who have a close relative (parent, brother, or sister) with this type of diabetes. Other factors that increase a person's risk are being Caucasian, having certain antibodies (islet cell antibodies) in the blood, and having certain viral infections (especially Coxsackie virus).

Currently, there is no way to prevent this type of diabetes, although research is working towards the creation of a vaccination to prevent the disease. If you have already been diagnosed with Type 1 diabetes, you can help prevent or delay the development of complications from diabetes by keeping blood sugar levels within a safe range. Treatment must include dietary and lifestyle changes that result in keeping blood sugar levels in a normal range with minimal insulin. Many Type 1 diabetics ignore their diet and simply adjust their insulin, which can lead to serious complications. There is *no* better way to prevent complications than by eating a well balanced diet, including plenty of fruits and vegetables, omega-3 fatty acid supplementation, and adequate fiber, *and* engaging in a regular exercise program. Of course, daily monitoring of blood sugar with proper adjustments of insulin dosage is a must.

TYPE 2 DIABETES

Between 90% and 95% of all diabetics in the United States have Type 2 diabetes. This number of diabetics, at present, is about 16 million in the United States and about 180 million on a world-wide basis. The number of cases of Type 2 diabetes is increasing rapidly, with the global number expected to grow to 230 million by 2015! Again, much of this increase is due to the rise in obesity—another global epidemic.

Type 2 diabetes develops when the cells become resistant to insulin. Insulin resistance occurs when the body's cells and tissues do not fully respond to the action of insulin, causing blood sugar levels to gradually rise out of the normal range. As a result, the body senses the abnormally high glucose level and produces more insulin. Because the cells are becoming increasingly insulin-resistant, a vicious cycle of slowly elevating blood sugars and the pancreas over-producing insulin continues until the condition eventually becomes diagnosed. The diagnosis may occur because of symptoms, but it is more likely that the abnormal blood sugar level will be found on a routine blood panel as part of a physical or a blood test done for some unrelated reason. There are *no* early signs of Type 2 diabetes. Unlike Type 1 diabetes, in which the body rapidly loses its ability to maintain a normal glucose level and produces symptoms that cannot be ignored, Type 2 diabetes develops over a number of years. It is estimated that at least eight million Americans have Type 2 diabetes and do not know it.

Certain ethnic groups are at an increased risk of developing Type 2 diabetes—specifically African-Americans, Hispanics, Native Americans, and Pacific Islanders. Genetics play a role, but research and population studies are *very clear*—the strongest risk factors for the development of Type 2 diabetes are obesity and a sedentary lifestyle. These two risk factors far outweigh the genetic link. In other words, if there is no family history of diabetes but are an obese couch potato, there is a high likelihood of developing diabetes! Conversely, if there is a strong family history of Type 2 diabetes but you maintain an active lifestyle and a normal weight, you will NOT develop diabetes. Clearly, there is no other disease that is so completely dependent on what you do (or don't do). Many diseases have a strong genetic tie or are connected to other factors out of our control (like environmentally-linked diseases). However, with Type 2 diabetes, you are in the driver's seat.

The number of cases of Type 2 diabetes has increased dramatically over the past 30 years. According to the annual report of the Center for Disease Control and Prevention, this type of diabetes has risen an alarming 70% since 1990. And, with each passing year, it is being diagnosed at astronomically increasing rates.

As stated above, Type 2 diabetes is most commonly seen in adulthood, after the age of 40. However, one of the more alarming aspects of this disease is that it is now being diagnosed in children as young as 10 years of age. In the early 1980s when I was first in medical practice, I never had a Type 2 diabetic in my practice that was under the age of 45, and most of them were in their 60's.

Today, more children than ever before are overweight at age two, very overweight at age four and obese at six years old! These obese children are usually very sedentary and eat diets shockingly full of processed and fast foods, which are appallingly deficient in vitamins, minerals, and fiber. Fifteen years ago, essentially 100% of children who were diagnosed with diabetes had Type 1 diabetes, which cannot be controlled. Today, estimates are as high as 25-40% for young diabetics (younger than age 18) who have Type 2 diabetes—a completely preventable disease!

Type 2 diabetes in a 12-year-old is one of the most frightening examples of the results of our 20th Century sedentary lifestyle and dietary excesses. I hope you are as shocked and saddened by this as I am. If you, your family, or friends are dealing with or at risk for diabetes—or are very overweight, there is hope.

Scientists have found that weight loss and modest adjustments to lifestyle can actually change the tendency toward the development of insulin resistance and Type 2 diabetes. Losing as little as ten pounds can result in a 10% drop in your blood sugar. Studies indicate that it is probably the dietary changes that cause this significant improvement from minimal weight loss. If the number of calories consumed each day is decreased, especially by limiting foods that stimulate the insulin response, the pancreas doesn't have to secrete as much insulin to work towards controlling blood sugar. If the caloric intake is consistently reduced and simple (insulin stimulating) sugars limited, your cells can gradually become more insulin-sensitive (normal) is reversed, and the tendency towards becoming diabetic. Just by adding fiber to your diet or walking three to four times per week, a significant improvement is made in blood sugar control.

Because such simple lifestyle changes can result in such a big health payoff, you might wonder why the number of Type 2 diabetics is increasing, rather than decreasing, as could reasonably be expected. There are two reasons.

First, many Type 2 diabetics aren't aware that such little changes can potentially reverse their health to a pre-diabetic state; and, second, most physicians tend to focus on pharmaceutical treatment, rather than lifestyle adjustments, but they are not trained to do otherwise. Unfortunately, most physicians graduate from medical school, complete a residency program, and never have even one credit hour in nutrition. A recent survey showed that two-thirds of U.S. medical schools do not have a core curriculum course on nutrition. At best, doctors' training on nutrition is weaved throughout certain courses, such as those dealing with the digestive system.

Although research clearly shows that Type 2 diabetes occurs as a result of obesity, a lack of fiber in the diet, and a lack of exercise, most physicians only give lip service to the lifestyle discussion. They may hand patients a pre-printed diet, refer them to a dietician, or send them to a class offered by their clinic. But all of these services, in today's managed care world, tend to be very limited or not available at all. What it comes down to is that you have to learn what to do to safeguard your own health, and then do it! Research is clear. Tight control of blood glucose levels will delay and usually prevent the complications that accompany diabetes. Blindness, kidney failure, dialysis, heart attack, and amputation are all preventable through dietary and lifestyle changes.

The line differentiating Type 1 and Type 2 diabetes is rather blurred today, because so many Type 2 diabetics require insulin along with oral medication to control blood sugar. This need for insulin occurs gradually over time, as cells become more and more insulin resistant from excessive intake of calories and high sugar foods. The non-pharmacologic treatment of both types of diabetes is essentially the same, requiring the same dietary and lifestyle changes.

Let me emphasize that if you currently have either Type 1 or 2 diabetes, see your physician regularly and continue to follow his (or her) advice on blood sugar monitoring and medication usage. Discuss medication with your physician. Make changes in your life that may reverse the progress of your disease (Type 2 diabetes), lessen the need for medication (both Type 1 and Type 2 diabetes) or delay/prevent complications of your disease (both Type 1 and Type 2 diabetes).

Talk to your physician concerning the dietary and lifestyle suggestions I make in the "Follow-up Preventive Prescription" section at the end of this chapter. If you are losing weight, your doctor should be aware so that he (or she) can monitor the probable adjustments needed to your medication. If you have Type 1 diabetes, improvements in your diet will probably result in less insulin requirements. Have your physician develop a sliding scale so dosage of insulin can be adjusted as you make improvements in diet and incorporate exercise.

Remember, if you have diabetes (Type 1 or Type 2), you are

the most important person in the treatment of that diabetes on a daily basis. If you don't have Type 2 diabetes, you have the power to stop from becoming a diabetic statistic. We can all work together to reverse this frightening epidemic!

FOLLOW-UP PREVENTIVE PERSCRIPTION

UTILIZE DIETARY AND EXERCISE CHANGES FOR IMPROVED HEALTH.

Dietary Recommendations

1. LOSE WEIGHT IF YOU ARE OVERWEIGHT. Obesity is clearly the most significant risk factor for Type 2 diabetes, but overweight Type 1 diabetics are increasing their likelihood of long-term complications. Being overweight means too many calories, too much insulin, and inadequate glucose control. (See Chapter 6 for weight loss advice and information.) Use soy protein-based meal replacements as the foundation of weight control. They are easy, health-enhancing, and can be used both to lose weight and to maintain permanent weight loss.

2. IMPROVE YOUR NUTRITION. Implement the following guidelines into your diet for maximum diabetic protection:

   a. DECREASE THE GLYCEMIC LOAD OF YOUR DIET. Glycemic index is a measure of how quickly a food becomes glucose in the bloodstream. It is based on a scale of 1 to 100, with a slice of white bread as the reference standard. While useful as a starting point, the Glycemic Index (see the Appendix) must be used with a few items in mind. Foods that may have a high glycemic index, such as Shredded Wheat (GI 97), can have a much lower glycemic load by being eaten with soymilk (GI 56) and a half-cup of fresh blueberries (GI 38). In general, adding soluble fiber and protein to your meal will result in a lower glycemic load. The lower the glycemic load, the lower the ultimate insulin response.

b. CONSIDER THE MEDITERRANEAN DIET. This diet focuses on generous amounts of vegetables, fruits, whole grains, and olive oil. Studies have shown that the monounsaturates in olive oil have the best benefit for diabetics in lowering their risk of atherosclerosis. Fish plays a more dominant role than meat, which increases the intake of healthy monounsaturated and omega-3 fatty acids.

c. AVOID WHITE FLOUR, WHITE BREAD, FRUIT JUICE. These foods cause a significant stimulation of insulin response, have minimal nutritional value, and tend to increase hunger.

d. EAT CRUCIFEROUS VEGETABLES AND GARLIC DAILY. Studies confirm that onion, broccoli, and garlic have beneficial effects on the immune and vascular system in diabetics.

e. DRINK GREEN TEA DAILY. Many studies have documented that polyphenol-rich green tea provides significant antioxidant and immune-enhancing benefits. I recommend at least two cups per day.

f. ADD FIBER, ESPECIALLY SOLUBLE, AIMING FOR 25-30 GRAMS PER DAY. Vegetables and fruits can provide the bulk of your daily fiber, although oat bran, guar gum, and pectins should be included as well. Optimum fiber intake helps manage diabetes, and also lowers the risk of colon cancer and diverticulosis and help to normalize cholesterol.

Supplement Suggestions

1. ESSENTIAL FATTY ACIDS. Supplementation of omega-3 fatty acids has been shown to help with peripheral

neuropathy, reduce the risk of stroke, protect against atherosclerosis, and reverse insulin resistance. Choose a high quality fish oil that contains both EPA and DHA; Optimum intake: 1500-3000 mg per day. *(NOTE:* Discuss usage of fish oil supplements with your doctor if you are on anticoagulants, such as warfarin (Coumadin) or have bleeding tendencies.*)*

2. CHROMIUM. Although rarely deficient in normal populations, it has been shown that a high percentage of diabetics (both Type 1 and 2) may be deficient in chromium. A recent large clinical trial showed good reductions in blood sugar, insulin, and cholesterol levels from chromium use. Food sources include most meats, brewers yeast, and whole grains. Optimum intake: 200-400 mcg per day

3. ANTIOXIDANTS. Vitamin C, vitamin E, and Alpha-lipoic acid should be supplemented in diabetics.

    VITAMIN C can slow the tendency for atherosclerosis and other oxidative damage in diabetics as well as support immunity and wound healing, both of which are compromised in diabetics. Best food sources are red peppers, citrus, and berries. Optimum intake: 1000-1500 mg per day.

    VITAMIN E is a potent fat-soluble antioxidant that works synergistically with vitamin C, has particular heart health benefits, and is difficult to get in adequate amounts in the diet. Optimum intake: 400-800 IU per day.

    ALPHA-LIPOIC ACID can be very helpful with the pain of diabetic neuropathy, and may also help with glucose uptake by cells. Food source is red meat. Optimum intake: 600-800 mg per day

4. MAGNESIUM. Deficiency of magnesium is common in diabetics, although the reason is not completely understood. Because of magnesium's role in glucose metabolism,

diabetics may need two times the recommended daily allowance. Food sources include green leafy vegetables, whole grains, and legumes (such as soybeans, lentils). Optimum intake: 400–500 mg per day.

5. A GOOD MULTIVITAMIN-MINERAL. Assure that your intake of zinc, folate, and all of the B vitamins is adequate by taking a good multivitamin-mineral supplement. This is especially important if you are on a weight loss program.

6. GYMNEMA. Gymnema sylvestre is an Ayurvedic herb that has been used in India as a diabetic treatment. It has been shown to lower glucose levels and may enhance insulin effectiveness. A recent study demonstrated that gymnema may actually decrease the taste of sweet foods, which could be helpful for weight loss in some individuals. Optimum intake: 400–600 mg per day in two to three doses.

7. GINGKO BILOBA. Gingko biloba is extracted from the leaves of the oldest tree on our planet to provide flavonoids and lactones that function as antioxidants, improve platelet and blood vessel function. Because of its effects on the circulatory system, gingko has been recommended for the peripheral vascular disease of diabetics as well as a general support to brain circulation and memory enhancement. Optimum intake: 40–60 mg three times per day. Extract should be standardized to 24% flavonoid glycosides. (*NOTE:* People using warfarin (Coumadin) or any blood-thinning medication should consult their physician before using).

EXERCISE & ACTIVITY ADVICE

Regular exercise, both aerobic and anaerobic (resistance weight training), have been shown to provide a number of short-term and long-term benefits for diabetics. These include, but are not limited to:

- Easier weight loss and lasting weight control

- Improved glucose tolerance and less tendency for insulin resistance
- Improved lipid profile—i.e. reduced cholesterol and triglycerides and increases in HDL, all of which will result in a reduced risk of heart disease.

My recommendations are as follows:

1. CHECK WITH YOUR PHYSICIAN before starting an exercise program if you are not currently exercising regularly.

2. TRY WALKING. An easy starting point is a commitment to walk 30 minutes five days per week. It is fine to split that into two 15 minute walks initially, but the long-range goal is to walk 30 minutes in one stretch. You will notice improved energy, better sleep, and easier mood control. Ultimately, a 45-minute brisk walk daily will provide you with more health benefits than imagined.

3. SUBSTITUTE OTHER ACTIVITIES FOR WALKING, if preferred. The goal is to *move* more rapidly than normal for 30-45 minutes per day. Choose an activity you like, and remember to vary what you do. Make your activity fun and social, and you will not view it as a chore, but a pleasant part of your day.

4. INCORPORATE WEIGHT TRAINING. Weight training is important, in conjunction with aerobic exercise. Weight lifting will help build muscle mass, which will increase metabolism and make weight control easier.

Other Helpful Methods

- Relaxation and stress management
- Yoga and Tai-chi

(See Chapter 8 for a discussion of these modalities)

CHAPTER 10

ARMED AGAINST
Autoimmune Disease

Points to ponder as you read:

- ✓ What are autoimmune diseases, and what are the symptoms?

- ✓ What causes autoimmune diseases and why are they becoming more common?

- ✓ If there is no cure for these diseases, what can be done to treat them?

- ✓ Is it possible to slow the progress of these types of disorders?

Have you ever heard of autoimmune diseases? Do you know of anyone suffering from an autoimmune disease? If you answered "no" to these two questions, you are in the minority. Autoimmune diseases are now the third most common category of illness in the United States, following heart disease and cancer. Take the following quiz to determine exactly how much you know about this group of serious illnesses, and then check your answers. Finding out the facts about autoimmune diseases may not only help you, but also a friend or family member.

Determining Your Autoimmune Acumen

1. This category of illness is called autoimmune because-
    a. it automatically occurs in anyone over age 50.

b. it is named for the Greek word for "self" and the immune system.

c. having one autoimmune disease makes you automatically immune from any others.

d. it is always treated using automated equipment.

2. An example of an autoimmune disease is-
    a. AIDS
    b. Cancer.
    c. Multiple sclerosis
    d. Influenza

3. The largest segment of the population affected by autoimmune diseases is-
    a. women
    b. men
    c. children
    d. minorities

4. Science tells us that autoimmune diseases-
    a. can be cured with drugs
    b. are never deadly
    c. tend to run in families
    d. affect very few people

5. Autoimmune diseases-
    a. are often life-threatening
    b. cannot be effectively treated
    c. are not diagnosed until they are serious
    d. need the lifelong care of a physician

6. Most autoimmune diseases are relatively-
    a. pain-free
    b. easy to diagnose
    c. harmless
    d. rare

ANSWERS TO "DETERMINING YOUR AUTOIMMUNE ACUMEN"

Question #1

This category of illness is called autoimmune because:

> b. it comes from the Greek word for "self" and the immune system.

The word "auto" is the Greek word for self. The immune system is a complicated network of cells and organ systems whose main role is to defend the body from infection, invading microorganisms such as viruses, bacteria, fungus, etc. Our immune system recognizes these "invaders" as abnormal and puts into action a destruction process. The viruses or bacteria are killed by certain white blood cells and then "swept out" by others called macrophages. Our immune system patrols our entire body looking for *any* abnormal cells—cells with improperly repaired DNA or toxic exposure that are leading to precancerous or cancerous changes. For unknown reasons, a person's immune system can suddenly identify some normal part of the body as "foreign" or "abnormal" and put into action these defense/destruction systems. This is what happens in the generation of an autoimmune disease. For instance, in Rheumatoid arthritis, the cartilage of joints is recognized as abnormal, and the immune system attacks certain joints, causing tremendous inflammation and even destruction of the joint.

Question #2

An example of an autoimmune disease is:

> c. Multiple sclerosis.

AIDS, cancer, and influenza all represent breakdowns and "underfunctioning" of the immune system, whereas autoimmune diseases are essentially overfunctioning of the immune system. AIDS involves a deficient immune system, due to the Human Immunodeficiency Virus (HIV) infecting the T-cells (particular cells in the immune system). The result is a gradual destruction of the immune system's ability to respond to any infections. Influenza is a mild breakdown in the immune system, leading to an infection with the influenza virus. An autoimmune disease, such as MS (multiple sclerosis), occurs when the immune system is "up-regulated" or over-stimulated. Autoimmune disorders are not contagious, so they cannot be passed from one person to another.

Some of the more common autoimmune diseases are as follows: *(These are listed in alphabetical order, not in order of their prevalence.)*

Alopecia Areata: The body's immune system attacks the follicles of hair shafts and can lead to areas of hair loss, from small "bald spots" on the head to larger areas of hair loss on the face or body. Alopecia totalis is a complete loss of hair on the body.

Crohn's Disease and Ulcerative Colitis: Current theory favors an immune system role in these inflammatory bowel disorders that result in serious malfunction of the colon and parts of the small intestine. Both of these diseases have a strong genetic component—i.e. tends to run in families.

Grave's Disease and Hashimoto's Thyroiditis: In both of these disorders, the immune system attacks certain cells of the thyroid gland, leading to significant disruption in the normal functioning of the thyroid gland. Grave's Disease is a form of hyperthyroidism (over-functioning of the thyroid) that occurs due to antithyroid antibodies. This is a serious disease that must be evaluated and treated promptly as it can lead to significant tachycardia (abnormal rapid heartbeat). Other symptoms include heat intolerance, anxiety, weight loss, and diarrhea. Hashimoto's Thyroiditis, on the other hand, leads to hypothyroidism (under-functioning of the thyroid gland). Symptoms include an enlarged thyroid, cold intolerance, weight gain, and dry skin.

Guillain-Barre Syndrome: This is a group of disorders that affect the peripheral nervous system, possibly due to an immune response to a viral infection. Nerves are progressively demyelinated, which leads to rapid onset of tingling and weakness of extremities. About one-third of Guillan-Barre patients may require mechanical ventilation due to the effects on the respiratory system. This syndrome can last from weeks to months, depending on its severity.

Insulin-Dependent Type 1 Diabetes Mellitus (once known as "Juvenile Onset Diabetes"): Type 1 diabetes is an immune-mediated disorder that may stem from a viral infection, resulting in destruction of the insulin-producing beta cells in the pancreas. Without insulin, the body cannot regulate blood sugar within a normal range, resulting in a life-long requirement for insulin injections. Many people with Type 1 diabetes use pumps to deliver insulin in addition to injections. Dietary management is extremely important with diabetes (see Chapter 9).

Systemic Lupus Erythematosis (also known as Lupus): This is a multisystem disease that develops due to antibodies against components of the cell nucleus. This disease can present itself in multiple ways, usually initially with fever, fatigue, facial rash, and muscle and joint aches. Lupus can be difficult to diagnose, and may ultimately result in involvement of heart, lung, kidneys, and nervous system. A high ANA titer (anti-nuclear antibody) is the hallmark of diagnosis.

Multiple sclerosis: MS is the most common nontrauma related neurological disorder in the United States. It is believed to be an autoimmune process that destroys some component of the myelin sheath that covers nerves. It is more common in the northern latitudes and is also, like Lupus, very difficult to diagnose due to the variety of ways in which it can occur. Because nerves are present throughout the body, the symptoms (and the disease process itself) relate to whatever area of nerves are affected. Visual symptoms, such as temporary loss of part of vision (optic neuritis), is a common presentation. Additionally, vague complaints of weakness, tingling, and even muscle pain brings many sufferers to the doctor. Most people with MS have flare-ups of their disorder, interspersed with periods when they have no symptoms. Others have a more progressive course.

Rheumatoid Arthritis: Rheumatoid arthritis is an inflammatory condition that affects certain joints, especially in the hands, although many joints may be involved. RA is marked by significant joint swelling and pain. This disease should be managed by a rheumatologist. Early and aggressive treatment can make a huge difference in limiting the joint destruction. Because powerful immune-suppressing drugs are often used, many of the difficulties associated with Rheumatoid arthritis are due to the treatment, rather than the disease.

Scleroderma: This syndrome occurs due to autoantibodies to cellular components called centromeres. The symptoms include diffuse thickening of the skin. Internal organs, including the esophagus and lungs, can be involved. Raynaud's syndrome, extreme sensitivity to cold, results in the fingers (and often the toes) turning blue, white and then, upon re-warming, very red. Raynaud's syndrome is present in virtually everyone with scleroderma, occurring due to involvement of the small blood vessels in the ends of your fingers and toes. Sjogren's Syndrome, which is a variant of systemic sclerosis (scleroderma) results in dry eyes, difficulty swallowing, and dry skin.

As illustrated above, autoimmune diseases can affect the body in many different ways. They can be serious and progressive, or temporary. They can be difficult to diagnose, and sometimes difficult to treat.

Question #3

The largest segment of the population affected by autoimmune diseases is:

      a. women.

Nearly 80% of the 8.5 million people with autoimmune diseases and disorders are women. This varies from condition to condition. With Lupus, the ratio is 9:1, women to men. Multiple sclerosis, on the other hand, is only about 2:1, women to men. If autoimmune diseases were listed together, instead of as separate entities, these conditions would be one of the top 10 causes of death for women under 65 in the United States.

Researchers have theories why women are more susceptible to these illnesses than men, although they have drawn no hard and fast conclusions. They do suspect, however, that hormones play a major role in the development of these diseases. Autoimmune diseases are most common in women of child-bearing age and certain autoimmune conditions are more likely to occur if the woman has had multiple pregnancies. Others are more commonly diagnosed during perimenopause and early menopause. The disease course itself may be affected by pregnancy. Women with multiple sclerosis and Rheumatoid arthritis enjoy a lessening of disease severity during pregnancy, while pregnant women with systemic Lupus may see their disease worsen.

Question #4

Science tells us that autoimmune diseases tend to:

    c. run in families.

The causes of autoimmune diseases are not known. However, according to Noel R. Rose, M.D., Ph.D., Professor of Pathology and of Molecular Microbiology and Immunology and Director of Autoimmune Research Center at The Johns Hopkins University, all autoimmune diseases show evidence of a genetic predisposition. That means that the genes people are born with contribute to their susceptibility for developing an autoimmune disease. For example, certain diseases, such as psoriasis, can occur among several members of the same family. This suggests that a specific gene or set of genes predisposes a family member to psoriasis. In addition, although individual family members with autoimmune diseases may inherit and share a set of abnormal genes, they may develop different autoimmune diseases. For instance, a daughter may have Lupus, a first cousin may have multiple sclerosis, and one of their mothers may have Rheumatoid arthritis. If you have any of these conditions in your family, you should definitely alert your physician to this fact.

It appears that even though you may carry a gene that predisposes you to develop autoimmunity, a "trigger" is required to unmask the tendency. This is often a viral infection (diabetes, Guillan-Barre, MS), but may also be an environmental toxin or other factor, such as exposure to fetal antigens during pregnancy. There may be dietary factors, as well, including iodine in thyroid conditions and excessive pro-inflammatory fats in the development of ulcerative colitis. As research into the human genome continues, along with autoimmune disease studies, hopefully we can help identify people with the genetic predisposition so they can lessen the likelihood of exposure to certain triggers. Much study still is needed.

Question #5

Autoimmune diseases usually:

d.   require the lifelong care of a doctor.

People who have been diagnosed with autoimmune diseases should be closely monitored by their primary care physician, with referral to sub-specialists as necessary. Although most autoimmune disorders cannot be "cured," there are many effective treatments. With appropriate treatment, most people with autoimmune disorders can live fairly normal, active lives. Treatment can be challenging because it is often aimed at suppressing the body's immune response to lessen the autoimmune process that is occurring. Side effects can include frequent illnesses, osteoporosis, peptic ulcer disease, and even higher prevalence of cancer. It is important for patients to be sure their physicians take the time to explain all aspects of treatment, including side effects, risks, and benefits. You may want to do research to make informed decisions about your health (see Chapter 19 for additional guidance).

Question #6

Most autoimmune diseases are relatively:

> d. rare.

While many of the individual autoimmune diseases are rare, as a group, they affect millions of Americans. Stephen J. Walsh, Sc.D., Associate Professor and researcher at the University of Connecticut Health Center, reports:

> *"Most of us know someone with an autoimmune disease, we just didn't know that the rare condition they have is part of a large group of similar diseases that afflict a relatively large segment of the population. Despite their common occurrence, the autoimmune diseases have not received the attention they deserve from public health officials because, taken as individual diseases, they don't seem all that common."*

Dr. Noel R. Rose sees autoimmune diseases as a major problem that needs a major response. He believes that autoimmune diseases need to be considered as a unified group to give them greater visibility. As stated earlier in this chapter, autoimmune diseases as a group are the third most prevalent disease in the United States. But, as Dr. Rose points out, individual autoimmune diseases are relatively rare, and most often are not fatal. They don't tend to garner the public's attention and thus, do not receive the funding they need. Research tends to focus on individual diseases. Possibly, we need to direct funds to study why 1) autoimmunity appears to be increasingly common, and 2) what environmental or dietary factors may be involved. If we could identify common triggers, the public could be educated and, possibly, some autoimmune diseases would not even occur!

Stephen Walsh agrees that additional resources should be committed to investigating autoimmune diseases—both the causes and potential cures. He specifically points to the need for regional registries of people diagnosed with autoimmune diseases. "No single hospital or university has enough patients with any one autoimmune disease to support effective evaluation of causes or treatments," says Walsh. "The creation of regional registries for cancer patients started in Connecticut in the 1930s had an enormous impact on our understanding of that disease. With a modest level of federal support, a similar program could be initiated for the autoimmune diseases."

Anthony S. Fauci, M.D., director of the National Institute of Allergy and Infectious Diseases, also believes that autoimmune diseases need to be spotlighted. He states, "The social and financial burdens imposed by these chronic, debilitating diseases include poor quality of life, high health care costs, and substantial loss of productivity."

If you or family members have been diagnosed with autoimmunity, you may want to become involved in the political process of lobbying for support. Contact one of the organizations below to find out how you can become involved in fund-raising and research efforts, etc.

NATIONAL INSTITUTE OF ARTHRITIS AND MUSCULOSKELETAL AND SKIN DISEASES

Phone Number(s): (301) 496-8188
(Information Office), (301) 565-2966 (TTY)
Internet Address: http://www.nih.gov/niams/

NATIONAL ORGANIZATION FOR RARE DISEASES

Phone Number(s): (800) 999-6673
Internet Address: http://www.rarediseases.org/

AMERICAN AUTOIMMUNE RELATED DISEASES ASSOCIATION, INC.

Phone Number(s): (800) 598-4668 (Literature Requests)
Internet Address: http://www.aarda.org/

Autoimmune diseases are certainly deserving of attention and study. As you become better informed about these diseases, recognize your own personal susceptibility, perceive environmental triggers that can stimulate disease development, and understand treatment options available to you or a family member, be better armed to protect yourself and your family against these debilitating diseases.

FOLLOW-UP PREVENTIVE PERSCRIPTION

SUGGESTED RECOMMENDATIONS FOR DEALING WITH AUTOIMMUNE DISEASE.

Dietary Recommendations:

It is clear that diet plays a role in immune function. Many autoimmune diseases have a strong inflammatory component and research is increasingly clear that diets rich in omega-3 fatty acids can provide natural anti-inflammatory benefits. B vitamins and protein deficiency can impair antibody formation and lessen the body's ability to respond to infection (a common trigger in autoimmunity). Low levels of antioxidant intake are frequently seen in individuals with autoimmune disorders. So, prudent guidelines would include everything mentioned in the "Follow-up Preventive Prescriptions" of Chapters Four and Five, including:

1. Eat at least seven servings of fruits and vegetables each day. Try to eat a wide variety—fresh or frozen are comparable.
2. Try to decrease the intake of fried and processed foods, as these are high in pro-inflammatory fats. Stir-fry with small amounts of olive oil instead. Drizzle olive oil (small amounts) and balsamic vinegar over salads instead of commercial dressings.
3. Eat fatty fish at least three times per week (including

halibut, wild salmon, or tuna). As many types of fish may have high levels of mercury, it is advisable for pregnant women to limit their fish intake to a few times per month. I recommend taking a supplement containing 500 mg of high quality fish oil, including both EPA and DHA.

4. Control your weight. Obesity may be a risk factor in the development of certain autoimmune conditions.

Supplement Suggestions:

1. (see no. 3 above) Omega-3 fatty acid supplements provide natural anti-inflammatory effects. Diets rich in omega-3 and containing less omega-6 intake may be a factor in the prevention of inflammatory conditions as well as helpful in their treatment. Omega-3 supplements have been shown to be very helpful in lessening symptoms associated with Rheumatoid arthritis, Crohn's disease, ulcerative colitis, and Lupus.

2. Multivitamin-mineral product to assure no nutritional deficiency—in particular B vitamins. This is important in regulating immune function.

3. Antioxidant supplement to assure a balanced intake, despite what the diet may bring. I recommend 1000 mg vitamin C, 400 IU vitamin E, and 20 mg zinc.

4. 400 IU Vitamin D is strongly recommended for Rheumatoid arthritis (RA). For multiple sclerosis (MS), at least 200 IU is suggested. Calcium supplements, either calcium citrate, calcium carbonate, or a combo in the range of 1000-1200 mg a day for people under age 40; increase to 1500 mg a day after age 40.

5. Add soy to the diet, including soy protein shakes and soy foods, to assure a healthy intake of vegetable protein sources, and to add to the intake of omega-3s. There is evidence that Rheumatoid arthritis sufferers may benefit from a vegetarian diet, and soy is absolutely the healthiest source of vegetarian protein. Soy isoflavones also help

protect bone mass. Loss of bone mass is a side effect of the treatment for many autoimmune disorders.

6. Glucosamine sulfate has been shown to lessen joint pain in both RA and osteoarthritis (OA). Several studies have shown some increase in cartilage thickness, although these have been in patients with OA, not RA. Stay tuned for more research in the area of alternative treatments for joint symptoms of autoimmune disorders. A trial of 500 mg glucosamine three times per day for a month or two is not unreasonable.

7. Stress reduction formula: ashwaganda, chamomile, gingko, and valerian are all herbs that may assist with feelings of stress, although few published studies exist. All of these herbs have had extensive usage with essentially no reports of toxicity.

8. Avoid Echinacea as it is an immune stimulant and may exacerbate the autoimmune process.

9. Melatonin and MS: The pineal gland (organ that secretes melatonin) has been implicated as part of the cause of MS, possibly due to dysfunction of this gland. Seventy percent of MS patients have been shown to have abnormal alpha-melatonin stimulating hormone levels. Pregnancy (which is associated with high melatonin levels) is a time when MS often goes into remission. Discuss the use of melatonin supplements with a neurologist.

10. Gingko biloba may be helpful in MS. I recommend beginning with 50 mg twice daily. Recent studies show improved effectiveness with intakes up to 240 mg per day. The addition of phosphatidyl serine, up to 50 mg per day, may help with protection of neurons.

11. Fiber supplements may be quite helpful for those with Inflammatory Bowel Disease (IBD). Begin with small amounts, two to three grams, and progress slowly. Soluble fiber will be better tolerated. Consider probiotics, such as live cultures of Acidophilus. There are many reports

of people with IBD benefiting from using aloe vera preparations, which has anti-inflammatory qualities. Be sure you are using an aloe that has the laxative alloin removed in the processing.

Exercise and Activity Considerations:

In general, there are no specific suggestions or precautions concerning autoimmune disorders that are specific for these conditions. I am a firm believer in regular physical activity for overall stress management and positive mental health. With chronic diseases, such as autoimmune conditions, continuing some type of activity can help with physical conditioning, strength, and flexibility, as well as lessening feelings of stress.

If you have Rheumatoid arthritis, your rheumatologist may very well provide specific suggestions and cautions, depending on which joints are inflamed. People with Lupus respond well to gentle aerobic exercise to lessen stiffness and muscle pains.

If you have MS, maintaining muscle strength can be assisted by a commitment to strength training and regular aerobic exercise. The keys are to:

1. Check with your physician as to any limitations.
2. Be gentle, but consistent.
3. Consider asking for a referral to see a physical therapist or occupational therapist to assist in developing a comprehensive program for strength and conditioning, tailored to your condition.

Other Thoughts:

Acupuncture may be helpful in multiple sclerosis and Rheumatoid arthritis.

Meditation, Tai-chi, and yoga have all been shown to be beneficial in stress reduction and in the alleviation of symptoms (especially pain and stiffness) in essentially all autoimmune disorders.

CHAPTER 11

FIBROMYALGIA AND CHRONIC FATIGUE SYNDROME
New Diseases or Signs of the 21st Century Lifestyle

Points to ponder as you read:

- ✓ What is fibromyalgia and how is it diagnosed?
- ✓ Is fibromyalgia treatable? Curable?
- ✓ How does fibromyalgia differ from Chronic Fatigue Syndrome?
- ✓ Can these conditions be prevented?

When Fibromyalgia and Chronic Fatigue Syndrome (CFS) are examined, it is easy to realize that with these two conditions, there is both good news and bad news.

FIRST, THE BAD NEWS...

Fibromyalgia is an arthritis-related disorder or syndrome. In 1990, the American College of Rheumatology defined fibromyalgia as - "unexplained widespread pain or aching, persistent fatigue, morning stiffness, and non-refreshing sleep"—conditions which are present for at least three months.

Pain is the most common and prominent symptom. It can be all over, or in one main region, but it is usually present in all four quadrants of the body (above and below the waist, and both the left and right sides.) Some people describe the pain as knife-like; some describe it as cramps, while still others describe it as flu-like—all-over aching. Although many people report pain in their joints, the pain of fibromyalgia is technically not in the joints, but rather in the muscles, tendons, ligaments, and tissue that connect to bones. Most individuals complain of aching and stiffness in areas around the neck, shoulders, upper back, lower back, and hip areas.

Fatigue is the next most common symptom. Nearly 90% of people with fibromyalgia have moderate to severe fatigue, which can range from listlessness, to exercise fatigue, to total exhaustion. About 75% of people with fibromyalgia have sleep disorders. Researchers are still trying to determine whether or not the pain causes the sleep disturbances, or whether the sleep disturbances contribute to the pain.

Fibromyalgia is often accompanied by mood changes. Although sufferers often report being "blue" or "down," only about 25% of people with fibromyalgia are clinically depressed (see Chapter 8).

Statistics show that more women are affected by fibromyalgia than men. Roughly 80% of those diagnosed are women, generally between the ages of 20 and 50, with fibromyalgia occurring most frequently in women of childbearing age.

This disorder is not reserved solely for adults. Recently, research has shown that fibromyalgia occurs in children, as well. It is also seems to run in families.

Misdiagnoses of fibromyalgia is common. One fibromyalgia patient remembers being told: "it [is] all in [your] head—take a pill—get counseling—get a hobby—get a life!"

There are no blood or x-ray tests that are abnormal in fibro-myalgia. The symptoms are wide-ranging, differing radically from one individual to another, and many symptoms overlap with other disorders. Many patients have no underlying disorders, while others who develop fibromyalgia may have existing conditions such as Rheumatoid arthritis, spinal arthritis, or Lyme disease. In addition, some sufferers have symptoms of irritable bowel syndrome, tension headaches, and coldness and numbness or tingling of the extremities.

Even though this disease is surprisingly common, there is no known cause. Sometimes trauma appears to be the catalyst, such as in a severe accident. Other factors that may contribute to fibromyalgia are extended periods of extreme psychological stress or biochemical abnormalities in the central nervous system, such as altered serotonin levels. Other research indicates that fibromyalgia may be triggered by something as seemingly minor as the flu.

Chronic Fatigue Syndrome, CFS for short, comes with its own bad news. Those who suffer from CFS feel a bone-weary flu-like fatigue that lasts for six months or more. This fatigue is not the result of another disease or condition, and it does not go away with adequate rest.

CFS is also diagnosed more frequently in women than in men, and occurs most often in Caucasians, between the ages of 25 and 50. It has been referred to as "yuppie flu," probably because of the high incidence of yuppies diagnosed with this condition. Whether this is because more yuppies get CFS or because more yuppies pursue a second and third opinion, sparing no expense to find out what is wrong, is not clear.

Like fibromyalgia, CFS can also be very difficult to pin down. The symptoms can be nondescript, as well as common, so it can be difficult to put together a diagnosis. Some who seem to suffer from CFS may actually have fibromyalgia. In fact, some scientific researchers theorize that fibromyalgia and CFS are actually one and the same disease.

It is not clear what causes CFS, but some doctors believe it is an immune system disorder (see Chapter 10). Some researchers feel it may be caused by exposure to the Epstein–Barr virus or the live rubella virus used in the vaccine for German measles. There is no known cure at this time.

NOW FOR SOME GOOD NEWS...

Even though fibromyalgia is chronic, it is not inflammatory, degenerative, or progressive. Patients may be reassured that the condition, while painful, does not damage tissues.

In addition, a simple diagnostic test has recently made diagnosing fibromylgia much easier. This test involves checking 18 specific points on the body for tenderness. These include points on the front and back of the neck, the chest and shoulders, the elbows, the hips and the knees. Those suffering from fibromylgia are highly sensitive in these areas. If such sensitivity occurs consistently, a diagnosis can readily be made.

The diagnosis for CFS has also been firmed up. If you have eight or more of the following symptoms for more than six months, explore with a doctor, the possibility of having CFS.

- Mild, but continuous sore throat
- Recurrent chills and fever
- Muscle weakness or discomfort
- Inability to concentrate
- Forgetfulness
- Sleep Disturbances
- Headaches
- Irritability
- Depression
- Joint Pain
- Excessive fatigue after exercise

Even though the causes of fibromyalgia and CFS are unknown and there are no cures at the present time, most cases can be managed. Fibromyalgia has been successfully treated with heat treatments, massage therapy, and supervised aerobic conditioning.

Exercise therapy has also helped fibromyalgia patients deal with muscle aches and stiffness. In addition, counseling is helpful in learning how to manage chronic pain.

Medications for better sleep and to relieve pain are also accessible. But care should be exercised with self-medicating. Stephanie A. Nagy, a certified therapeutic Recreation Specialist working with mental health and substance abuse patients, makes the following points:

- Due to pain and depression, people sometimes self-medicate with alcohol, opiates, illicit drugs, antidepressants, or even Tylenol.
- Approximately 25% of the people in treatment for drug abuse secondary to chronic or acute pain conditions (i.e - accident or surgery) are there due to self-medicating or becoming addicted to or dependent on pain medication. In reality, some of these patients have fibromyalgia.
- Some people do legitimately need medication, but over-doing it will not help.
- If current prescribed medication is not helping, do not try to self-medicate. Instead, contact a healthcare professional for assistance.

CFS can also be managed through exercise programs and medication. Alternative treatments, such as vitamin therapy and acupuncture, can also be tried.

The important thing to remember about these conditions is that they can be managed with patience and effort. Diana Karol Nagy, a sufferer of fibromyalgia and an *About.com* guide on Fibromyalgia and Chronic Fatigue Syndrome, remembers that after she was diagnosed with fibromyalgia, it took her a long time to get her health care regimen into place. Today, though, she has her fibromyalgia under control. Her secret?

"I became educated and finally realized that in order to have a successful treatment plan, I had to take charge of my own health care," Nagy reports. "I was on medication for a long time, but I didn't like how it made my head feel. Today, I try to get enough sleep, eat well, get a weekly massage, take walks when I can, and try to keep my life in balance."

Through this self-care, Nagy is able to manage her fibromyalgia and keep it from taking control of her life.

After carefully reviewing the symptoms for fibromyalgia and CFS, if they seem familiar and yet, diagnostic tests rule out these two diseases, maybe it is simply "21st century lifestyle" that is causing problems.

To understand this term, consider the properties of a rubber band.

Take hold of opposite sides of a rubber band, stretch it out tight, and then release it; the rubber band snaps back to its original shape. However, if the rubber band is wrapped around a stack of papers, stretched tight and left for a period of time, say a month or so, the rubber band will lose some elasticity and, while it would become smaller after being removed from the papers, it would fail to snap back to its original shape, leaving it stretched out. If this same rubber band were left stretched tight around the stack of papers for a year or more, the rubber band would lose most of its elasticity and become almost brittle. When attempting to remove it, chances are the rubber band would snap in two.

Compare the rubber band to a 21st century lifestyle. Today, life is hectic, fast-paced, plugged-in, and connected. The former long distance commercial that encourages—"reach out and touch someone"—is now out of date, as today you rarely find yourself out of touch in any manner.

For example, you come down with a case of stomach flu and are unable to go into the office. No problem! Thanks to internet connections, work files are downloaded at home in between bouts of vomiting.

The boss, a micro-managing control freak, has a family event that takes him out of the office just as the final phases of a business plan are winding up. No problem! Thanks to email, the boss can efficiently continuing nagging and managing via cyberspace from his laptop.

You're out of town on a special project for work, and can't attend that board meeting to make a presentation. No problem! Thanks to teleconferencing and video-conferencing capabilities, you stay connected to the home office, while still supervising that special project, thereby increasing productivity.

In recognizing the many ways to be plugged in and connected, it is easy to get a vision of life as a rubber band, being stretched ever tighter until there is no elasticity left. If this is your life, it may explain your sleep problems, tense, achy muscles, mind-numbing fatigue, and forgetfulness. The good news is that the methods to successfully treat fibromyalgia and CFS can also help with the hectic, fast-paced life of today.

Diana Nagy states that a person with a chronic illness often focuses only on the body. While this makes sense, she also recommends working with personal health care professionals to determine what course of treatment is right: medication, massage or physical therapy, healthy eating, and/or exercise. However, she adds that focusing only on the body has to change. The mind also needs to be fed and expanded, keeping busy with other activities: work, school, volunteer work, or informal learning. Nagy cautions against "over doing it" and states that time and stress management are also very important. Her final words of wisdom, that I fully support, are when having a really rough day, go to "Plan B," which is, "when all else fails – go to bed!"

The final good news is that whether facing fibromyalgia or chronic fatigue syndrome, or just trying to make it through another fast-paced difficult day, you can take control of your choices and manage your life. And, remember, "When all else fails – go to bed!" Tomorrow is another day.

FOLLOW-UP PREVENTIVE PERSCRIPTION

SELF DIAGNOSIS

If you think you or someone you know may be suffering from fibromyalgia or chronic fatigue syndrome, make a list of the symptoms listed above. Keep a log or diary of how you feel. If, over a period of a month or more, your symptoms match those for fibromyalgia or chronic fatigue syndrome, contact a health care provider for information. Keep asking questions until you get all the answers you need.

CHAPTER 12

EATING DISORDERS VS. DISORDERED EATING

Points to ponder as you read:

- ✓ What is "disordered eating?"
- ✓ What are the different types of eating disorders and how are they diagnosed?
- ✓ How can you find professional help to overcome a diagnosed eating disorder?
- ✓ What are the consequences of untreated (or undiagnosed) eating disorders?

Can you relate to any of the following scenarios?

- After skipping breakfast and working through lunch, you come home from work, ravenous, and head to the kitchen to whip up that nutritious meal you promised yourself to make. On the way to the fridge, however, you notice the cherry pie on the counter that you bought in a weak moment yesterday at the grocery store. You think to yourself, "Nutritious meal in half an hour or cherry pie now?" You decide that a small —very, very small piece—can do no harm. Two TV shows and half a cherry pie later, you are stuffed and realize that the nutritious meal is now merely a memory.

- You got a copy of "*Dr. Burns Celebrity Diet*," a favorite of starlets everywhere, with guaranteed quick weight-loss results. You have been following the diet to the letter—eating watercress soup for breakfast and lunch, and a salad with lemon and half a chicken breast for dinner for nine days, 23 hours, 17 minutes, and 54 seconds, and you are so sick of watercress soup and so hungry that the dog's kibble looks tempting. But if you can just hang on for four more days, you will surely have lost the 25 pounds in two weeks that the diet promised, and then you can go back to eating anything (and everything) you want.

- You and your family eat so many meals in the living room in front of the television. The kids have started referring to it as the dining room and have now suggested it would be more convenient to get rid of the end tables and move in the fridge.

- With a hectic schedule and frantic lifestyle, gulping down food is now an art. Your finely-tuned, eating-on-the-run skills have developed to the degree that you can consume any—and I do mean any—meal in less than 15 minutes flat. A specialty is eating on the road, having mastered "knee driving" so that you can eat anything, even tacos, without spilling food down the front of your clothes.

- You have developed a "saint or sinner" approach to nutrition. When you are good (as in eating healthy, well-balanced meals), you are very, very good; but when you are bad (as in eating your way through the candy aisle at Albertsons), you are awful. You have had more "last meals" than the convicts on death row. Your recurring behavior is to feel disgust with yourself at overeating and plan tomorrow to begin dieting anew. But first there is one last, blow-out meal with every fattening food you can think of.

- After looking at the models on the covers of fashion magazines and then looking at yourself in the mirror, you determine you are in desperate need of improvement. Totally unaware of the two hours with a hair stylist, an hour in makeup, and numerous photographic "tricks of the trade" used to give a model her glamorous appearance, you decide that will power is all that's needed to make you as stylish as any model out there. You may need to starve yourself, but that is a small price to pay to look like a supermodel.

If you can relate to any of the above, you have disordered eating and need to make some changes. Now! It might be amusing to read about poor eating habits, but there is nothing funny about what poor eating habits can do to the body and its health.

After 25 years of listening to women patients, I have come to believe that a majority of women in America today have a disordered view of eating, of body image (what a healthy body should really look like), and of the role eating food plays in the health process. (Men also have problems with eating, but because they are acceptable in larger sizes, they can usually eat as they want for a longer time before their eating habits affect their health.) Women, who essentially live on a diet (be honest now—-if you are on a diet more than you're not, I'm talking to you), are at risk for weight gain (despite extreme dieting), poor metabolism, frequent illnesses, depression, osteoporosis, and, last but certainly not least, the development of anorexia or bulimia.

In the 1960's, women's magazines began putting very thin women on their covers—holding them up as "the standard" by which American women should judge themselves when they look in the mirror. By 1965, many young girls were going on starvation diets, grapefruit diets, and popcorn diets so they could look like Twiggy, the young, emaciated, British model, who later admitted she had been anorexic for years. Mothers would suggest that daughters try their diet in order to "prevent weight gain." Fathers and brothers would tease daughters and sisters about "thunder thighs" or "chubby faces." And what was the result? The beginning of a vicious cycle of "yo-yo dieting."

Those women, who were the teens and college-aged girls of the 1960's, are now in their mid-40's to early 50's. Despite 35 years of trying to be thin, more than 60% are seriously overweight to obese. To add insult to injury, many are having to dealing with the after-effects of 35 years of malnutrition (or at least under-nu-trition). From years of an inadequate supply of essential vitamins, minerals, and phyto-nutrients in their diets, these women are now being diagnosed with osteoporosis, auto-immune disorders, de-pression, and fibromyalgia, and look older than their years.

Since the unhealthy eating practices inspired by the models of the 1960's are still flourishing today, it's important to learn from the mistakes of the past. Ask yourself, and answer honestly, the following question:

While focusing on a number on the scale, have you been guilty of jeopardizing your health?

If the answer is yes, it is important to realize that change is necessary now! Re-read chapters 4, 5, and 6 and make a firm commitment to make some much-needed changes to protect your health.

If, however, the problems you have with eating and food are deeper, more intense, and more serious than those described above, rather than disordered eating, you may be suffering from an eating disorder. This is a very serious and sometimes, fatal dis-ease.

There are many diseases, disorders, and problem conditions involving food, eating, and weight. In the context of our dis-cussion here, however, "eating disorders" will refer to anorexia nervosa, bulimia nervosa, and binge eating (also known as com-pulsive overeating).

ANOREXIA NERVOSA

Anorexia is often thought of as a disease of the young. How-ever, many women continue to suffer from varying degrees of this disorder into middle age. While adolescence is definitely a high-risk period for anorexia, there are many women who, having experienced this condition in adolescence, continue to suffer with the condition in to adulthood, keeping it hidden or relapsing into the old habits when experiencing a crisis.

The exact cause of this disorder is not known, but social attitudes towards body, appearance, and family factors play a role in its development. The condition usually occurs in adolescence or young adulthood, and is more common in women than in men, affecting 1 to 2% of the female population and only 0.1 to 0.2% of males.

Anorexia is seen mainly in Caucasian women who are high academic achievers and have a goal-oriented family or personality. Some experts have suggested that conflicts within a family may contribute to anorexia. For example anorexia may be a subconscious way for a child to draw attention away from marital problems, and bring the family back together.

Anorexia is generally diagnosed as self-induced starvation. A woman who is anorectic wants to be as skinny as possible and expresses an aversion for food. The desire to lose weight becomes an obsession. No matter how thin a woman with this illness may get, she thinks she is too fat. She literally has a distorted body image. The most obvious danger with anorexia is death by starvation, but there are other risks involved. A woman who has been anorectic for a number of years stands a much higher risk for developing osteoporosis and gastrointestinal disorders, among other conditions. Anorexia also weakens the heart, as in the case of Karen Carpenter, the results of which were fatal.

An anorexic person may have some or all of the following characteristics:

- Refuses to maintain normal body weight for age and height
- Weighs 85% or less than what is expected for age and

height
- Denies the dangers of low weight
- Is terrified of becoming fat
- Is terrified of gaining weight even though s/he is markedly underweight
- Develops skeletal muscle atrophy
- Has severe loss of fatty tissue
- Experiences low blood pressure
- Has dental problems from self-induced vomiting
- Has blotchy or yellow skin
- Is usually "in denial," refusing to recognize that they have an eating disorder
- Reports feeling fat even when very thin

In young girls with anorexia, menstrual periods do not begin at the appropriate age. In women, menstrual periods stop and men experience low levels of sex hormones.

In addition, anorexia nervosa can include depression, irritability, withdrawal, and peculiar behaviors such as compulsive rituals, strange eating habits, and dividing foods into "good/safe" or "bad/dangerous" categories. An anorexic may have low tolerance for change and new situations. She may fear growing up and assuming adult responsibilities and an adult lifestyle, being overly engaged with, or dependent on, parents or family. For an anorexic, dieting may represent avoidance of, or ineffective attempts to cope with the demands of a new life stage, such as adolescence. It allows a person to subconsciously and literally "disappear," rather than face a feared scenario.

BULIMIA NERVOSA

A bulimic can have any or all of the following behavior and thought patterns:

- Binge eats
- Feels out of control while eating

- Vomits, misuses laxatives, exercises, or fasts to get rid of calories consumed
- Goes through a cycle of binging, dieting, and binging again
- Falsely believes self-worth requires being thin

Additionally, bulimics often engage in self-destructive behavior, such as shoplifting, promiscuity, alcohol and drug abuse, or compulsive shopping with out-of-control credit card spending. Even though bulimics put up a brave front, they are often depressed, lonely, ashamed, and empty inside. Friends may describe them as competent and fun to be with, but inside there are guilty secrets. Bulimics hurt, feel unworthy, and have great difficulty talking about their feelings, which almost always include anxiety, depression, self-doubt, and deeply buried anger. Impulse control is a problem, as evidenced by the self-destructive, risky behaviors listed above. A bulimic acts with little consideration of consequences. Weight may be normal or near-normal unless suffering from anorexia, as well.

BINGE EATING

A binge eater is someone who:

- Eats frequently and repeatedly
- Feels out of control and unable to stop eating during binges
- May eat rapidly and secretly, or may snack and nibble all day long
- Feels guilty and ashamed of binge eating
- Has a history of diet failures
- Tends to be depressed and obese

People who have a binge eating disorder do not regularly vomit, over-exercise, or abuse laxatives. They may be genetically predisposed to weigh more than the cultural ideal (which, at present, is exceedingly unrealistic), so they diet, make themselves hungry, and then binge in response to that hunger. Or they eat for emotional reasons—to comfort themselves, avoid threatening situations, and/or numb emotional pain. Regardless of the reason, diet programs are not the answer for bingers. In fact, diets almost always make matters worse.

The first step to overcoming any eating disorder is to admit there is a problem. It is difficult to admit to any eating, exercise, or body image disorder and that treatment is needed. However, taking those first anxious or fear-ridden steps to get help will also give you hope!

Finding and getting the right professional help is essential. If you or someone you care about exhibits eating disorder behaviors, as described above, seek medical help immediately. There are a variety of treatment options available—individual therapy, group therapy, nutritional support, psychiatric care, outpatient, inpatient, and residential care. Start with your primary care physician and seek a referral to a specialist.

In addition, the following guidelines can help:

- DON'T DIET. It sounds simplistic, but if no one ever dieted, there would be no anorexia nervosa or other eating disorders. Instead of dieting, design a meal plan that gives the body all the nutrition it needs for normal growth and health. If healthy weight is the goal, limit (but don't eliminate) the intake of fatty and sugary foods, and refined carbohydrates. Instead, eat lots of whole grains, fruits, vegetables, and enough dairy and protein foods to maintain strong bones and healthy muscles and organs.

- EXERCISE SENSIBLY. Try to get 30 to 45 minutes of exercise or physical activity three to five days a week. Unless a coach or trainer is supervising, anything more rigorous is excessive.

- TRAIN THOUGHTS AWAY FROM FEELING FAT. When you start to get overwhelmed by "feeling fat," instead of dwelling on appearance, consider how life would be better if you were actually thinner. What would you have that you don't have now? Friends? Self-confidence? Love? Control? The admiration of others? Their acceptance? Success and status?

Realize that being unhealthily thin will bring none of these things, only a fragile illusion of success that has to be constantly reinforced with even more weight loss. All of the above items are legitimate goals of healthy people, but working to achieve them directly is much more effective than focusing on losing weight. If weight loss brought happiness, then starving Third World children would be ecstatic with joy.

- DEVELOP A REALISTIC BODY IMAGE. Recently on a syndicated game show, the question was asked, "What should a mother hide from her teenage daughter in order to protect her health?" Although the celebrity contestants came up with some bizarre (and rather frightening) answers, the correct answer was also a little surprising.

"What should a mother hide from her teenage daughter in order to protect her health?" Fashion magazines. The host of the show explained that a perfect, pencil-thin, "body beautiful" woman featured in fashion magazines gives girls a distorted image of their own bodies and fosters unrealistic expectations of how they should look.

Accept that your body shape is determined in part by genetics, and that you may never have a totally flat stomach. Even if very thin, your internal organs will give you a certain roundedness, especially after eating, and additionally, if people in the family tend to store fat in the midsection.

- GET HELP IF YOU SLIP. The road to recovery for those suffering from eating disorders is often long and hard. No one travels it gracefully. There are many slips, trips, and lapses.

Those who eventually do recover learn to pick themselves
up when they fall, brush off the dust, and keep going. By so
doing, they keep a temporary lapse from turning into a full-
blown relapse.

If you feel yourself slipping back into unhealthy habits, call
your therapist and schedule an appointment. Returning to counseling in no way means failure. It only means it's time to re-evalu-
ate and fine-tune your recovery plan.

• REALIZE EATING DISORDERS CAN BE DEADLY.
  These disorders do not go away by themselves. Ongoing eating
  disorders, left untreated, can lead to tragic consequences. The
  following are signs of severe complications tied to eating
  disorders. These are conditions where hospitalization may be
  required.

  • Severe dehydration, possibly leading to cardiovascular
    shock
  • Electrolyte imbalance (such as potassium
    insufficiency)
  • Cardiac arrest related to the loss of cardiac muscle and
    electrolyte imbalance
  • Severe malnutrition
  • Thyroid gland deficiencies which lead to cold
    intolerance and constipation
  • Appearance of fine, baby-like body hair
  • Bloating or edema
  • Decrease in white blood cells which leads to increased
    susceptibility to infection
  • Osteoporosis
  • Tooth erosion and decay from self-induced vomiting

Another factor to keep in mind according to research is that
some individuals, suffering from an eating disorder may have a
genetic flaw. This flaw, in combination with lifestyle factors, can
predispose some individuals to develop eating disorders and these

conditions may run in families. If one family member develops an eating disorder, genetics combined with environment may be the basis for other members to develop similar problems.

The most critical thing to keep in mind with eating disorders is that they are treatable. If you suffer from one of the disorders described above, get help. Life does not have to be controlled by problems with food. Those who eventually do recover learn to pick themselves up when they fall and keep going. It isn't easy, and change won't happen immediately. Remember disorders don't develop overnight, but through perseverance, hard work, and never giving up on yourself, recovery can be accomplished. Eating disorders can be beaten, and you can be the one to do it!

FOLLOW-UP PREVENTIVE PERSCRIPTION

SEEKING PROFESSIONAL HELP

In trying to find a therapist to help with an eating disorder, consider the following information from the Eating Disorder Referral and Information Center (Edreferral.com).

Contact a professional referral service. Professional organizations maintain referral lists of qualified therapists. For instance, you could look up an organization for psychiatrists or psychologists. These organizations can help make an appropriate match according to the specific problem and the therapist's expertise. If a therapist receives any complaints, the referral service is available to evaluate and resolve the dispute. If consistent problems occur, the therapist will be removed from the service. Most referral services require therapists to maintain the highest level of professionalism, and also perform extra screenings before referring them.

Do not accept the first therapist contacted, unless the rapport is immediate and comfortable. Talk to at least three therapists, and keep in mind that a call returned quickly does not imply that the therapist is a good one. It may seem preferable to see a therapist that is busy and popular, but a therapist's expertise cannot be determined with a quick returned phone call. Talk to each therapist on the phone, and determine whether there is a sense of comfort before committing to treatment.

Before calling a therapist, decide if you want a same-sex therapist or one of the opposite sex. If you are apprehensive about therapy, then choose the sex of the therapist with whom you feel most comfortable.

Next, find out how much you can afford for therapy. If therapy is once a week, then figure out how much you can afford to pay for four sessions in a month. If you have insurance, contact the carrier and obtain in writing what they cover. For instance, find out if you have to see a specific therapist on their list, or if you have to see a particular type of therapist. Ask the carrier how much they pay for each office visit, and how many sessions they will cover. Also, ask about annual and lifetime pay-out limits.

When ready to contact a potential therapist, here are some questions to ask on the phone. Ask if he has a few minutes to talk about therapy. If he is not available at that moment, ask when a call would be more convenient. If he is too busy for even this brief introductory talk, ask whether he is accepting new clients and when the first available appointment could be made. If it is too long a wait for an appointment, then ask for a referral to another therapist. The average wait is usually less than a week, although occasionally, with very busy therapists, it can be up to six months.

Does the therapist limit his practice to a particular type of client? For example, does the therapist do individual, family, or couples therapy? What type of therapy does he use? What type of experience, training, and license does the therapist have? Will the therapist read your history before the first session? How long are the sessions, and how often does the therapist generally schedule sessions for? In addition, of course, what is the fee and will the therapist accept your insurance and how are co-payments handled? (Co-payments are the amount paid by the client beyond the insurance payment). Ask the therapist about a "sliding fee scale," a fee that "slides" or varies according to the client's ability to pay or based on their monthly income.

Has the therapist ever had a license revoked or suspended? Has he ever been disciplined by a state or professional ethics board and, if so, would he be willing to discuss it? (Call the state licensing board to check out his license, credentials, and any ethical violations).

If anything negative results from these questions, tell the therapist that you want to talk to a few other potential therapists, and will call back if an appointment is wanted. Give yourself some time to think over and digest your feelings about the phone conversations. Then choose a therapist and make an appointment for an initial trial session. The first session will help you decide if you want to work with this therapist.

After leaving the first session, assess carefully how you feel. Was the therapist open to the manner in which you presented your history? Did you get a sense that you could be comfortable with this therapist? Did you feel a sense of connection? Remember that each therapist creates a different environment and decide if the atmosphere felt right. Can this therapist be trusted? Did the therapist push too quickly for you to reveal things that were uncomfortable? Were your needs heard? Did the therapist behave in a professional manner? Did the therapist explain how therapy works and were goals set? Did you feel comfortable about the goals that were set?

There are a lot of excellent therapists, and you have the right to find the one that fits your needs the best. Remember, the therapist is there to serve you.

CHAPTER 13

CHRONIC DIETING
Silent Thief of Health
and
The Resultant Osteoporosis
Nightmare in Young Women

Points to ponder as you read:

- ✓ What is meant by the term "chronic dieting?"
- ✓ How can chronic dieting affect health?
- ✓ Why should worry about osteoporosis at age 25?
- ✓ What health problems stem from osteoporosis?

Anyone who lives in Seattle will say it rains . . . a lot. On the plus side, this accounts for abundant green trees, lush vegetation and gorgeous, breathtaking scenery. On the minus side, it also accounts for rain-saturated hillsides, swirling flood waters, and mudslides.

Several years ago, residents on a high Seattle street, along the top of a hill with spectacular city views, were anxiously wondering if their very expensive homes would end up sliding down the hill. This concern was based on the collapse of hundreds of feet of land, lying below their front yards. There had been thick growth all the way down the hillside but, because of continual rains, the ground became so saturated there was no place for the water to go. Springs began bursting from the ground underneath the thick vegetation, which made the land extremely unstable and, eventually, did cause a slide.

Imagine the feelings of insecurity if, standing on the deck, you looked down and saw that much of the land below you, land that you once considered part of your home's foundation, had been washed away. It's hard for a home to remain upright and stable if part of the foundation is gone.

To have a home go sliding down a hillside would be devastating. However, there is a similar type of foundation erosion that is far more critical. It occurs in the body. This erosion, rather than being triggered by torrential rains, is fostered by chronic dieting.

The sad truth is that the majority of women in America have spent their lives dieting, often starving themselves, hoping to emulate cover girl models. This first became a phenomenon in the Roaring Twenties when being thin was "all the rage." It returned with a vengence in the 1960's when Twiggy burst onto the modeling scene. Soon, there were stories of young girls and women going on starvation diets, trying to achieve a body that was skeletal—one that had also been achieved by anorexia and bulimia. Many supermodels of today admit that they have to starve themselves to keep the body shape and size required by the modeling agency. And this is the standard to which too many young girls and women hold themselves (see Chapter 12).

Chronic dieting causes erosion that is far more insidious than the erosion of land during excessive rains. This erosion takes place inside the body due to a lack of necessary nutrients—day in, day out, month in, month out, resulting in a complete devastation of health if not caught in time.

One of the most significant and disabling effects of chronic dieting is osteoporosis. Osteoporosis is a disease often considered an older woman's disease. But while there are many older women suffering with the collapsed vertebrae, stooped posture and chronic back pain associated with this disability, it is now not uncommon to see a 25-year-old with a wrist fracture because she too has osteoporosis. Currently, the age group with the largest increase in hip fractures is women in their 40's! Although this is shocking, diet trends and the increasing percentage of women (and very young teenage girls) who are, essentially, always on a diet point to a problem that will become much worse and more prevalent over time.

CHRONIC DIETING

Chronic dieting greatly impacts bone strength and silently erodes good health.

Chronic dieting is a subtype of disordered eating (see Chapter 12).

Actually, the name says it all: Chronic means habitual or frequent recurrence. Dieting means to eat or drink less according to a prescribed rule. Therefore, a chronic dieter is someone who frequently or habitually restricts the amount of food and drink in their diet. This leads to several, potentially serious health issues.

First, many chronic dieters choose to go on diets that are not based on principles of good nutrition. A chronic dieter often selects a diet because it looks easy, is "in fashion," or comes recommended by a best friend. The word "diet" is often connected with the words, "short-term" and "failure," because that is what occurs with essentially all diets.

Because most diets are unbalanced, a person can't stay on one for long. The body almost always rebels. Weak and half-starved, the dieter goes off the diet and back to old eating habits, and usually regains the weight lost—along with a few more pounds! A month or two later, disgusted with out-of-control eating, the person is on to another, better, newer, quicker-results diet.

Again, because the body's nutritional needs are not being met, within a few weeks, the diet is again discarded, and old eating habits resumed. Soon the weight creeps back on because, for many people, going "off the diet" can be like "falling off the wagon" is for an alcoholic. "Off" status justifies binge-eating all the rich, empty–calorie foods that were strenuously resisted during two weeks of meals consisting of half a grapefruit and two boiled eggs. In addition, the dieter feels tired all the time, which leads to bypassing exercise. The more sedentary, the more weight gained. The vicious cycle of chronic dieting continues.

Please understand that each time a diet is followed that does not meet the body's protein needs, more lean muscle than fat is lost. When returning to old habits, more calories are eaten than needed, and only fat is regained. After many cycles of dieting, precious lean muscle mass is lost that determines metabolism. The less muscle available, the slower the metabolism. The higher the body fat, the lower the metabolism.

To understand how this works, let's look at two different women, both of whom are 5'5" and weigh 145 pounds.

The first woman, Jennifer, is an active gal who plays tennis and goes to Pilates twice weekly. She has rarely been on a diet, choosing to exercise and eat sensibly for weight control. A body composition analysis on Jennifer shows that she has 120 pounds of lean muscle with 19% body fat. She is in excellent shape (wears a size 6) and is burning over 1900 calories at rest—the resting metabolic rate (RMR).

Susie is the same height and weight as Jennifer, but her numbers are far different. She "lives" on a diet, and has done so since she was 16 years old. Her body composition shows a lean muscle mass of 105 pounds with 32% body fat. She squeezes into a size 10 (on a good day) and her RMR is only 1150 calories. Even if Susie exercises one-and-a-half hours at the gym (and how likely is it that Susie has this much time or energy?) she would probably only burn an average of 450 calories, which means she will have to eat less than 1100 calories per day in order to lose an average of one pound per week. It also means that Susie will have to eat even less calories on the days she doesn't exercise or isn't at the gym for an hour and a half.

Two women—same height and weight: the non-dieter is a smaller size and has a higher metabolism, which means she can eat more without gaining weight, and still look great. The other woman looks far heavier (fat takes up far more space than muscle) and has to eat fewer calories in order to not gain weight. There is also no way to supply her body with the necessary nutrients.

Sadly, Susie is not only having problems with the outside of her body, but she's having problems on the inside as well. With chronic dieting, calcium is being leached out of her bones, her immune system is becoming less resistant to both infections and chronic diseases (due to inadequate antioxidants and essential fatty acids), she is at increased risk of becoming anemic (because of inadequate iron & B vitamins), she may be weakening her heart muscle (from inadequate protein), and the list continues.

Susie's prognosis does not have to be yours.

Refer back to Chapter Six, where there is a "perfect solution" for the Susie's of the world. No one should ever be on a diet, as we understand this term today. But everyone can and should make a commitment to eat healthfully and to exercise (move) every day. It's important to follow an eating plan—not diet, high in protein, low in calories, and enriched with vitamins and other supplements. This type of eating plan will actually rebuild and permanently increase muscle mass and metabolism. Susie's problems do not have to be yours. The trap of chronic dieting can be broken.

A house remains upright because of a solid foundation; and a body remains upright for the same reason. However, a house's foundation is concrete and a body's foundation is skeletal. One thing science has proven beyond doubt is that bones need calcium to be strong; and if, through poor eating, the bones do not receive adequate amounts of calcium, vitamin D, and other necessary nutrients, the bone structure is undermined.

WHAT YOU SHOULD KNOW ABOUT CALCIUM

If you have forgotten your parents' admonition to "drink your milk," you only have to walk through a supermarket and see all the calcium-fortified juices, cereals, and other products to realize that calcium is something that, to paraphrase a commercial, "does a body good."

However, if you are using calcium-fortified products, thinking you are taking good care of your bones, think again. Next time you buy some calcium-fortified orange juice, check out the amount of calcium in one eight-ounce serving. There is a very small percentage of the daily amount of calcium needed in each serving. Calcium-fortified juices and other products are not intended to be a major source of calcium. "Calcium-fortified" is, in fact, a marketing scheme. The public knows that calcium is essential. "Calcium-fortified" on a label is a marketing strategy to get people to buy more of a particular product. Don't be taken in by advertising and labeling. Make sure to get an adequate daily intake of calcium through natural sources to prevent bone loss and reduce the risk of osteoporosis.

Knowing a few facts about bones will explain why osteoporosis occurs. The bone structure is made up of both calcium salts and phosphate salts, which form hydroxyapatite crystals, held together in a "matrix" of collagen. These hydroxyapatite crystals give bone its amazing strength and ability to withstand stress. Collagen, the main protein of skin, tendons, and cartilage, also provides flexibility to bones.

When viewed through a microscope, bone structure resembles a sponge. Cortical bone makes up 80% of the skeleton and resembles dense sponge. Cancellous bone, the other 20%, is found in the interior of the bone, resembles "loose sponge," and is more metabolically active. The skeletal mass is constantly losing cells, remodeling cells, and building cells. Therefore, the skeletal mass you have today will be 100% changed in a little over one year! Consequently, if an eating plan is inadequate in bone-supporting nutrients, the cancellous bone will become even less dense, which is the beginning of the road to osteoporosis.

Calcium is an essential nutrient for bones and teeth, using about 99% of the calcium in the body. The remaining 1% is essential for many cellular functions, including the maintenance of proper electrolyte balance in the heart muscle and regulation of heart rhythm. Calcium also aids in clotting and is essential for proper nerve transmission. It helps maintain normal blood pressure and, therefore, plays a role in preventing hypertension (high blood pressure).

In order to perform the above-described functions, the cells must have calcium on demand. Bones serve as a reservoir of calcium, responding to the various needs of the body. People with an inadequate intake of calcium, such as chronic dieters, will require their bones to "give up" calcium in order to keep the heart pumping properly, nerves transmitting normally, etc.

The amount of calcium an individual needs is dependent on dietary factors, including the amount of protein and sodium eaten on a daily basis. People with low intakes of protein (such as in the traditional Asian diet) will have lower calcium needs.

Conversely, in the United States where our protein intake is higher, calcium tends to be lost from the bones. This is another concern regarding the high protein diets that are currently in vogue. It is believed by most experts (and confirmed in studies) that these diets are both low in calcium and stimulate increased calcium excretion (leading to increased calcium loss from the skeleton). Excellent data from the Framingham Study shows over a period of many years, diets high in fruits, vegetables, potassium, and magnesium are associated with preservation of bone mass in both men and women. Other nutrients that aid calcium absorption include vitamin D, copper, zinc, manganese, silicon, and boron.

A high phosphorus intake tends to favor bone resorption (loss). There is good evidence that chronic excessive intake of carbonated beverages (extremely high in phosphates) will lead to bone loss as well as demineralization of teeth. Just think of the impact of soda machines that are on almost every school campus. A study completed by Grace Wyshak of the Harvard School of Public Health (HSPH) and Harvard Medical School (HMS) was published in the June 2000 issue of the Archives of Pediatric and Adolescent Medicine. This study checked girls in two different suburban Detroit high schools for risk of fracture. The researchers examined 15- to 17-year-old girls and found they were already showing signs of bone loss. Why? The study proved a clear correlation between the intake of sodas and the likelihood of fracture. Follow-up BMD (Bone Mineral Density) studies confirmed lower T-scores in the girls who drank significant amounts of carbonated beverages per day, compared with girls who drank far less sodas. (A T-score is a scale where any women's bone density can be compared to other women her age and also to the average 25-year-old woman the peak of bone density.)

The news from this study is alarming because the body begins to build bone mass in infancy and continues to do so throughout childhood into young adulthood, reaching a peak between the ages of 25 and 30. During these formative years, it is obviously important to get the proper amount of calcium, vitamin D, and other nutrients to ensure strong bone formation to reach maximum density. After the ages of 25 to 30, everyone (both men and women) needs to continue to provide their bodies with these necessary nutrients in the recommended amounts for life, but during the formative years it is critical.

This can't be emphasized enough. When the body does not get the calcium it needs, bones begin to deteriorate. This is the start of osteoporosis. It leads to a weakened bone structure, which in turn leads to an increased risk for fractures. Since these effects may remain undetected and painless in the early stages, osteoporosis is the "silent thief."

Unfortunately, as this disease progresses, it no longer remains silent. It causes bones to become weak, fragile, and susceptible to fracture. Osteoporosis affects regions of the spine, as well as the hip and wrist. It leads to collapse of vertebrae in the spine, leading to loss of height, a chronic "stooped" appearance, and severe pain.

The symptoms of osteoporosis can truly devastate a sufferer's quality of life. Deformity often causes loss of self-esteem, disability, and may force a patient to give up activities that previously brought enjoyment. Hip fractures are one of the most disabling events for older women. Many women go from leading happy, independent lives to being confined in a nursing home (while recovering from surgery to repair their fractured hip). At this point, the likelihood of secondary complications, including pneumonia and stroke, is very high. Thus, osteoporosis is not only a leading cause of disability, but of premature death.

Increasing dietary calcium intake, as well as ensuring proper intake of other bone-supporting nutrients, can help prevent theft of calcium from bones, stopping osteoporosis before it has a chance to start. The best way to increase dietary calcium is to utilize calcium-rich foods in an everyday nutritional program. Because most people do not take in adequate calcium by food sources, calcium supplements are extremely prudent for all women and men who do not consume dairy products.

The new NIH Consensus Statement has raised the recommendations for daily calcium intake beginning in childhood. Teens and young adults, male and female (ages 11-24), are recommended to take 1200-1500 mg calcium per day. Adults between the ages 25 and 65 are encouraged to get 1000 mg calcium per day for health. Once women reach menopause, if they are not using estrogen, they should increase their calcium intake to 1500 mg per day, as should all men and women over the age of 65. The

National Academy of Science suggests that all adults consume 1200 mg of calcium per day, and some experts recommend up to 2000 mg daily for postmenopausal women. It is easy to see why osteoporosis is such a health threat, when the typical American woman consumes less than 600 milligrams of calcium per day.

Calcium isn't just good for bones. There are several valid studies that show a reduction of symptoms in PMS (premenstrual syndrome), especially moodiness and sweets cravings, by taking both calcium and magnesium in recommended daily amounts. So, ladies, here's a way to be less moody, have less cravings, and be good to your bones!

Most Americans do not achieve the RDA of calcium because of misconceptions about which foods are calcium-rich, and just how much of these foods is needed to supply daily requirements. For instance, a single eight-ounce glass of 2% low-fat milk only contains 288 mg of calcium, and many women avoid dairy products altogether because of the fat content. But, achieving the RDA of calcium is not hard to do if low-fat or nonfat dairy products and cheese are eaten, along with green leafy vegetables and almonds. Below is a suggested eating plan for a calcium perfect day.

Breakfast

Soy Protein Smoothie
- 2-3 scoops vitamin-mineral enriched soy protein powder
- eight-ounces low-fat soy milk
- ½ cup blueberries

Lunch

- Vegetarian tossed salad with lots of greens and raw veggies, including broccoli florets, cubed low-fat cheese, sliced almonds, and dressing made from fat-free plain yogurt

Dinner

Tofu Stirfry
- 1 cup cubed tofu
- 1 cup spinach
- 1 cup broccoli
- ½ cup sliced onion
- ½ cup red bell pepper cooked in 1 tablespoon olive oil
- Serve over ½ cup brown rice

Dessert

- 1 cup of apple slices
- dipped in eight-ounces vanilla fat-free yogurt

The above eating suggestions provide the daily calcium needs. But it is also clear that most Americans simply don't fulfill their calcium needs through their eating choices. This is why supplements are so important for all who do not eat at least 3 to 4 servings per day of calcium-rich foods.

Look for supplements that provide both calcium and vitamin D in divided dose form. Since the body cannot absorb more than 500 mg at a time, keep that in mind when considering supplements. Calcium citrate is better absorbed than calcium carbonate, but only 60% as opposed to 40%, and the citrate form is more bulky, which can make for very large tablets to swallow. A blend of citrate and carbonate is best, along with 400 IU vitamin D. (It is now understood that both men and women over the age of 65 should increase their vitamin D intake to at least 600 IU, as they no longer make vitamin D efficiently. Vitamin D is usually produced in the skin through sun exposure. People who spend little time outdoors should be sure to supplement with extra vitamin D, no matter what their age.) It is preferable to take a calcium supplement at the end of a meal, as the decrease in pH (more acid) related to eating will favor increased calcium absorption.

CHRONIC DIETING AND LACK OF OTHER BONE ESSENTIAL NUTRIENTS

Let's take a look at other essential bone nutrients that chronic dieting can be depleted in.

Vitamin K

While most people know vitamin K is essential for normal blood clotting, certain metabolites of vitamin K are also essential for bone health. The exact role is not clear, but people on chronic warfarin (low vitamin K state) are at increased risk of osteoporosis. The Nurses' Health Study showed women who were in the lowest quartile of vitamin K intake had the highest incidence of hip fractures.

Boron

Boron affects calcium balance by reducing calcium loss in the urine. Boron is found in beans, nuts, legumes, beer and wine, and green leafy vegetables. Boron supplemented via a multivitamin is wise, especially if the eating plan does not regularly include it. Chronic dieters, who would not tend to be eating the above on a regular basis, should be sure their multivitamin preparation contains at least 150 micrograms.

Fluoride

Fluoride is found extensively in soil. Many municipal water supply systems are also supplemented with fluoride. There are a number of studies now confirming that high dose fluoride, along with adequate calcium intake, increases bone density and reduces hip fractures.

Phytoestrogens

Diets rich in soy appear to be bone-protective. It is believed to be the isoflavone content that confers the protection from fractures and helps to preserve bone mass. Animal studies have shown that isoflavones diadzein and genestien directly stop bone demin-eralization. Studies in postmenopausal women have shown in-creased bone density with diets rich in soy protein and low in fat. The recommended amount of isoflavones is 30-50 mg per day.

At the start of the chapter, we discussed the risk of a home sliding down a hillside. We can all understand what a frightening prospect that would be. What I want you to realize is that the loss of strong, healthy bones carries far worse consequences. If you are a chronic dieter, stop now! Take a nutritional, common-sense approach to eating, making sure to give the body all the calcium and other nutrients it needs.

You have the power to stop chronic dieting from silently stealing your health.

FOLLOW-UP PREVENTIVE PERSCRIPTION

KNOW THE RISK FACTORS AND TAKE APPROPRIATE STEPS TO COUNTERACT THEM.

Risk Factors For Osteoporosis:

1. Small build, low body weight (below 125 pounds)
2. Caucasian or Asian female
3. Family history
4. Smoking
5. Excessive caffeine (more than five cups per day)
6. Excessive alcohol
7. Sedentary lifestyle
8. Poor diet (as in chronic dieting)
9. History of eating disorders, anorexia, bulimia, and compulsive overeating
10. Prolonged amenorrhea (lack of menstrual period—

often seen in gymnasts, long distance runners, and ballerinas)

11. Excessive consumption of carbonated soft drinks (diet *and* regular)

Medications That May Increase Calcium Loss:

- Corticosteroids
- Lasix
- Antiseizure medications
- Antacids with aluminum
- Warfarin (Coumadin)
- Cholestyramine

Healthy Bones Dietary Recommendations:

PROTEIN—Try to limit excessive animal protein intake, which increases calcium excretion in the urine. Provide at least 30 mg isoflavones (generally three servings of soy foods) per day.

CALCIUM—Combined sources from diet and supplements should total 1200 mg per day under age 50 and 1500 mg per day over age 50 (for both men & women)

GREEN VEGETABLES—Asparagus, cabbage, broccoli, romaine lettuce, and other leafy greens all supply vitamin K. Broccoli is also a reasonable non-dairy source of calcium

LIMIT intake of salt, sugar, caffeine, soft drinks, and alcohol

Supplement Suggestions:

CALCIUM—see above

VITAMIN D—400 IU/day; increase to 600 IU/day over age 65

MAGNESIUM—400 mg/day (*NOTE*: if suffering from kidney disease, check with your doctor.)

VITAMIN C—cofactor in collagen formation (part of

bone matrix) 500-1000 mg/ day

OMEGA-3 FATTY ACIDS—1000 mg per day (*NOTE*:
If you are taking blood-thinning medications, check
with your doctor.)

ZINC—30-456 mg/ day

BORON—3 mg/ day

COPPER—1 mg/ day

Exercise/Activity Considerations:

There is a clear correlation between weight-bearing exercise
and activities, and higher bone density. There are abundant reasons to be as active in life as possible. Prevention of osteoporosis is
just one more reason to be active each and every day!

Other:

All women age 40 and up are urged to review carefully the
risk factors to determine their personal osteoporosis risk. Discuss
with a physician when to have a bone density test. Also, if Bone
Mineral Density is in the osteoporosis range, discuss the use of the
appropriate medications.

CHAPTER 14

NEW HORMONE CHALLENGES
for the 21st Century Woman

Points to ponder as you read:

- ✓ Is PMS something that just has to be lived with?
- ✓ Can endometriosis be cured?
- ✓ Is surgery the only option for fibroids?
- ✓ What are the real risks of hormone replacement therapy and how do you find the right treatment?

Women today are living radically different lives than their female ancestors. Modern diets and lifestyles are dramatically changed and and so are our modern bodily functions. There is probably no part of our bodies more impacted than our hormones. Evolutionarily, our hormonal system is designed to facilitate pregnancy and lactation. It is not designed to be menopausal, to deal with stressful lifestyles, to withstand environmental toxins (many of which affect hormonal function), or to cope with unhealthy diets that tend to increase estrogen levels and activity leading to many estrogen-related conditions, including endometriosis, uterine fibroids, fibrocystic breast disease, and all the gynecologic cancers—cervical, ovarian, uterine, and breast.

The science of "women's health" is amazingly new. Until the 1980's, there were almost no studies looking at the difference between men and women—in health or in disease. We know the anatomical differences, of course, but not the functional ones. Specific hormonal issues were just not studied, in part, because it was considered unethical to do research on women for fear they would become pregnant and be adversely affected by the research parameters. Even drugs such as hormones and oral contraceptives were initially tested on men and on animals so as not to cross this artificial barrier related to research on women.

We are just now beginning to see studies that examine how drugs work in women as opposed to men. Consequently, we are still in the earliest stages of learning the "why's"—not only of specific female functions, but of the many diseases that have different courses in women compared to men.

For example, Rheumatoid arthritis. This disease is four to six times more likely to occur in a woman than a man. Lupus (SLE) occurs nine times more frequently in a woman. In fact, essentially all auto-immune disorders occur more frequently in women than they do in men. Lots of theories exist, but there are no solid, scientifically-verified reasons as to why this is so.

With that said, here is my philosophy as it applies to women's health.

In general, women know their bodies very well. Women are far more in tune with their bodies than men are. That is why women are also far more likely to seek out a medical opinion about changes, about something that is perceived to be abnormal, and about figuring out if what is happening is truly normal. Our modern medical paradigm tends to lead us to believe that normal functions of menstruation, pregnancy, and menopause are somehow abnormal and in need of treatment. A multitude of over-the-counter products are on the shelves of pharmacies and grocery stores for dealing with menstruation. The normal fluctuations of the menstrual cycle, or even menstruation itself, are to be manipulated, treated, and prevented. A few years back, the

FDA declared that menopause was a disease and as such, natural products could not be labeled as being beneficial for menopause as that would be paramount to a disease treatment claim. How ludicrous it is to declare a perfectly normal transition of life as disease!

Our mindset must shift to focus on the dietary and lifestyle changes needed to promote optimum functioning of all body parts and systems. Do not just put your life in the hands of a doctor to "fix"—via drugs, surgery, or other treatments. Be willing to take control of your own life. Look at the body as a precious resource, to be treasured and pampered. (By that, I am not referring to pounds of chocolate and frequent shopping trips - although I truly am a "shop till you drop" kind of gal!)

Let's specifically examine some of the stages of life that are part of a woman's health.

MENSTRUATION AND PMS (PREMENSTRUAL SYNDROME)

The normal menstrual cycle is 28 days on average, although some are as short as 21 days and others as long as 35. During the first half of the cycle, there is a gradual rise in both estrogen and progesterone hormones. Ovulation occurs on day 14 (approximately), with day 1 being the first day of menstruation. During the second half of the cycle, progesterone rises quicker than estrogen. It is essentially the fluctuations and the interrelationship of hormone balance that leads to the symptomatology known as PMS. Increased hunger, cravings—along with moodiness, sleep disturbance, depression and anxiety, fluid retention, and abdominal bloating are all symptoms that are described as being premenstrual. Some form of PMS is experienced in about 60% of all women. At least 40% of women seek medical care for PMS; while 10% have severe symptoms.

Let's examine the different symptoms and discuss treatment.

But first, there will be no pharmaceutical recommendations. The treatment of bloating with diuretics, or anxiety with Xanax only leads to medicinal side effects without addressing the imbalances that lead to the symptoms themselves. The symptoms of premenstrual syndrome result from an imbalance—excesses of one or the other—between the two types of hormones (estrogen and progesterone) or external factors, such as stress. Our diets dramatically effect our hormones—both in levels and in relative balance. Stress, lack of physical exercise, and life events (positive and negative) can also cause hormonal changes resulting in PMS.

It is important to determine what symptoms are truly related to your menstrual cycle. Chart your symptoms over a three-month time span to determine patterns. Begin the chart on day 1—first day of menstruation—to day 28, or the last day of the menstrual cycle. Note down other aspects of your life during this time—stresses, vacation, illnesses, dietary changes, intercourse—along with actual physical symptoms.

There are specific triggers that accentuate the symptoms of PMS. Fortunately, there are also lifestyle and dietary adjustments that can be made to alleviate symptoms. The one exception to this is severe depression during the second half of the menstrual cycle. If you suffer from this type of depression, you may have Premenstrual Dysphoric Disorder (PMDD). In addition to dietary and lifestyle changes, discuss the symptoms with a physician to determine if further treatment is warranted. There are studies showing that certain drugs (SSRIs) that affect serotonin levels may work well for this disorder. Additionally, there is an apparent connection between Seasonal Affective Disorder (SAD) and PMS. Many women notice worsening of symptoms for both disorders in the fall and winter months. In treating SAD, light therapy seems to decrease depression, cravings, weight gain, and fatigue.

PMS Triggers

The following are conditions or behaviors that have led to

exacerbated PMS symptoms:

1. Excessive intake of caffeine. This contributes to blood sugar swings, causing irritability.
2. Excessive intake of refined carbohydrates, sweets, etc. This contributes to blood sugar swings.
3. High dairy intake, especially high-fat varieties. This can contribute to magnesium deficiency.
4. Being overweight. This contributes to high levels of circulating estrogen.
5. High meat, high-fat diets. This contributes to high estrogen levels.
6. Low levels of antioxidants, especially vitamins C and E and selenium. The theory behind this trigger is that the liver cannot properly metabolize estrogen when antioxidants are deficient.
7. Magnesium deficiency. This causes increased cravings and may affect metabolization of estrogen.

Program for PMS "Treatment"/Prevention

The following tools will help you deal better with the symptoms of PMS and may actually help prevent them from developing:

1. Eat a balanced diet with plenty of servings of fruits and vegetables (at least seven servings combined). Try to eliminate saturated fats, especially trans-fatty acids, as well as all white sugar and white flour products.
2. Add sources of omega-3 fatty acids and essential fatty acids into your diet in a healthy balance. This means increasing your intake of cold water fish (salmon, halibut, and mackerel), eating 7–10 almonds a day, and sauting vegetables in olive oil.
3. Eliminate caffeine. Remember colas, chocolate, and tea contain caffeine, not just coffee. Try to limit intake to one or two servings per day between day 1 and 14, with no servings between day 14 and 28 of the menstrual cycle.

4. Exercise. The endorphin response of moderate exercise can greatly lessen PMS symptoms. As little as a 20- to 25-minute brisk walk three to four times per week can be adequate.

5. Supplement with the following:
   a. Multivitamin-mineral
   b. Fish oil supplement—at least 500 mg 3-4 times per day
   c. Magnesium—400-800 mg per day.
   d. Calcium-vitamin D—at least 1000 mg Ca/400 IU Vitamin D per day

6. Try natural progesterone creams (tablets are also available—but must be from a natural source). Progesterone is associated with calm and tranquility. Synthetic forms of progesterone must be metabolized in the liver. The metabolites are what cause certain bothersome side effects, such as oily skin, depression, and even weight gain. With synthetic progesterone, the treatment can actually worsen the symptoms! But this is not the case with natural progesterone, especially the creams, which are absorbed through the skin and do not require the liver to metabolize them. 2% progesterone cream can be purchased over the counter. One-quarter to one-half ounce applied to soft, non-sun exposed skin daily from day 7 to day 28 can greatly reduce symptoms of PMS, in conjunction with dietary and lifestyle changes.

7. Reduce stress. Meditation, relaxation methods, yoga, etc. can all assist with balancing the biochemistry. There are several published studies validating that effectiveness of these practices.

DYSMENORRHEA

Dysmenorrhea is not the same as PMS, though many women experience both. At least 60% of all women experience dysmenorrhea, which is moderate to severe menstrual cramps. Some women are incapacitated to the point of staying in bed for a day or two. While PMS occurs before the onset of the menstrual flow (and is usually relieved at that point), dysmenorrhea begins with the onset of menses. Some women experience cramping up to a day before menstrual flow begins. For most women, dysmenorrhea is something they have to deal with as teens and young adults, but it tends to lessen or disappear after pregnancy occurs.

If you have not had menstrual cramps and you begin having them, be sure you let your doctor know, as new onset of cramping can signal other problems such as endometriosis. Most of the dietary and lifestyle suggestions made for PMS also work for lessening dysmenorrhea. When your life and your diet are balanced, there will be less suffering due to these menstrual disorders.

ENDOMETRIOSIS

Endometriosis, which is the growth of endometrial tissue outside the uterus, is an increasingly common disorder in our modern world. The reason for this is not entirely clear. In part, it may be because laparoscopies have become more common for a variety of reasons, and this is the primary and definitive method to diagnose endometriosis. Some women, who are diagnosed with endometriosis on laparoscopy have no symptoms at all, while in others the symptoms are quite severe. There is a significant correlation between endometriosis and infertility, although they are not believed to be directly connected as in cause and effect. Dr. Christiane Northrup, author of Women's Bodies, Women's Wisdom and The Wisdom of Menopause, believes that both endometriosis and uterine fibroids are the result of poor diet and blocked pelvic energy. When a woman's inner emotional needs are in conflict with what is expected of her in the world, a cascade of events occurs, resulting in endometriosis or fibroids. Endometriosis has been called the "career woman's disease" because of the frequency with which it is seen in women who have delayed child-bearing due to careers. There is no proof, however, that pregnancy will resolve endometriosis.

Although we do not know what causes endometriosis, the three most common theories are: 1) retrograde menstruation (but this occurs intermittently in all women), 2) exposure to external estrogen-like compounds or environmental toxins, such as dioxins and many food additives, and 3) autoimmunity. Others believe that women are born with endometriosis, and that it worsens depending on stress, dietary factors, external factors, etc.

The predominant symptom of this condition is pain—-often severe, disabling, and unrelenting in the second half of the cycle. Untreated or unrecognized, endometriosis can lead to scarring, cysts, and infertility. As with many of the illnesses we've discussed, endometriosis tends to run in families.

Treatment for Endometriosis

The following are suggested treatments for endometriosis:

1. Implement dietary changes that decrease estrogen excess and increase series 1 eicosanoids. This includes taking a good source of essential fatty acids rich in omega-3s (previously discussed) and minimizing the intake of margarine and hydrogenated oils.
2. Avoid meat and limit dairy, both of which are high in arachidonic acid, which seems to increase pain.
3. Eat two servings per day of cruciferous vegetables, including broccoli, cabbage, and cauliflower.
4. Eat at least two servings daily of soy foods, such as soy protein powder in a smoothie/shake, tofu, etc.
5. Aim for at least 25 grams of fiber per day, eating fruits, vegetables and whole grains. Shredded Wheat or oatmeal are the best grains because they have no refined carbohydrates.
6. Supplement with the following:
   a. Multivitamin-mineral preparation
   b. 100 mg each of the B vitamins riboflavin,

thiamine, and pyridoxine.

    c. Magnesium—400 mg per day, divided doses

7. Examine your life for problems. Dr. Northrup suggests that if you examine your emotional needs, competitive and control issues as in your business and personal life, whether there is adequate sleep, etc., you may find the answers to improving life and greatly reducing the symptoms of endometriosis.

8. Surgery and medication (hormones that essentially trigger menopause) should be reserved for severe cases that do not respond to the above. Complete surgical removal of endometriosis tissue, however, will result in a cure. The hormones (such as Danazol and GnRH agonists Lupron and Synarel) have many side effects, but may be necessary for some.

UTERINE FIBROIDS

Fibroids are benign tumors in the uterus. Between 25 to 50% of women have fibroids, although not all are symptomatic and may only be found on a routine pelvic exam. Fibroids are the most common cause of hysterectomies and account for one-third of all hospital admissions for gynecologic reasons. Fibroids can become quite large, causing bleeding, urinary frequency, and pelvic pain. A hysterectomy is recommended when the size of fibroids is rapidly increasing or the symptoms are unrelenting. However, there are other alternatives. As with endometriosis, uterine fibroids develop, in part, due to estrogen dominance. As with the dietary and lifestyle suggestions listed above for endometriosis sufferers, women with fibroids (even quite large ones) can avoid hysterectomy by changing their diets, dealing with emotional stresses, and losing weight (if obese). Being overweight is one risk factor that is different for uterine fibroids than with endometriosis.

In addition to the suggestions for endometriosis, here are some lifestyle suggestions specifically for fibroids:

1. Aerobic exercise at least 25 minutes 3-4 times per week. Brisk walking, cycling, or swimming is advised.
2. Weight loss, if necessary, can decrease estrogen dominance in the body. (See Chapter Six for specific advice.)
3. Castor oil packs to the lower abdomen three times per week to increase circulation and healing. This is especially helpful if combined with meditation and imagery focused on stress reduction.

PREGNANCY

While pregnancy is clearly a normal part of life and not a disease, it is a "condition" that has risks. These risks can be life-threatening for the mother, such as toxemia and placental abruption. These risks can also be potentially life-endangering for the baby, as in those conditions just listed, as well as problems like placental insufficiency and various labor and delivery challenges. Pregnancy is a time when diet, lifestyle, stress management, and a "minimalist" approach to intervention are important and well-supported by the medical establishment (the same ones, I might add, who rush to medicate and "treat" in most other circumstances).

Because pregnancy is such a life-changing event for women, it is a good time to "take stock" of your diet and lifestyle. I would suggest you choose your physician even more carefully than you might for your general care. Your physician should be your partner in the process of pregnancy, labor, delivery, and postpartum care. Select someone you feel very comfortable with and whom you feel communicates well with you. Write down your questions before each visit to be sure you get all the information you need.

The baby is an excellent "parasite," taking from mom what he or she needs. (The bad news is that this "parasitic" state continues long after birth—usually for at least 18 to 22 years!) If mom's nutritional intake is not adequate during pregnancy, it is mom's bones that will weaken (insufficient calcium intake), mom who will be anemic (if iron stores are low), and mom who may lose muscle mass (if protein intake is inadequate). Taking a good prenatal vitamin-mineral preparation, eating 3 to 4 servings of low-fat dairy, and being certain to eat at least 60-70 grams of protein per day is a good base to start from. An extra 300 calories per day are necessary, from an energy and calorie standpoint (not the doubled calories that some women gravitate towards). You should aim for a weight gain of about 25 pounds. More than that increases your risk of gestational diabetes, hypertension, toxemia, and complications during labor and delivery.

This is a time in life when you need to smile, enjoy, revel in the ability to help create a new human being, and focus on pampering yourself with good nutrition, regular exercise (discuss the particulars with your own physician), and plenty of sleep! Speaking as someone who knows, you will need that sleep after the baby arrives!

PERIMENOPAUSE, MENOPAUSE, AND BEYOND

Menopause is defined as the cessation of menses due to the ovarian function ceasing to produce follicles, and the resultant lack of menses for 6 to 12 consecutive months. The average age for natural menopause is 51 in the United States, with an overall range of 40 to 60. Surgical menopause occurs when the uterus is removed (hysterectomy) for whatever reason. If one or more of the ovaries are left, a woman will continue to ovulate (and potentially experience symptoms related to her menstrual cycle), but will not actually menstruate.

Perimenopause is the relatively new term that describes the transition phase into menopause. The ovaries usually do not stop functioning abruptly, but rather experience a slow decline over 2-10 years. During perimenopause, women may experience menstrual changes, including heavier and more frequent periods, inter-menstrual spotting, or less frequent periods. Hot flashes, mood swings, and sleep disturbance may begin to occur. All of this takes place because of the gradual decrease in the natural production of progesterone, followed by a gradual decrease in estrogen production.

Around age 40, women will begin to notice changes in their menstrual cycles. My experience with patients has been that perimenopause brings on a magnification of whatever your menstrual cycles have been. In other words, if you have tended towards heavy periods, they usually become heavier, closer together—often with more premenstrual symptoms. If you have had pretty normal cycles with few complaints, perimenopause for you will probably consist of irregularity of your cycles. A period may be missed, or the flow will be lighter or shorter. You may begin with hot flashes sooner than the woman with the heavy flow.

Thin women will often go through menopause a year or two earlier than heavier women. Progesterone production declines first (before estrogen), which is the reason why menstrual changes usually occur before hot flashes and sleep problems. Thus, progesterone supplementation is the best treatment when menstrual irregularity occurs. I would recommend a 2% natural progesterone cream. Pro-Gest is a good choice and is readily available. Apply as directed—usually ½ tsp. to soft skin (where there is not much fatty tissue) once to twice daily between day 10 and day 28. Remember day 1 is the first day of menstruation. You should notice, within two cycles, lighter and shorter menstrual flows, possibly a cessation of the mid-cycle spotting that often occurs. (*NOTE*: if there is spotting or significant changes in your cycle after age 40, it is wise to see a physician for an endometrial sampling to evaluate the uterine lining.)

It is also a good idea to begin using (if you are not already) soy and other phytoestrogen-containing foods. Soy is the best source of phytoestrogens, with population studies in Asia as well as controlled studies in the United States and Europe that validate the usefulness of soy foods to control vasomotor symptoms that accompany perimenopause. The typical Asian diet provides between 100 and 200 mg per day of isoflavones, while the typical American diet contains less than five mg per day. Note that the breast cancer risk of women in Asia is less than one-quarter of the risk of American women—including women of Japanese decent. It is likely that soy is protective against the development of breast cancer; and there is no evidence that regular consumption of soy in any amount will increase the risk of breast cancer in pre- or post-menopausal women. Current evidence also suggests that 60-100 mg per day of soy isoflavones may benefit vertebral bone health and reduce cardiovascular disease risk. The heart health benefit includes a lowering of LDL cholesterol (the "bad" cholesterol) and a mild lowering of blood pressure. It is believed that the isoflavone component of soy protein also helps to lessen hot flashes and night sweats.

Consume at least two servings of soy per day for all women (men, too). As hot flashes and night sweats increase, increase the amount of soy as well. Use soy milk, tofu, miso, soybeans, and lentils for at least two servings per day. Additionally, isolated soy protein powder (for shakes and smoothies) can be a great source of isoflavones. Supro 670 from Protein Technologies is a high-quality soy protein with a reliable supply of isoflavones.

Other phytoestrogen sources include black cohosh, dong quai (aka Angelica sinensis, "Tang Kuei"), and red clover.

BLACK COHOSH (CIMICIFUGA RACEMOSA) may not have any direct estrogen effects, but may work through other neuro-endocrine pathways. If this can be validated, black cohosh will be a great option for breast cancer survivors as they deal with menopausal symptoms. Take 40-80 mg per day, in two divided doses, less if three-four servings of soy foods are being eat every day. In addition, black cohosh has also been validated for assisting in reducing headache, dizziness, palpitations, and sleep disturbance.

DONG QUAI (ANGELICA SINENSIS) has been used in traditional Chinese medicine for centuries as a uterine/general women's health tonic. Western-based studies, however, are few and far between. Dong quai is known to have smooth muscle re-laxation effects and, thus, may be helpful for general muscle aches as well. Teas or tablets with the powdered root should be used. Use at least one gram per day, and it is best taken at night.

RED CLOVER (TRIFOLIUM RATENSE) is a popular supplement today and is a rich source of all four major phyto-estrogens. Used in combination with soy isoflavones, it has been shown to reduce hot flashes. Herbalife's Woman's Choice is an excellent source of phyto-estrogens, initially one supplement per day and increasing to two per day as a woman transitions from perimenopause to menopause. Woman's Choice contains a nice blend of soy isoflavones, red clover, and black cohosh.

Other supplements that have been found to help with the symptoms of perimenopause to menopause include:

ST. JOHN'S WORT. This herb is comparable to Prozac for the treatment of mild to moderate depression. Depression is often experienced by women in perimenopause to menopause as they adjust to the changes in their bodies. It has also been shown to help lessen the sexual side effects of women who are using a prescription antidepressant. Caution is necessary, though, due to herb-drug interactions. Discuss this herb with a doctor if any pre-scription medications are taken. If St. John's Wort is being used, the dose is 300 mg three times per day—it must be standardized to 0.3% hypericin and 3-5% hyperforin. It may be the hyperforin that is most important in determining benefit.

GINGKO BILOBA. This herb has been shown in a number of studies to improve and protect long-term memory, both in the young and old. Gingko increases blood flow to the brain and is a potent antioxidant. Use 100 mg per day to start. Look for stan-dardization of the glycosides and terpenes. (*NOTE*: Avoid using if prescription anti-coagulants are being taken.)

ABOUT HORMONE REPLACEMENT THERAPY (HRT)

In response to the evidence of increased incidence of heart disease after menopause, physicians began routinely prescribing hormone replacement therapy (HRT), or estrogen replacement therapy (ERT) if a hysterectomy had been done, in the belief that this would decrease a woman's chance of developing heart disease, Alzheimer's disease, and osteoporosis. A number of studies validated an increase in risk of breast cancer with HRT (and ERT), but the benefits were felt to outweigh the risks. That was the feeling until the results of the landmark Woman's Health Initiative were published in JAMA (Journal of American Medical Association) in July, 2002.

This study, which included over 16,000 women, clearly linked the usage of HRT, a combination of estrogen and progesterone, with an increased risk of breast cancer, heart attacks, blood clots, and strokes. A June 2003 analysis of data from the Women's Health Initiative study indicated that breast cancer in women taking the estrogen-progestin pills may be harder to detect (probably because of an increase in breast density making mammograms harder to read) and even more aggressive.

Another reason for doctors prescribing hormone replacement therapy, other than to relieve menopausal symptoms, was to prevent Alzheimer's disease and senile dementia. But recently there has been bad news about HRT in this area, as well. The results of another arm of the Women's Health Initiative found that combined HRT in women 65 and older doesn't prevent dementia, and, in fact, may actually increase one's risk. The study's lead investigator, Dr. Sally Shumaker of the Wake Forest University School of Medicine reports, "What we found is that women in the combination hormone replacement therapy had twice the risk of developing dementia as compared to women on placebo."

The study followed more than 4,500 women over four years, testing the theory that the combined estrogen/progestin therapy might help stave off the dementia and memory loss that often accompanies old age. Dr. Shumaker says what they found "was exactly the opposite – that combination therapy significantly increased harm." New data from the same study also suggests that HRT does nothing for sleeping difficulties or mental outlook either, as was once thought.

This new research has lead most doctors to now feel that HRT is best reserved for short-term usage to help provide relief from severe perimenopausal symptoms. As always, however, discuss your personal situation with a physician, weighing the risks and benefits for your particular health scenario. We know that the likelihood of developing osteoporosis is lessened with the use of ERT/ HRT, but adequate calcium, regular weight-bearing exercise, and paying attention to minimizing other risk factors (as discussed in Chapter 13) will also help to avoid this disorder. There are now "bioidentical" types of hormone preparations that are more similar to our natural hormones. While there is preliminary data that these preparations do not have the same risks as conventional hormone therapy, there are no long-term studies available as yet.

Recently, the Food and Drug Administration approved a new low-dose variety of HRT, but urged that it be taken only for the shortest possible duration. The FDA also announced new labeling requirements for estrogen and estrogen with progestin products, after reviewing data from the Women's Health Initiative study that raised concerns about the risks of using the popular pills. FDA Commissioner Scott McClellan said the agency was issuing revised consumer labeling to reflect the study findings and requiring all makers of estrogen and estrogen with progestin products, including patches and topical medications, to update their product labels. The new labeling requirement includes a warning highlighting the increased risks for heart disease, heart attacks, strokes, and breast cancer.

Commissioner McClellan also emphasized that post-menopausal women who are confused about whether to continue HRT should consult their health care provider about what's best for them. He said, "There are risks and benefits that women need to consider in their individual circumstances. Women should consult their physicians and find the therapy regimen that works best for them."

If you and your physician decide that benefit can be obtained from the use of prescription hormone therapy after menopause, here are my recommendations.

- Try to use bioidentical forms of both estrogen and progesterone (estrogen is needed only if the uterus has been removed).
- These bioidentical hormones have several advantages, including less negative effects on blood pressure, cholesterol, and triglyceride levels, less likelihood of causing clotting problems, and probably less risk of developing breast cancer (as seen with other forms of HRT and ERT).
- 17-beta Estradiol in tablet, patch, or vaginal ring is probably the best. Use the patch if there is a history of high triglycerides or are a risk of blood clots.
- Micronized progesterone, in oral capsule or as a troche (a slowly dissolving lozenge), is a good plant-based option. Good quality natural progesterone creams are another alternative, as discussed previously.

So, are there alternative solutions to HRT for the challenges of menopause? Absolutely!! While there clearly needs to be additional research in this area, there is enough evidence to support the use of soy and certain botanicals to help deal with some of the transitional challenges. And, there are clearly health-enhancing, age-defying lifestyle and dietary modifications that you can do to feel great, no matter what your age!

Embrace womanhood — with all its joys, challenges, and uniqueness. Read, be aware, ask questions. Enroll your physician as a partner in your health process. Utilize dietary changes and life-style modifications to help lessen the symptoms and progression of hormonally-mediated challenges that women can have.

There are a lot of choices out there, and few of them are truly definitive. Medicine is a work in progress, and always will be. The state of knowledge is constantly evolving, and each new discovery either supports our current beliefs or threatens to overturn them.

The best advice? Remember you are in charge of your health. Research, study, and investigate options that feel right for you. Don't take someone else's opinion as the final word. Keep looking and keep asking questions, until you find what is best for you.

FOLLOW-UP PREVENTIVE PERSCRIPTION

GENERAL GUIDELINES FOR HEALTHY HORMONES IN THE 21ST CENTURY WOMAN:

Dietary Recommendations

Focus on eating whole foods and less processed foods. Make a commitment to decrease intake of refined foods, and saturated and hydrogenated fats. Use a drizzle of olive oil and plenty of balsamic vinegar on salads. For a treat, have a nice-sized piece of whole grain or rustic bread dipped in (not drowned in) olive oil and balsamic vinegar. It is a true taste sensation. Have a big salad with plenty of different color vegetables every day. Try to have red, yellow, bright green, dark green and purple in every salad. Vary your choices. Try a few slices of kiwi or orange to add a new taste. Be creative and enjoy!

Commit to eating vegetarian-based meals (soybeans, lentils, tofu, pinto or kidney beans, etc.) at least two days per week and eat cold water fish at least twice per week. It is incredibly easy to begin most days with a soy protein-based shake or smoothie. Mix in a serving of 15-20 grams of soy protein in unsweetened soy milk, add 1 cup of fresh or frozen berries, and blend for a nutritious, filling, and tasty way to start the day.

If there is a high risk of breast cancer in the family, limit alcohol to three to four drinks per week. If you smoke, quit! Be wise regarding caffeine intake. Try substituting green tea for coffee. Its health benefits include antioxidant protection, heart health protection, and reduced risk of breast and colon cancer.

Supplement Suggestions

Review the section or sections of this chapter that are relevant. Notice that there are many botanicals that can be helpful for different hormone-mediated conditions—herbs and botanicals tend to have balancing and "modulating" effects. Balance is an important key to a woman's hormonal health. I also strongly suggest discussion of natural supplement usage with your physician. Many physicians are still learning about supplements and progressing to better acceptance of an integrative system of medical care. It's important to tell a physician everything you are taking, including supplements, over-the-counter products, homeopathic products, etc. to assure that the total picture of your health is being presented.

Supplements for women of all ages should include:

MULTIVITAMIN-MINERAL PRODUCT—preferably one that is formulated to be taken in divided doses for best absorption and utilization.

CALCIUM—Recommended dosage of 1000 mg per day up to age 40; 1200-1500 mg per day after age 40. Take a preparation that provides at least 400 IU vitamin D as well—this amount may be partially found in your multivitamin tablet.

MAGNESIUM—400-600 mg per day, may be included in calcium supplement.

ANTIOXIDANTS—A combination product is fine—

look for some combination that provides 10-25,000 IU mixed carotenoids, 500-1000 mg vitamin C, 400 IU vitamin E, 50-200 micrograms selenium as a minimum. Additionally look for alpha lipoic acid (100 micrograms per day) and pycnogenol 50-100 mg per day.

Exercise Encouragement

I am clearly a strong advocate of regular exercise—both "cardio" (aerobic) and weight training (anaerobic)—for everyone. Women really need to incorporate some form of weight training, especially as they reach age 40 and beyond to prevent muscle loss, improve balance and strength, and protect bone mass. (*NOTE:* Take caution if you are very overweight or have cardiovascular disease. Talk with a medical professional to develop a plan for exercise.)

Remember to make exercise fun and enjoyable. Find a partner to walk with and walk fast enough to make conversation just a bit "breathless." Look for advertisements or websites about various run and walkathons that are organized to support various causes, such as breast cancer research, AIDs research, finding a cure for leukemia, etc.

Check out some of the websites listed below:

Walkathon For Breast Cancer
www.breast cancer.net

The Susan G. Komen Walk
www.breastcancerinfo.com

American Cancer Society
www.cancer.org

Walkathon for Diabetes
www.jdrf.org/support/walk_to_cure.php

www.goodworks.net/checklist.html

By getting involved with one of these organizations, you will not only improve your own health through physical exercise, but you will also have the joy of raising money to improve the health and lives of others, as well.

CHAPTER 15

THE VICIOUS CYCLE
of Digestive Disorders

Points to ponder as you read:

✓ What causes ulcers?

✓ How can you deal with reflux problems?

✓ Who needs a gluten-free diet and why?

✓ Why is fiber important and what are the health risks of eating a low fiber diet?

The picture to the left is a diagram of the digestive tract. The digestive tract begins in the mouth and ends at the anus. The main purpose of the digestive system is to break down the nutrients you

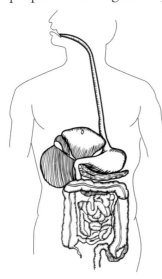

put into your mouth into sub-components that can be absorbed through the mucosal lining of the stomach and upper small intestines, and pass through, what is not absorbed or not needed, for excretion. Once absorbed into the bloodstream, these nutrients, the amino acids, fatty acids, glucose, vitamins, minerals, and phyto-nutrients (plant nutrients), drive the myriad of functions that keep you alive at the cellular level.

The process of digestion actually

begins in the mouth. Once food or drink reaches the tongue, the salivary glands secrete digestive enzymes that start the process of digestion and metabolism. Absorption of nutrients begins in the stomach, which is lined with acid-secreting and mucous-producing cells. These cells break food down into components. The pancreas then secretes many digestive enzymes, and the liver secretes bile and bile salts which contribute to the process of breaking foods (and supplements) into their component parts. Some nutrients are not absorbed until they reach the upper small intestines (called the duodenum). This part of the stomach and upper intestines is normally a very acidic environment, which is necessary for digestion. Part of the food, primarily undigestible fiber, both soluble and insoluble, is not absorbed and continues to migrate through the intestines into the colon (also known as the large intestine). In the colon, there is ongoing digestive processing of "the remains" of what was eaten. Ultimately, the stool that is excreted is the end result of the processing of food and drink. Ideally, we eat and absorb what we need and pass through what is left. But, largely due to the changes in our diets over the past 50 years, and the use of various medications that impact digestive function, doctors diagnose and treat digestive complaints more than any other single type of problem.

The following is an overview of the common types of digestive disorders that exist.

Beginning at the top of the digestive system, we see primarily dysfunctions in digestion—from chronic indigestion, hyperacidity (too much stomach acid), reflux problems (gastroesophageal reflux and hiatal hernia), and ulcers. The other main types of disorders related to the lower digestive area include irritable bowel syndrome, diverticulosis, ulcerative colitis, and Chrohn's disease. There are also disorders of absorption, such as Celiac disease.

Let me emphasize, before we go into the specifics of these diseases, to always discuss what you are doing or what supplements are being taken with your physician, if you are under regular care. I do want you to be aware that many digestive disorders are functional, meaning that they can be largely controlled by changes made to the diet, stress level, fluid intake, etc. Medications are greatly over-prescribed in the area of digestive disorders because the complaints are common and have bothersome symptoms. Thus, there are a large number of medications from which to choose. But, in my medical experience, an integrative approach is often the most effective in dealing with these oftentimes complicated scenarios.

PEPTIC ULCER DISEASE AND GASTRITIS

Peptic ulcer disease is a common and complicated disease, the treatment of which has changed significantly over the past 20 years. An ulcer occurs in the stomach or duodenum when mucosal protective factors are overwhelmed. This can be as a result of infection with a bacteria called Helicobacter pylori (H. pylori), usage of non-steroidal anti-inflammatory drugs (NSAIDs), a prolonged over-stressed condition, or a combination of all these factors. Alcohol usage, smoking, sleep deprivation, and other medications, such as those used in chemotherapy, can also increase one's risk of developing an ulcer or gastritis. Gastritis is defined as abdominal pain due to excessive acid production without the presence of an ulcer. NSAIDs, including over-the-counter ibuprofen (Motrin), naproxen (Alleve), and aspirin, as well as countless prescription versions, greatly increase one's risk of developing these conditions. Once H. pylori was discovered in 1983, much of the treatment of these conditions became focused on treating this bacteria, although clearly it is not the sole cause of ulcer in anyone. At least 70% of people who are infected with H. pylori do not have any documented ulcer or even any GI symptoms. It is estimated that stress contributes to at least 30 to 65% of all ulcers.

The most common symptom of ulcer or gastritis is pain in

the upper abdomen—usually right in the midline below the diaphragm and above the umbilicus. Pain can be increased or alleviated by eating. Awakening during the night with pain can signify a duodenal ulcer. Other symptoms include nausea, vomiting, blood in the stool, or loss of appetite. If these conditions are present and have not been evaluated by a physician, make an appointment to be seen. If the pain is severe, increasing, and/or you vomit blood (can look like "coffee grounds" or be bright red) or notice dark tarry-looking stools, be seen as soon as possible. Once a diagnosis and appropriate medical treatment is underway, begin integrating the following diet and lifestyle changes into the recovery plan.

Nutrition

It was once believed that eating a spicy diet contributed to, or even caused, an ulcer. Although we know now that this is not the case, it is prudent to pay attention to whether or not certain foods aggravate symptoms. Certain spices may bother you; and caffeine and alcohol can both stimulate acid production, which may increase pain or nausea. Also, keep in mind that diets high in animal protein and saturated fat seem to be associated with increased prevalence of ulcer.

On the other hand, there is evidence that both fiber intake and eating a diet with plentiful fruits and vegetables will decrease one's risk of developing an ulcer. In fact, diets high in fiber have been shown to reduce the risk of duodenal ulcers by up to 50%. Yogurt has also been shown to be helpful, along with berries, green tea, legumes (such as soy and lentils). Red wine also seems to inhibit the growth of the H. pylori bacterium.

Supplements

CHAMOMILE—the extract has been shown to inhibit ulcer formation and may promote ulcer healing. Dosage: Tincture works best: 1–4 ml of a 1:5 tincture.

LICORICE ROOT (DEGLYCYRRIZIANATED LICO-RICE DGL)—Licorice has been used traditionally to prevent and treat ulcers. It appears to stimulate mucous production in the stomach which provides protection from the effects of the acid present in the stomach. Dosage: 5-10 g/day of powdered root; extracts containing 200-400 mg glycyrrhizin.

Stress Management

Relaxation techniques, meditation, imagery, hypnosis, and yoga can all be ways of reducing and managing stress.

GASTROESOPHAGEAL REFLUX DISEASE (more commonly known as GERD)

GERD, or gastroesophageal reflux disease, is a condition caused by chronic reflux of acid into the esophagus. Normally, there is a barrier—the gastro-esophageal (G-E) junction and lower esophageal sphincter (LES)—that keeps the very acidic contents of the stomach from moving upward back into the esophagus. The barrier is important because the acid from reflux can lead to nausea, indigestion, chest pain, and difficulty swallowing (dysphagia). Over time, GERD can lead to ulcerations in the esophagus and an increased likelihood of esophageal cancer. The symptoms, especially if pain is a predominant symptom, can be mistaken as being heart-related chest pain or even a heart attack. Other symptoms that people may experience include chronic hoarseness, cough, or sore throat.

If nature has given our bodies a barrier to stop reflux, why do some people's lower esophageal sphincter refuse to work properly? There are several reasons.

By far, the most common reason is weight gain. When weight is gained in the abdominal area, the internal organs are "displaced," leading to a pushing upward of the stomach against the diaphragm. This, in turn, leads to reflux and the development of a hiatal hernia.

Pregnancy can also cause symptoms of GERD—more pronounced in shorter women (less room for the enlarging uterus) and in women who gain more than the recommended 25 pounds during pregnancy.

Certain medications also seem to relax the sphincter, including calcium-channel blockers (treatment for hypertension and certain heart conditions), anti-anxiety medications such as Valium and Xanax, and non-steroidal anti-inflammatory medications. In addition, substances such as nicotine, caffeine, and alcohol all tend to increase the likelihood of developing GERD (and hiatal hernias) because of increasing acid production in the stomach.

Dietary and lifestyle modification is the key to alleviating the symptoms of GERD, as well as beginning the process of reversing whatever damage has occurred in your esophagus and LES. If you are currently suffering with GERD, it does not mean you will have a chronic problem. The good news is that this aspect of your health is largely controllable.

1. Lose weight. See Chapter Six for advice on not only losing weight, but keeping it off forever.
2. Quit smoking. Nicotine gum and patches are helpful in the physical withdrawal period, which technically lasts about three to four days, although using the patch or gum will be helpful for several weeks. After a month, you are completely dealing with the emotional addiction and the actual habit. Human beings do not change habits easily, and smoking is one of the most difficult ones to give up.
3. Decrease the intake of caffeine (coffee, tea, colas, and chocolate).
4. Avoid eating large meals ever, and never eat within three hours of retiring for sleep for the night.
5. Elevate the head of the bed by approximately six inches.
6. Try drinking a good quality aloe vera juice on a daily basis.

Look for the IASC (International Aloe Science Council) seal to assure quality and adequate active components to assure effect. Although the scientific data is not extensive, there is a long history of usage dating back to ancient Egypt and the Greek physicians Hippocrates and Aristotle. Begin with two ounces, three times a day. Increase gradually to four-six ounces, two to three times per day. I have drunk aloe vera juice since 1990. The combination of dietary changes and aloe resolved a three-year battle with hyperacidity and documented gastric ulcers. I haven't had any symptoms in over 13 years.

7. Initially, acid suppression therapy may be needed. Discuss this with your physician. Prilosec, Pepcid, Zantac, or Prevacid are the usual pharmaceutical recommendations. Zantac and Pepcid are now available as over-the-counter medications. It is important to note that these medications are recommended for use for six to eight weeks—not forever. The dietary and lifestyle suggestions listed above are the mainstay of treatment and prevention of GERD.

CELIAC DISEASE—AKA GLUTEN ENTREROPATHY

Celiac disease is a digestive disorder of the small intestine that results from a hypersensitivity reaction to gluten—the protein component of certain grains, including wheat, barley and rye. There is new evidence that points to oats not being one of these triggers. The damage results in flattening the absorptive surface of the villi leading to malabsorption of many nutrients. The disease is genetic in origin, although breast-fed babies have a much lower risk of developing celiac disease. It is generally understood that celiac disease requires some environmental trigger to unmask, such as a virus (adenovirus) or food additive. Emotional stress also appears to be a trigger. Celiac disease seems to be associated with other autoimmune conditions; however, it is not clear, at present, whether this is a primary or secondary autoimmune process.

Celiac disease is diagnosed with a small bowel biopsy, although this would not be considered unless there was a strong family history or there were certain antibodies present in blood tests. Many of these symptoms are also present in irritable bowel disorder—a more common but less serious disorder (discussed next) and inflammatory bowel disease (Crohn's Disease and ulcerative colitis). If any of the following symptoms are present, alert your physician:

- Chronic diarrhea
- Recurring abdominal bloating and pain
- Unexplained weight loss, especially associated with GI symptoms
- Pale, foul-smelling stool
- Unrelenting fatigue
- Recurrent aphthous ulcers (chronic ulcerations, including canker sores) in the mouth

Diagnosing celiac disease is difficult because some of its symptoms are similar to those of other diseases, including irritable bowel syndrome, Crohn's disease, diverticulosis (see below), chronic fatigue syndrome (see Chapter 11), and depression (see Chapter 8). Recently, researchers discovered that people with celiac disease have higher than normal levels of certain antibodies in their blood, specifically antigliadin and antiendomysial.

The mainstay of treatment is to follow a gluten-free diet, that is to avoid all foods that contain gluten. For most people, following this diet will stop symptoms, allow healing of existing intestinal damage, and prevent further damage. Improvements begin within days of starting the diet, and the small intestine is usually completely healed—meaning the villi are intact and working—in three to six months on average.

The gluten-free diet is a lifetime requirement. Eating any gluten, no matter how small an amount, can potentially lead to damage of the villi in the small intestine. A gluten-free diet means avoiding all foods that contain wheat (including spelt, triticale, and kamut), rye, barley, and possibly oats (try very small amounts of oat to see how you react) or, in other words, most grains, pastas, cereals, and many processed foods.

Despite these restrictions, people with celiac disease can eat a well-balanced diet with a variety of foods, including bread and pasta. For example, instead of wheat flour, you can use potato, rice, or soy flour. Or, buy gluten-free bread, pasta, and other products from specialty food companies. Plain meat, fish, rice, fruits, and vegetables do not contain gluten, so people with celiac disease can eat as much of these foods as they like.

Following a gluten-free diet is complicated, but will become a way of life if you have this condition. People with celiac disease have to be extremely careful about what they buy for lunch at school or work, what they eat at cocktail parties, or grab from the refrigerator for a midnight snack. Eating out can also be a challenge as the person with celiac disease must scrutinize the menu for foods with gluten and question the waiter or chef about possible hidden sources of gluten, such as additives, preservatives, and stabilizers found in processed foods (as well as medicines and mouthwash). If ingredients are not itemized, check with the manufacturer of the product. Keep in mind, however, that with practice, screening for gluten will become second nature.

A dietitian, a health care professional who specializes in food and nutrition, can help you learn about the gluten-free diet. Also, support groups are particularly helpful for newly diagnosed people and their families as they learn to adjust to a new way of life. With as close to 100% adherence to a gluten-free diet as possible, you can live a normal and healthy life.

IRRITABLE BOWEL SYNDROME

Another extremely common digestive disorder is irritable bowel syndrome or IBS. IBS accounts for approximately 12% of all visits to primary care physicians and about 50% of all referrals to gastroenterologists. IBS is not actually a disease, but rather a functional problem with the digestive process—top to bottom. In other words, there are no pathological or biochemical changes to explain the symptoms. It is twice as likely to be a problem for women, as it is for men. The main dysfunction is in the colon, which appears to have abnormal peristalsis in IBS. Peristalsis refers to the contractions that occur normally, in rhythmic fashion, moving undigested matter through the small intestines into the colon, where further processing results in fecal matter being eliminated as a bowel movement. People with IBS may have overly reactive nerves in the wall of their colons, which can result in a variety of symptoms. Changes in diet, lack of sleep, and stress appear to be the major triggers of this condition. Symptoms include gassiness, bloating, abdominal discomfort, and alternating bouts of constipation and diarrhea. Some people tend towards just constipation or just diarrhea, but the great majority of folks have alternating bouts of both.

It is not clear whether specific foods are triggers, whether food intolerances play a role in the etiology of the disease, or whether it is just a manifestation of stress and diet. Fiber definitely plays a role in the treatment of IBS, as does foods that are "calming." We do know that IBS is an extremely common condition with fibromyalgia (see Chapter 11).

IBS is diagnosed using a series of criteria called the Rome II Criteria, shown below. Clearly, before you can be conclusively diagnosed with IBS, other causes of these symptoms must be excluded. Your physician will have you looking for hidden blood in the stool and/or give you a referral to a gastroenterologist for a colonoscopy or sigmoidoscopy as dictated by your age, family history, etc.

Rome II Criteria for Diagnosis of IBS

Presence of abdominal pain or discomfort for at least three months (total) of the past 12 months, along with at least two of the following three features:

1. relief of symptoms with a bowel movement; and/or
2. onset of symptoms associated with a change in frequency of stools; and/or
3. onset of symptoms associated with a change in appearance of stools.

Treatment for IBS involves an integrative approach with diet, stress management, botanicals, and fiber all playing a role. Pharmaceuticals are strongly discouraged for IBS, as they tend to have side effects and can cause a reliance on the drug, which is not curative. Dietary and lifestyle changes can be very effective in decreasing symptoms and flares without the risks associated with drugs.

Diet

As stated earlier, food sensitivities and intolerances may play a role. Eating a healthy diet, with a broad range of fruits, vegetables and grains, low in saturated fats and including a balance of vegetarian and animal sources of proteins is advised. Wheat, wheat gluten, dairy products, caffeine, citrus, and sweets are all possible offenders. It is important to pay attention to your body and determine what foods, beverages, etc. may bother you. Try eliminating a certain food for at least two weeks, then re-introduce it and see if symptoms recur. Keeping a food diary is a good idea to help narrow down the potential foods that may bother you. Fiber supplements (avoid wheat bran) and probiotics are often helpful. My favorite combination includes a mixture of probiotics and fiber—fructo-oligosaccharides, arabino galactan, and guar gum.

Botanicals

There are a wide variety of botanicals, including fiber sources, that are recommended and widely successful with IBS.

CARMINATIVE HERBS. Ginger, peppermint and fennel can be helpful to aid in digestion. Chamomile, goldenseal and angelica (also known as dong quai in Chinese medicine) are natural anti-spasmodic agents that relax the muscle wall of the colon.

BULKING AND OSMOTIC AGENTS. Cascara sagrada, psyllium seeds and husk, senna and aloe vera give the stool a consistent size and improve peristalsis (movement of stool/feces through the colon).

Mind-Body Medicine

Since a majority of patients with IBS report flares related to significant emotional stresses, the use of mind-body techniques is an important part of the integrative approach to managing IBS. You be in charge of your life, not your bowel tendencies. If there is depression or anxiety, use biofeedback, hypnotherapy, or guided imagery to assist with stress management. Yoga and Tai-chi can also be extremely helpful.

INFLAMMATORY BOWEL DISEASE

Inflammatory Bowel Disease (IBD) refers to two chronic, relapsing diseases, Crohn's disease and ulcerative colitis. These disorders are both mediated by genetic, dietary, and environmental factors that result in inflammation in the small intestine and/or colon. They tend to be initially diagnosed between the ages of 15 and 30. Ulcerative colitis is distributed equally between men and women, but Crohn's disease is about twice more likely to occur in a female than a male. With these conditions, there appears to be a defect in the immune cells in the intestinal tract that leads to inflammation and tissue damage in the intestinal wall. Crohn's disease usually affects the ileum, the lower one-third of the small intestine, but it can affect any part of the digestive tract, from the mouth to the anus. Ulcerative colitis affects only the colon. People with either of these disorders have symptoms that include significant abdominal pain, along with diarrhea and weight loss. There is usually blood in the stool, and anemia can occur if there is significant ongoing bloody stool. Ulcerative colitis usually is first diagnosed in young adulthood, but Crohn's can manifest itself in childhood. If it does, delay in normal development can occur due to malabsorption of nutrients.

Nutritional complications such as deficiencies of proteins, calories, and vitamins are well documented in Crohn's disease and ulcerative colitis. These deficiencies may be caused by inadequate dietary intake, intestinal loss of protein, or poor absorption (malabsorption).

The other significant complications to be aware of are osteoporosis and colon cancer, the latter being associated primarily with ulcerative colitis. There is much active research in the area of developing drugs that target the immune system, as the immune response is a key component of inflammatory conditions. Treatment should focus on minimizing long-term complications and controlling symptoms with a minimum of risk. Diet and lifestyle modification, along with drug therapy is usually indicated. The majority of people with IBD can live fairly symptom-free with minimal flares, if a true integrative approach is taken, and they commit to being consistent in following the measures prescribed.

A treatment plan for IBD should include the following measures.

Adequate Protein & Calories

Adequate intake of calories and protein is essential. Calories should ensure a minimum of 90% of ideal body weight and approximately 0.5-0.75 gm of protein per pound of body weight, depending on how much weight needs to be regained. Up to 1 gm of protein per pound of body weight may be necessary in malnourished individuals. Vegetarian protein sources, especially soy, poultry and lean cuts of meats, are the best choices.

Adequate Fiber

While adequate fiber is considered important, make changes

very slowly. Adding too much roughage too quickly may cause a flare up of symptoms. Fresh fruits and lightly steamed vegetables are most advised. Be cautious with cereal grains, especially wheat, rye, and barley. Oats tend to be better tolerated.

Avoid Dietary Triggers

Become aware of foods and beverages that may be irritants and trigger symptoms and/or full flare ups. Caffeine, refined sugar and sweets, dairy products, corn, and gluten are common irritants. Another important part of the diet to look at is fats. Our western diets are high in omega-6 oils that tend to cause inflammation (pro-inflammatory) and low in omega-3, which are naturally anti-inflammatory. In Paleolithic times, our diets provided a ratio of 2:1 omega-6:omega-3. Today's western diets tend to be up to 10:1 omega-6:omega:3. One of the theories as to why there are so many more inflammatory and autoimmune conditions today is the pro-inflammatory diet we consume. Decrease vegetable oils high in omega-6 (corn, safflower, and sunflower) and animal saturated fats and increase the intake of cold water fish, olive oil, and flaxseed to prevent or decrease inflammation.

Utilize Supplements

VITAMINS & MINERALS

Because so many micronutrients are malabsorbed in IBD, supplementation is essential, especially of the B vitamins and fat-soluble vitamins (A, D, E and K). Supplementation with the minerals zinc, copper, and manganese are important for their cellular functions in energy function and metabolism. People with IBD tend to be very deficient in antioxidants (we're not sure whether this is an intake problem or an increased use situation), so supplement with a variety of vitamin, mineral, and botanical antioxidants. My favorite combination includes vitamins C, E, mixed carotenoids, selenium, and schizandra berries for liver protection.

OMEGA-3 FATTY ACIDS

It is prudent to assure better balance of omega-6:omega-3 by using a fish oil supplement daily. Be sure yours provides 500 mg fish oil per capsule with a balance of EPA and DHA. Research has yet to clearly define just what that ratio should be. Take at least 1000 mg per day, up to 3000-4000 mg per day is fine—especially if you do not consume salmon, tuna, mackerel etc. regularly. Sauté vegetables in small amounts of olive oil, and use olive oil and balsamic vinegar on your salads rather than commercial salad dressings, as they tend to be high in omega-6 oils.

HERBS & BOTANICALS

Ginger, turmeric and boswellia are well validated anti-inflammatory herbs. Ginger: up to 1.5 grams per day, divided. Turmeric: 300-400 mg 2-3 times per day. Boswellia: 350 mg 3 times per day.

Aloe vera juice is one of the most commonly used botanicals in people with IBD. It is soothing and healing. Be sure to find a type that removes the alloin and latex in the leaf lining, as it is a strong laxative.

MIND-BODY THERAPY

As with all the other digestive disorders and diseases discussed in this chapter, management of stress is critical. Your emotions and intestines are closely linked neurologically. Therefore, relaxation methods, meditation, yoga, Tai-chi, hypnosis, etc. can be most beneficial.

CONVENTIONAL THERAPY

Pharmaceuticals are the mainstay of therapy. Surgery may be necessary if more conservative management is not successful. People with Crohn's disease are more likely to require surgical intervention than those with ulcerative colitis. Pharmaceuticals include the following:

- REMIKADE—ANTI-TNF. Cells affected by Crohn's disease contain a cytokine, a protein produced by the immune system, called tumor necrosis factor (TNF). TNF may be responsible for the inflammation of Crohn's disease. Anti-TNF is a substance that finds TNF in the bloodstream, binds to it, and removes it before it can reach the intestines and cause inflammation.

- ANTIBIOTICS—FLAGYL AND CIPROFLOXACIN. Antibiotics are now used to treat the bacterial infections that often accompany Crohn's disease, but some research suggests that they might also be useful as a primary treatment for active Crohn's disease.

- NATALIZUMAB. Natalizumab is an experimental drug that reduces symptoms and improves the quality of life when tested in people with Crohn's disease. The drug decreases inflammation by binding to immune cells, preventing them from leaving the bloodstream and reaching the areas of inflammation.

- 5-AMINOSALICYLATES (AZULFIDINE AND PENTASA). These are the mainstay to prevent recurrences in both UC and CD. They are anti-inflammatory in nature.

- CORTICOSTEROIDS. Used in both UC and CD in moderate to severe disease to prevent tissue damage.

DIVERTICULOSIS

Diverticulosis is present in at least 35% of people in the western world by age 50, and in at least 65% of all people by age 80. This is due to low fiber dietary intake, which results in high pressure within the colon from low stool volume leading to pouching out of the wall of the colon. These pouches are called diverticula. They can be asymptomatic, but they can also lead to pain, bleeding, infection (diverticulitis), and intermittent bloating and gassiness. Pain tends to be left-sided. If infection occurs (diverticulitis), fever, chills, and nausea can also be present, and if that is the case, it is very important to be seen, evaluated, and generally treated with antibiotics. Untreated, abscesses, perforations, and obstruction can occur.

Though not unequivocally proven, the dominant theory is that diverticulosis is caused by a low-fiber diet. This is supported by the fact that the condition was first reported in the United States in the early 1900s, which is about the same time processed foods, containing refined, low-fiber flour, were introduced into the American diet.

Fiber is the part of fruits, vegetables, and grains that the body cannot digest. Some fiber dissolves easily in water (soluble fiber). It takes on a soft, jelly-like texture in the intestines. Some fiber passes almost unchanged through the intestines (insoluble fiber). Both kinds of fiber help make stools soft and easy to pass and prevents constipation. Constipation, which makes the muscles strain to move stool that is too hard, is the main cause of increased pressure in the colon. The excess pressure might be the cause of the weak spots in the colon that bulge out and become diverticula.

The standard treatment for diverticulitis is a high-fiber diet. The American Dietetic Association recommends 20 to 35 grams of fiber each day. The Institute of Medicine published guidelines in 2002 recommending 25-30 grams per day for women and 30-35 grams per day for men. The table below shows the amount of fiber in some foods that can easily be added to the diet.

AMOUNT OF FIBER IN FOODS

Fruits

apple	1 medium	=	4 grams
peach	1 medium	=	2 grams
pear	1 medium	=	4 grams
tangerine	1 medium	=	2 grams

Vegetables

acorn squash, fresh, cooked	¾ cup	=	7 grams

asparagus, fresh, cooked	½ cup	=	1½ grams
broccoli, fresh, cooked	½ cup	=	2 grams
brussels sprouts, fresh, cooked	½ cup	=	2 grams
cabbage, fresh, cooked	½ cup	=	2 grams
carrot, fresh, cooked	1 cup	=	1½ grams
cauliflower, fresh, cooked	½ cup	=	2 grams
romaine lettuce	1 cup	=	1 gram
spinach, fresh, cooked	½ cup	=	2 grams
tomato, raw	1	=	1 gram
zucchini, fresh, cooked	1 cup	=	2½ grams

Starchy Vegetables

black-eyed peas, fresh, cooked	½ cup	=	4 grams
lima beans, fresh, cooked	½ cup	=	4½ grams
kidney beans, fresh, cooked	½ cup	=	6 grams
potato, fresh, cooked	1	=	3 grams

Grains

bread, whole-wheat	1 slice	=	2 grams
brown rice, cooked	1 cup	=	3½ grams
cereal, bran flake	¾ cup	=	5 grams
oatmeal, plain, cooked	¾ cup	=	3 grams
white rice, cooked	1 cup	=	1 gram

Source: United States Department of Agriculture (USDA). USDA Nutrient Database for standard reference.

Your doctor may also recommend taking a fiber product such as Citrucel or Metamucil once a day. These products are mixed with water and provide about 2 to 3½ grams of fiber per table-spoon, mixed with eight ounces of water.

Diverticulitis can be a very serious condition. However, keep in mind that a simple thing, such as adding more fiber to the diet, can keep the condition under control.

There are many more digestive disorders and problems that could be discussed. But remember that this vicious cycle can be broken and relief found. Digesting food needed to live does not have to be a painful and unhealthy process. Whatever disorder you might suffer from, there is help. Study, research, and ask questions of health care professionals. You have the means to make life healthier and better for yourself.

FOLLOW-UP PREVENTIVE PERSCRIPTION

FIND ROOM FOR MORE FIBER

Since several health conditions are related to problems with the colon, and since most of these conditions can be alleviated by eating more fiber, make a commitment to do so. Look at the list of fiber in foods. Make a commitment today to add some of these foods to the diet tomorrow. Remember, you need 20 to 35 grams of fiber daily. Make sure that fruits, vegetables, and whole grains are a part of your diet. Your body will be glad you did.

CHAPTER 16

ALCOHOLISM AND SUBSTANCE ABUSE
Crying Out for Help

Points to ponder as you read:

✓ How big a problem is alcohol and substance abuse in America today?

✓ How do you know if you have a problem with alcohol or other addictive substances?

✓ What other addictions are there besides alcoholism?

✓ What is a very real problem with nicotine gum?

Imagine with me for a moment that you have inherited a fortune from a long, lost relative. You find out that this fortune is huge, making you a multi-billionaire. (If we're going to dream, we might as well dream big!) Now, let's suppose that a man comes up to you, right after you have gotten this fortune, and makes you this proposition. If you will turn over total control of your fortune to him, he will make all the decisions about your money. You will only be able to spend what money he wants you to spend, when he wants you to spend it, on only those purchases he approves. How many would think this is a good deal? For most of us, the thought of turning over that vast fortune to the control of someone else would be unthinkable. And, yet millions of Americans surrender control of something far more valuable than money every single day. They give up total control of their lives to addiction.

The Substance Abuse and Mental Health Services Administration (SAMHSA) conducted a survey in 1999, surveying thousands of households across America on the subject of drug abuse. The results were both alarming and disturbing. The following is what was discovered:

- Approximately 4% of Americans (8.5 million), ages 12 and over, meet the criteria for alcoholism
- Almost 15 million Americans use illicit drugs, and almost 4 million of those would be considered drug dependent
- Among teens ages 12-17, nearly 11% have used illicit drugs
- Over 110,000 Americans die of alcohol-related medical conditions

Looking at the above results, it is easy to realize that substance abuse and dependence are major threats to public health in America. Statistics also show that up to 80% of alcohol abusers under the age of 30 will abuse another drug as well, and 80% of cocaine abusers are also alcoholics. The tally of deaths from illicit drug use is 20,000 each year; while nicotine use results in 400,000 deaths annually. When you also consider that in the year 2000, 17,126 deaths were the result of drunk drivers and another 100,000 deaths were alcohol-related, it is clear that "Houston, we have a problem" (alcohol statistics compiled by Arthur Hu in "Death Spectrum: Top Causes of Deaths in the USA").

It is estimated that drug and alcohol use costs nearly $300 billion annually in the United States, which is almost one-quarter of our entire health budget! Nearly one million Americans are actively involved right now in a specialized treatment for either drug or alcohol abuse. There is no doubt that addictions and addictive behavior is one of the major problems facing Americans today.

ADDICTIONS IN GENERAL

An addiction is defined as a compulsive need for and use of a habit-forming substance or habit-forming behavior; also a persistent compulsive use of a substance known by the user to be harmful. In other words, there is difficulty avoiding this behavior or substance, no matter how harmful or detrimental it may be. Experts tell us that addiction tends to be so consuming that it affects not only an addict's behavior, but also his thoughts and feelings. This is partially because substances like alcohol and nicotine interfere with the natural chemistry of the brain, and it is also because the experience of addiction, as a whole, has an effect on a person's perceptions, attitudes, and personality.

Sometimes, we have a tendency to downplay addictions, unless people can actually die from them. For instance, most of us would recognize that a heroin addiction could lead to an overdose or a nicotine addiction could lead to lung cancer, and that these would be serious consequences. But, even addictive behaviors such as gambling, that do not involve substance abuse, still work in a manipulative partnership with the brain's own chemistry and can result in significant damage, both physically and emotionally.

The depth of the psychological impact of an addiction depends on a person's mental health before becoming addicted and the ongoing circumstances of their life. This means if you are unemployed, homeless, and physically unwell, your psychological health is likely to suffer more than if you have a home, a job, and a supportive family. If the addiction itself is physically damaging to the brain, such as in alcohol abuse, long term psychological harm may result. And, of course, when brain damage occurs, there is no guarantee that it will be reparable, even if the addictive behavior ceases.

Not everyone who becomes addicted has precisely the same experience. However, there are certain psychological symptoms that most addicted people suffer sooner or later, either all at once or in clusters. People may begin to look for treatment when these start to become severe, because of the growing inescapable impact of the addiction's harmful consequences.

The psychological effects of addiction can be divided into those that relate to feeling and those that relate to thinking. These thoughts and feelings may bear a close relationship with addictive behaviors that may result from and/or lead to the thoughts and feelings. For example, an addicted person may avoid others. This leads to a feeling of isolation. He may at the same time feel ashamed of feeling unable to cope, and of the addiction that is causing this. To deal with the feeling, he takes more of the drug. His relationship with the drug excludes people. So people avoid him. The result is increased isolation, and on and on, into a downward spiral.

It is also important to realize that the psychological effects of addiction are not only experienced by the person who is addicted. Unfortunately, addictive behaviors also have an impact on anyone personally involved with the addict, such as families, friends, and colleagues.

FEELINGS ASSOCIATED WITH ADDICTION

Many of the feelings experienced in addiction derive from a sense of being unable to gain control of oneself. Some feelings, like shame and guilt, come from an addict behaving in ways that are at odds with their personal values and beliefs. For instance, a compulsive gambler may have difficulty living with the knowledge that he has stolen money from his loving, trusting grandmother to gamble away.

Below are some of the feelings addicts can experience:

- Depression—Ranges from feeling very down and helpless to the extreme of suicidal.
- Anxiety—Ranges from feeling generally fearful to

loss of trust and paranoia.

- Low self-esteem—May become self-loathing; links to shame and guilt.
- No confidence—A state of mind related to anxiety and depression.
- Anger—From touchy and irritated to explosive, often blaming others for one's behavior.
- Boredom—The pattern of addiction becomes relentlessly, tediously the same.

THOUGHTS ASSOCIATED WITH ADDICTION

Many of the thought patterns of an addict are defensive and work to protect the addiction. Some are responses to the stress of the lifestyle of addiction, while others are the results of physical damage done by the addiction itself, as in drug or alcohol use.

Below is a sample of thoughts and experiences that affect an addict's mind:

- Dependency—Believing others are responsible and therefore should work towards "fixing" you.
- Denying reality—Convincing oneself and attempting to convince others that the addiction is not as bad as it actually is.
- Obsessive—Overwhelming focus on the substance or behavior.
- Grandiosity—Thinks that his/her concerns are more important than anything or anyone else.
- Self harm—Ideas about ways to relieve or escape the suffering.
- Memory and concentration impairment.

BEHAVIORS ASSOCIATED WITH ADDICTION

Behaviors tend to reflect the consuming relationship with the drug or need of choice. They postpone positive changes and facing up to reality, which make them ultimately self-defeating. In many instances, behavior is simply about avoiding the discomfort of withdrawal.

The following are some of the behaviors an addict may exhibit:

- Avoidance—Isolating; not taking responsibility
- Controlling—Including various kinds of manipulation and even violence
- Betrayal—Anyone can be sacrificed because the addiction comes first
- Self harm—Deliberate acts for relief or punishment
- Deceiving—Deception of self and others to stay ahead of consequences

SPECIFIC ADDICTIONS

Alcoholism

According to the American Society of Addiction Medicine, alcoholism is a "primary, chronic disease with genetic, psychosocial, and environmental factors influencing its development and manifestation." Some of the health consequences of excessive alcohol consumption include:

- high blood pressure
- gastritis and esophagitis
- alcoholic hepatitis and cirrhosis
- diabetes
- gout
- depression/anxiety
- seizures
- dementia
- breast cancer
- traumatic injuries
- impotence

- anemia
- multiple types of nutritional deficiencies
- pneumonia and a high incidence of other infections, especially sexually transmitted diseases (STDs)
- giving birth to a baby who has "fetal alcohol syndrome"

And the list goes on and on.

Treatment of Alcoholism

The most effective treatment of alcoholism requires a team approach, ideally at a licensed intensive outpatient or inpatient program that specializes in the treatment of alcoholism. The careful use of pharmaceuticals, along with certain psychological support measures, results in the least negative physical effects and the shortest hospital stay.

There are two phases to alcohol recovery: 1) the acute withdrawal phase and (2) the recovery and relapse prevention phase. Because acute withdrawal can be quite dangerous in someone who is a long-term alcohol abuser or has been on a significant binge, I recommend that the acute phase of withdrawal be handled by a specialist. If the problem is severe and/or long-standing, an inpatient stay of at least 14 days is helpful to have the person "take a break" from the realities of their life that have led to alcohol dependency.

With the alcohol recovery process, it is important to take it one day at a time. Recovery is a long and slow process. Alcoholics Anonymous and ALANON are two organizations that can be very helpful and supportive in alcohol recovery and relapse prevention.

Nicotine

Nicotine is a psycho-active substance that can be found in cigarettes, cigars, pipe tobacco, chewing tobacco, and snuff. Nicotine is extremely addicting, although it is believed that there are a number of different psycho-active substances in tobacco that provide an additional addictive effect. The physical effects of nicotine usage include increased heart rate and blood pressure and general feelings of energy. Agitation, euphoria, and calmness are all reported as feelings associated with nicotine.

Surveys show that at least 80% of smokers want to quit, 35% attempt to quit in a given year, but only 5% are able to quit without some sort of intervention. The scientific research is exceedingly clear—smoking is the leading cause of lung cancer and contributes to an increased risk of most other types of cancer, as well. In addition, smoking is one of the three main risk factors for the development of heart disease. There is now a Surgeon General warning on the side of cigarettes and other nicotine-containing products stating that smoking is harmful to your health, including causing an increased risk of birth defects—along with the other dangers just listed. Smoking also greatly increases one's risk of developing chronic respiratory problems, including emphysema and chronic bronchitis. While cigarette smoking causes the majority of the adverse health effects of tobacco, chewing is also hazardous, causing oral cancer in particular, as does tobacco smoking via cigars or pipes.

In addition, we now know that smoking also harms others. There are definite health risks from passive smoking, not to mention smoking during pregnancy, which adversely affects fetal development.

And, yet, with all the scientific information documenting the health damages associated with smoking, we all know someone who smokes, who would like to quit, and yet can't seem to. Mark Twain once said that it was easy to give up smoking . . . he had done it hundreds of times.

A gentleman and his wife were both chain smokers. She was diagnosed with lung cancer. The cancer was caught in the beginning stages, and her prognosis was very good. However, despite the fact that that she knew smoking was threatening her life, she continued to smoke several packs a day, as did her husband. On the day of her funeral, her husband lit up a cigarette to help calm his nerves.

Treatment of Nicotine Addiction

When someone stops smoking, acute withdrawal begins quickly, and generally lasts three to five days. Symptoms include agitation, insomnia, restlessness, and difficulty concentrating. The best interventions for smoking cessation include pharmacologic and psychological support. Pharmacologic replacement of nicotine via patches, inhalers, or gums should be slowly tapered over three to eight weeks for best results. The addition of a calming type medication is an option for those who are agitated and nervous. Bupropion (also known as Zyban) is available from your physician, if appropriate. (Zyban is contra-indicated in someone who is trying to withdraw from alcohol along with smoking.) Valerian is an herbal alternative for the anxiety and restlessness that often occurs with nicotine withdrawal. Used in homeopathic preparations, lobelia is also an aid to stop smoking, although there are essentially no published double-blind studies.

In my experience, the use of transdermal nicotine (Nicoderm patches) is associated with the highest success rate and the least likelihood of ongoing addiction (to the nicotine replacement). I have had patients who struggled for years to stop the nicotine gum (Nicorette)!

Illicit and Prescription Drugs

In addition to the difficulties associated with alcohol and nicotine addictions, new problems arise with the use of illegal substances. Users have to keep a constant eye on maintaining their supply and finding ways to pay for it. This often means bein involved in some form of illegal behavior, either to obtain money to pay for the drugs or in the actual procurement of the drugs (always illegal—with the exception of marijuana for medical purposes allowed in some states).

Unfortunately, people can also become dependent upon prescription drugs. This often begins innocently, with the appropriate prescribing of a pain medication after an injury or surgery, or the prescription of an anti-anxiety medication for someone dealing with an acute trauma. Most often, however, these drugs are sought out by people with addictive tendencies, who have previous experience with the effects of certain classes of psychoactive drugs.

Whether someone is using illegal or legal drugs, there are similar signs and behavioral changes:

- Abrupt changes in work or school attendance, quality of work, work output, grades, and discipline
- Unusual flare-ups or outbreaks of temper
- Withdrawal from responsibility
- General changes in overall attitude
- Deterioration of physical appearance and grooming
- Wearing of sunglasses at inappropriate times
- Continual wearing of long-sleeved garments, particularly in hot weather, or reluctance to wear short-sleeved attire when appropriate
- Association with known substance abusers
- Unusual borrowing of money from friends, co-workers, or parents
- Stealing small items from work, home, or school
- Secretive behavior regarding actions and possessions
- poorly concealed attempts to avoid attention and suspicion, such as frequent trips to storage rooms, restroom, basement, etc.

Some of the more common illicit drugs being abused are cocaine, marijuana, and inhalants.

Cocaine Dependence

Cocaine is a central nervous system stimulant. Initially euphoria is experienced, although chronic use leads to tolerance and eventually depression from depletion of a particular neurotransmitter (dopamine) in the brain. People can suffer cocaine intoxication, which can be life-threatening if extremely high blood pressure or heart arrhythmias occur. Cocaine withdrawal usually lasts from three to seven days, consisting of extreme irritability and depression. There is no FDA approved treatment protocol for cocaine withdrawal or for prevention of relapse. Various antidepressants have been studied, without convincing results.

Marijuana (aka Cannabis) Dependency

Marijuana usage became quite common amongst teens and young adults in the 1960's and 70's. This era of people are now in their late 40's to early 60's, and a certain percentage of them continue to use. Marijuana smokers are highly likely to abuse other drugs, most commonly alcohol. Chronic users may note personality changes, have difficulty concentrating, experience paranoia, and memory loss. Alcohol use causes an additive effect.

Studies clearly validate that driving performance is affected by marijuana; and alcohol usage will only aggravates this condition. Chronic marijuana users may develop some of the same chronic lung diseases that tobacco smokers develop, such as asthma and chronic lung disease. As with cocaine dependence, there are no approved treatment protocols for marijuana withdrawal or relapse prevention.

Inhalants

Inhalants are widely available products, such as gasoline, adhesives, cleaning fluids, and paint thinner. As a group, they are the fourth most common drug abused by adolescents. These substances are incredibly dangerous, but very attractive to youngsters who are looking for an "easy" euphoric high or hallucinogenic experience. Because these substances contain volatile substances that become gases, there are a wide variety of physical responses that can occur. These include agitation, confusion, disorientation, and sedation. These effects can occur rapidly and are fatal more often than most people are aware of.

Treatment of Drug Abuse

Treatment is dependent on the substance. Acupuncture and transcendental meditation have been studied in the setting of alcohol and various substance withdrawal programs and both have been shown to be helpful in preventing relapses. Yoga, with its combination of breathing techniques, postures, and meditation can assist with stress management. This is important because life stresses are one of the triggers for relapse into addictive behavior.

It is no secret that drug addiction is very difficult to overcome. Most drug abusers require professional help to break free of their habit. Certainly, if the abuse involves opiates (heroin, methadone, and other narcotics), withdrawal, rife with possible complications, should only be attempted under supervision by trained professionals.

Whatever addiction you or someone you care about may be fighting, there is help available. There are numerous organizations and medical facilities dedicated to helping the addict find his way back, as well as offering counseling and support to his family members. Sometimes an addict has to hit "rock bottom"—experiencing the most devastating realities of his addiction, before he will seek help. But, once an addict can bring himself to admit he has a problem, there is always hope.

 FOLLOW-UP PREVENTIVE PERSCRIPTION

CHECK OUT THE FOLLOWING "THREE C's."

If you or someone you know might have a problem with substance abuse, consider the American Psychiatric Association's diagnostic criteria for alcoholism or other addictions:

- CONTROL: once an addict begins using the substance of choice, there is no control or feeling you can stop or quit.
- CONSEQUENCES: An addict continues to drink or use the drug despite negative consequences (work problems, deterioration of relationships, and negative health effects)
- COMPULSION: There is a gradual increase in the amount of usage, the frequency of usage, and the preoccupation with this usage (things go from bad to worse).

The following suggestions will not cure an addiction, but they will strengthen the addict to better fight his particular battle.

Dietary Recommendations

While there are no specific foods that will prevent addiction or relapses to alcohol and substance abuse, a balanced, complete nutritious eating plan is a lifestyle choice that will help. There is good substantiation of improvement of mental health when certain foods are included in the diet. Conversely, mental health may suffer when certain other foods are included regularly. A study done in Great Britain, sponsored by BBC Health, showed a definite link between food and mood. Foods that tended to negatively impact mood included sugar, caffeine, alcohol, and chocolate (sorry, ladies). Foods that seemed to positively affect mood included vegetables, fruits, oil-rich fish (e.g. salmon), and water.

We know that our intake of omega-3 fatty acids (which make up a substantial part of the brain) has greatly declined since Paleolithic times. It is theorized by many mental health experts that this decline in omega-3 intake (and concomitant increase in omega-6 intake) may be part of the explanation of the increase in violence and evil deeds in our modern world.

My recommendations include:

1. Regularly partake of a variety of fresh fruits and

vegetables—at least two servings of fruit and five servings of vegetables per day.

2. Eat omega-3 rich fish at least three times per week (or supplement—see below). Good fish choices include wild salmon, halibut, shrimp, or mackerel.

3. Avoid sweets on a regular basis, as blood sugar fluctuations can be a trigger for individuals with addictive tendencies.

4. Drink plenty of water—at least six to eight glasses. Mild and chronic dehydration can also be a trigger for cravings (and overeating).

5. Minimize caffeine intake, especially if feelings of anxiety or insomnia are present.

Supplement Suggestions

1. Take a quality multivitamin mineral preparation, one that is formulated to be taken two to three times a day.

2. Take an Omega-3 supplement, 500 mg of a blend of EPA and DHA per capsule. Look for one that includes the RDA of vitamin E.

3. Valerian may be helpful in dealing with anxiety, and St. John's Wort may be helpful with mild to moderate depression. However, there are no clinical studies using valerian or St. John's Wort in the setting of addiction.

Activity Encouragement

Exercise is a known stress reliever and can help in lessening the craving for a particular substance or behavior. The release of endorphins in the brain, in response to moderate physical activity, provides some of the "positive feelings" that are needed in dealing with relapse prevention (see Chapter 7).

Other Modalities

Acupuncture, meditation, yoga and other mind-body therapies, plus the Twelve Step programs are all good choices if you or a loved one is dealing with addictive behavior. There are reasonable studies using acupuncture and transcendental meditation in preventing relapse with alcohol and other substances. There are fewer studies with yoga, guided imagery, and hypnosis as sole therapies, but all of these modalities can be effective combined with other treatment approaches (especially addiction treatment centers).

CHAPTER 17

A LEGACY FOR OUR CHILDREN
Diet and Lifestyle Leading to Adult Diseases

Points to ponder as you read:

- ✓ What is the number one health concern for children in America today?
- ✓ What health risks do obese children face?
- ✓ What are the major factors that have led us to this epidemic of obese and overweight children?
- ✓ How can parents make a difference in these trends?

What kind of legacy can we leave our children? What sort of role model do we want for our children, as well as others around us? Most of us who are between 35 and 55 (the Baby Boomers) grew up in families where the mom stayed home and the dad was the bread winner for the family. Families in the 60's and early 70's tended to eat as a family most nights, with eating out an exception to the weekly dinner routine. School lunch programs were limited, and most children brought their lunch to school. I attended Catholic schools from kindergarten to 12th grade and could count on two hands (possibly one) the number of times I ate a school lunch, rather than the lunch my mother made. I had a peanut butter and jam sandwich, an apple, and a small thermos of milk almost every day. My lunch variety was based on a change in fruit, the occasional treat of a cheese or tuna sandwich, and the rare event of a small bag of chips or raisins. My nickname was "beanpole," as I was always taller than most of my classmates and on the slender side. Growing up, I can only remember a handful of children who were overweight.

Today, life is much different for most of our children. Most mothers now work outside of the home, as do the fathers. Divorce is far more common, and children are often juggled between two households. As most men are generally less interested and less competent "chefs" and women are too tired to cook a meal after a long day at work, children end up eating a high percentage of their meals from convenience packages, take-out containers, or fast food restaurants. Mom is too busy getting ready for work and juggling all the needs of a family in the morning to worry about breakfast or making lunches. The overwhelming majority of children today eat whatever is on the school lunch menu or whatever they can buy from the vending machines that are now on almost all middle and high school campuses. Many high schools today contract with the local fast food establishments to provide school lunch fare. That means high school students, on a daily basis, are choosing lunch from McDonalds, Burger King, Taco Bell, or Pizza Hut! Between classes, many students have the option of grabbing a soda from a hallway vending machine. On the way home from school, thanks to a convenience store on every other corner, a teenager can pick up a "Big Gulp" or its equivalent, a 32-ounce cola which provides 540 empty calories, 320 mg of caffeine, and 44 teaspoons of sugar.

Taking these factors into account, it is no wonder teenagers vacillate between being irritable and lethargic. The sugar and caffeine provide a "rush" of energy and a spike in blood sugar. Two hours later, after blood sugar has plummeted and the caffeine is metabolized, the student is ready for a nap, when he should be studying.

Recently, Dr. David Satcher, the U.S. Surgeon General, issued his "state of the health of the nation" address, where he virtually declared war on obesity, emphasizing that it is the number one health concern in America today—for Americans of all ages. As of 2002, 62% of American adults were overweight to obese, with an alarming 38% being obese (and thus facing the dramatically increased likelihood of many chronic diseases). The American Academy of Pediatrics has also recently addressed this subject, affirming that, since we have seen the prevalence of overweight to obese children in the U.S. double in the past 10 years, childhood obesity is the number one problem facing children today. They also stress that for pediatricians and family physicians providing medical care to children, this should be the single most important issue on which they focus. When we realize that obesity generates 117 billion dollars in annual medical bills and triggers 300,000 premature deaths each year, it is easy to see why medical experts consider this a health crisis and feel the problem needs immediate attention.

The statistics regarding weight problems among children are horrifying. Not only have the number of overweight and obese children doubled between 1992 and 2001, but the number has tripled over the last 25 years. In the past, the issues parents dealt with regarding their children's health focused on diseases like chickenpox or conditions like Little League elbow. Today, we diagnose children and adolescents with hypertension and elevated cholesterol levels. Today's parents are being told by their pediatrician that their overweight 11-year-old son has type 2 diabetes or their 16-year-old daughter has osteoporosis. While our diets are fostering obesity and obesity-related diseases, our society pressures girls to be thin and perfect like actresses and models. We have a generation of malnourished, overweight kids and growing numbers of malnourished, anorexic and bulimic young girls (see Chapter 12).

Weight problems in children have led to a 50% increase in the diagnosis of Type 2 diabetes in just the past 10 years. This obesity-related disorder used to be known as adult onset diabetes mellitus (AODM), because it was seen as an adult disorder. In my practice, until the 1990's, all of my patients with non-insulin dependent diabetes were age 45 and older. A child with abnormal blood sugars had insulin-dependent diabetes, now called Type 1 diabetes. The definitions and characteristics of these two diseases have changed fairly dramatically in the past 15 years, essentially because of our diets and the alarming increase in obesity in children. Type 2 diabetes brings with it an increased risk of coronary artery disease, other circulation problems such as chronic nerve pain (called peripheral neuropathy), and several types of kidney disease which can ultimately lead to the need for dialysis and kidney transplant. And all of this occurs simply because children, teens, and young adults are overweight and eating diets that are high in refined sugars and saturated fat, and low in fiber.

As discussed in Chapter 13, conditions like osteoporosis were formerly associated with women 70 years of age and older. But, today, it is not at all uncommon to have bone-density tests reveal dangerously low bone densities in young gymnasts, ballerinas, and anorexics, leading to an increased risk of fractures and even a loss of height from collapse of their vertebrae. That fact, in itself, is not surprising because we know that very low body weight and body fat can lead to this occurring in youngsters. Today, however, we are seeing bone thinning in normal and even overweight teens and young adults.

There are many reasons for this trend, but one of the recently recognized causes is the dramatic increase in consumption of carbonated beverages. Today's youth drink three times the amount of soft drinks and less than half as much milk as 20 years ago, and experts firmly believe that there is a connection between soft drink consumption and bone thinning. The main theory involves the high phosphate content of sodas, which "leaches" calcium out of the bones and demineralizes teeth. A study by Grace Wyshak in Archives of Pediatrics & Adolescent Medicine in 2000, demonstrated a clear correlation between the risk of fractures and consumption of carbonated sodas in otherwise healthy high school girls. A Harvard School of Public Health author and researcher writes: "Calcium and calcium supplementation have been found to increase bone mineral density. Osteoporotic fractures may be affected by diet and activity in young women. Adolescence is a critical period for bone mass formation. Adolescence is a prime population for early prevention of osteoporosis with calcium intake and avoidance of behaviors that may be counter-productive to increasing bone mass."

Elevated cholesterol and triglyceride levels are also commonplace issues for today's children. This is alarming because elevations in blood lipids are a prime risk factor in the development of heart disease. Overweight kids show elevated levels of C-reactive protein in their blood stream, which is predictive of increased risk of heart disease and stroke.

For millions of years, human beings have been raising families on this planet. In just the last decade or two, however, we have managed to dramatically and negatively impact the health of our children through poor diet and lifestyle choices. It is time to pay attention to the details of our lives and our children's lives. We need to turn the tide of this terrible trend and begin to reverse these frightening statistics.

NUTRITION

The single most important factor affecting the health of children is the food they eat—and the foods they don't eat. Most experts believe that the single element of the American diet that is most harmful to our children is fast food consumption. In an article entitled, "Marketing of Fast Food and Sugar-Sweetened Beverages to Children: Is it Promoting Obesity?" Cara B. Ebbeling, Ph.D. asserts that the unprecedented weight gain and prevalence of overweight and obesity among children and teens in the United States is the result of a "toxic environment," which is characterized by an overabundance of fast food and sugar-sweetened beverages. She writes:

> Over the last few decades, increased consumption and sales of unhealthful fast food has paralleled the rising prevalence of obesity. In the late 1970's, children consumed 17% of their meals away from home, and fast foods accounted for only 2% of total calorie intake. By the mid- to late-1990's, the proportion of meals eaten away from home nearly doubled to 30%, and fast food intake increased to 10% of total calorie intake. Likewise, per capita daily soft drink consumption increased from six ounces to over 17 ounces for boys and from five ounces to almost 12 ounces for girls between 1965 and 1996.

Now is the time for a moment of self-evaluation. Have you been guilty of rushing your children out the door in the morning, hurrying by a McDonalds where you pick up an Egg McMuffin or sausage biscuit that your child chokes down on the way to school? Have you ever come home late and tired, without the least desire to cook, and decided to drop by KFC to pick up the Fried Chicken Family Pak for dinner? (See Chapter 4 to find out how many calories and fat grams you also decided to pick up for your family.) Take a moment and add up how many fast food meals your children consume in an average week. How many trips do you make to a fast food drive-thru? How many pizzas do you order in? Keep in mind that if your child is a consumer of the school lunch program, you also need to calculate in what they are eating there. A typical hot school lunch program serves hot dogs, pizza slices, fried fish sandwiches, and nachos. In some school lunch programs, ketchup is counted as a vegetable!

As discussed earlier in this chapter, our middle and high school sons and daughters are choosing between various fast food choices at lunch, with plenty of sodas and high sugar snacks available in vending machines on campus and convenience stores on the way home. Many football field scoreboards carry large advertisements for soda companies; and many high schools depend on money from these companies to help fund athletic programs. It's ironic that companies, who sell beverages with absolutely no nutritional value that contribute to obesity, low bone density, and hyperactivity, subsidize our children's sports activities.

Dr. Ebbeling believes that these unhealthy eating trends have been driven, at least in part, by marketing strategies of the fast food and soft drink industries. Children are exposed to thousands of television advertisements per year, many of which are for fast foods and sugar-sweetened beverages. When tested by being exposed to 30-second commercials for the same, is it any wonder that young children would later select an advertised food given the options. Thus we see the basis for Dr. Ebbeling's beliefs.

Let's look at fast food commercials. How many advertising campaigns, specifically targeting children, link fast foods and beverages with toys, games, movies, and collectibles? And, if your child doesn't want to go to a fast food place to pick up the latest toy, maybe he is moved to go there because of the pleasant environment.

Think about the messages commercials portray. Everyone at fast food establishments is in a really good mood. It's a fun place. One of the fast food restaurants even names its child's takeout a "Happy Meal," and its most recent slogan is "Put a smile on." There's no question what message this company is trying to get across. And what child would not want to have Ronald McDonald for a friend; and, for that matter, what parent would not want him for a babysitter.

Fast food commercials also create an emotional connection with their food. Your little league team is slaughtered on the baseball diamond, and you have never felt like such a loser! No problem. After you go out for pizza, you will feel great. It's a rainy day, you're bored, or you're feeling lonely. Once again, no problem.

After you go out for fast food, all will be right in your world once again. When it is considered that behavioral experts say emotional eating is one of the triggers that leads to obesity, you can see why equating fast food consumption with pleasant emotions is extremely unhealthy.

The aim of fast food commercials is not just to have children clamoring to go out to eat, but they also want parents to feel guilty if they don't go. The message these companies are trying to get across is: good parents love their children enough to take them out for fast food. One particularly offensive commercial shows a mother coming home from work. Sensing that her son has missed her and needs to talk, she tells him they are going out for dinner. The scene then shifts to mother and son in the fast food restaurant, happily eating French fries and sharing ketchup, as they talk and laugh and catch up on each other's lives. The implication being that a good parent, who loves her child, takes him out to eat so she can give him her undivided attention. When, in reality, the good parent is one who loves her child enough to provide nutritious meals that will help him lead a healthy and happy life. A more perfect picture of a loving parent, would be one in the kitchen, fixing a nutritious meal for her family, while the child sits at the kitchen table doing homework and talking. Parental attention, despite what the fast food commercials would have you believe, does not have to be steeped in fat and calories to be effective and loving.

Dr. Ebbeling also makes the point that progressively larger fast food meals may be contributing to the pediatric obesity epidemic. She is referring, of course, to the ever popular "super-sizing" of portions. Dr. Ebbeling shares these enlightening, yet disturbing facts:

> *…the fast food industry offers consumers the choice to "super size" portions for a minimal increase in cost over what is charged for smaller servings. At McDonald's Restaurant, the "super size" serving of fries at 610 calories contains 3 times more calories than the*

small serving, which has 210. The Big Mac and Big N' Tasty with Cheese sandwiches [both packing a whopping 590 calories] contain approximately twice the calories of a classic hamburger (280 calories). In the 1950's, a standard serving of Coca-Cola was 6.5 fluid ounces, and servings marketed as "king size" were 10 to 12 fluid ounces. Currently, McDonald's beverages range from child size (12 fl oz / 110 calories) and small (16 fl oz / 150 calories) to large (32 fl oz / 310 calories) and "super size" (42 fl oz / 410 calories). Serving sizes at other major fast food restaurant chains have similarly increased.

Read this account of a child's response to fast food marketing:

"I was taking my 10-year-old son and his friend to a Mariner's baseball game. On the way, we stopped by a fast food place to get a hamburger. My son's friend, who is overweight, asked if he could have the triple cheeseburger with bacon. He pointed out that this sandwich was on sale, and that it was only in the restaurant for a limited time. He also wanted to super-size it all, and he definitely did not want a diet drink. When the food came, I was appalled. Behind a mountain of French fries, was a HUGE burger. This sandwich had three hamburger patties covered with cheese, topped with three strips of bacon, dripping with a special sauce made from mayonnaise. As I watched this 10 year old child eat every single morsel of this meal, a meal that provided more fat and calories than any adult should consume in an entire week, I understood very clearly why this boy was overweight. And, it wasn't surprising that the triple cheeseburger with bacon (which should have been nicknamed the "Heart-Attack Special") was only there for a limited time. If too many loyal customers ate a steady diet of these burgers, the restaurant's clientele would be dropping like flies."

Clearly, from the evidence above, it is vital to your child's health to limit his consumption of fast food. Fast food should definitely be the rare "exception" in an eating plan, rather than the "rule."

But, just taking fast food out of your child's diet is not enough. You need to replace it with healthy, nutritious meals and snacks. I am certainly sensitive to the challenges facing our families today. Most homes have two working parents, who are often commuting some distance to work, and really feel too tired in the evening to prepare any kind of meals. But, as you have read in this chapter thus far, it is imperative for the collective health of our nation as well as the individual health of our children to take control. Jim Rohn, a business and personal philosopher, says: "For things to change, you must change". Here are some guidelines and tips to help you and your child benefit from a commitment to improved nutrition:

PLAN MENUS. Let your children help plan out a week's worth of menus. Start out by planning just dinners, but, by the second month, include breakfast and lunch in your planning, as well. For dinners, let everyone include a favorite food at as many meals as possible. Discuss with your children why you feel it's important to have more vegetables and fruits with your meals and less refined sugars. If your child is buying school lunch, look critically (through your newly "nutritional-savvy" eyes) at the menu and decide if this is how you want your child to eat! If it is the typical school lunch fare, you should try to transition your child to taking lunch to school. You may be surprised at how enthusiastic he will be about this prospect. Talk to your child about eating foods that will protect him from getting a cold, give him more energy for riding his bike after school, and the ability to concentrate better in class. Every time I have talked on nutrition to elementary and middle school children, I am amazed at how interested they are in the topic and how many misconceptions they have about various foods. (If you need to brush up on principles of nutrition, re-read Chapters 5 and 6).

NO FORCED FEEDING. Try letting children (over the age of five) serve themselves. Do not insist they eat everything on their plate. I still remember my mother chiding us to eat every bite because "there are starving children in India." I never quite understood the relevance of that to me having to eat liver that made me gag! Many overweight adults trace the roots of their overeating to childhood and being forced to clean their plates, whether they were hungry or not. Infants and toddlers will generally eat only when they are hungry and will stop when they are full. Some days they eat only meat, and other days they only want vegetables. There are probably internal signals telling them what their body needs more of, at a particular time. By the time we are school age, we have been programmed to eat at a certain time (family dinner time) whether we are hungry or not. If we want dessert, we must clean our plate (which is a double whammy for weight control). And speaking of dessert, why does dessert have to be cookies or ice cream? Try fresh fruit, served sliced with a dollop of vanilla lowfat yogurt, or air-popped popcorn with a dusting of paprika and tossed with a small amount of olive oil. Get creative, and help children learn to enjoy new and healthier tasty treats!

LET KIDS HELP. Let children help prepare dinner by giving them age appropriate tasks. Even young children can help. Set them on a chair or stool at the table with some pre-cut raw vegetables. Let them arrange the veggies on a tray around a bowl of low-fat dip. Letting a child prepare meals with you will also give you an opportunity to share nutritious cooking knowledge, such as why we grill instead of fry or demonstrating how to steam vegetables.

STOCK UP ON THE GOOD STUFF. Keep your kitchen stocked with healthy foods. If you don't buy "junk food", you will eliminate one place where your child can eat it. If your child looks at a well-stocked pantry, refrigerator, and freezer, and says, "There's nothing to eat," what he means is there are no empty, high fat, high sugar calories to consume. Take that comment as a compliment, and know that you are on the right track.

PLAN FOR A SNACK ATTACK. After-school snacks should be readily available as children tend to come home from school famished. If all they can find is Oreo cookies and potato chips, guess what they will eat? Be sure to have your kitchen stocked with healthy snacks. Both my son and daughter really loved the fruit smoothies that I often made as after-school snacks. I would mix (for two servings) eight ounces of lowfat fruit-flavored yogurt, a banana, 1 cup of frozen strawberries, 1 cup of fresh orange juice and 3-4 ice cubes. "Mommy's Special Drink" is still a favorite of my son—even though he is now a strapping 6'2" 24-year-old! Other nutritious staples good to have on hand are applesauce, low-fat Jell-O and pudding cups, cut-up veggies, and fresh fruit.

GO BACK TO THE TABLE. Make eating a family gathering. If you are eating dinner in front of the television, strongly consider moving dinner back to the dining room or kitchen nook (where there is NO television). Make dinner a leisurely, pleasant experience. One night a week, make dinner an event. Use the good china, crystal, and silverware on the people that matter most. Let your children experience elegant dining. This will have the added benefit of providing an opportunity to teach more formal table manners so they will not embarrass you on those occasions when you dine at a fancy restaurant or have your husband's new boss over for dinner!

EXERCISE AND PHYSICAL ACTIVITY

With obesity having doubled in children over the past 20 years, it's not surprising to discover that activity levels in children have greatly reduced. Our children are the victims of a 20th century lifestyle, sitting for hours in front of a television or computer screen. Children, just like adults, are eating more and exercising less. The amount of time spent in front of the television directly correlates with the likelihood of obesity in our children. Experts have discovered that if your child has a TV in his bedroom, he will be three times more likely to become overweight or obese. If your child's idea of exercise is standing up to put in a new video game or searching the couch cushions for the remote control, you've got a problem.

Keep in mind that most children who are content with a sedentary lifestyle have parents who are content with a sedentary lifestyle. In other words, couch potatoes spawn little spuds. So, as with nutrition, the solution to the problem of lack of exercise lies with the parents.

Encourage your children to be active. Olympic medal speed-skater Apollo Ohno, stars in a "verb" commercial, sponsored by the Center for Disease Control. This public service ad shows kids doing their favorite verbs, such as running, swimming, jumping, hiking, biking, etc. The idea behind this advertisement is to en-courage kids to find their favorite "verb" and be active.

Here are some additional ideas to help you and your children get off the couch and start moving:

- BUY ACTION GIFTS. For instance, a great birthday present to hopefully inspire your child to be more fit would be a bicycle, roller blades, a tennis racket, a basketball and freestanding hoop, a skateboard, or a scooter. If you live where it's cold, ice skates, skis, or a snowboard are a great gift.

- HAVE ACTIVE BIRTHDAY PARTIES. By this I do not mean having a group of children running around like wild banshees. I mean parties based on activities. For instance, instead of a pizza party, arrange a party at the rollerskating rink, swimming pool, or iceskating rink.

- ENCOURAGE SPORTS. Give children the opportunity to sign up for sports teams or lessons. Let them have the chance to play on a soccer or baseball team. Or, if team sports don't appeal to your child, let her take tennis, diving, golf, dance, or judo lessons. Give children experience with sports and activities, so they will have a chance to find a "verb" to enjoy for a lifetime.

- BE AN ACTIVE FAMILY. Instead of renting a video and eating a big bowl of popcorn drizzled with butter, go on a family bike ride or a hike. Pack a healthy picnic lunch, and divide it up into backpacks for family members to carry. Join the local YMCA or gym as a family and go to workout together.

- ADD ACTIVITY TO FAMILY TRADITIONS. For instance, after Thanksgiving dinner, instead of settling on the couch for eight straight hours of football and/or a nap, go on a family bikeride or a walk. Make the walk or bicycle ride as much a part of the tradition as the meal. It will be a great way to share activity with family members while working off some of calories.

- MODEL AN ACTIVE LIFESTYLE FOR CHILDREN. Instead of driving around in the supermarket parking lot for 15 minutes, trying to get a spot as close to the door as possible, park on the edge of the lot and walk to the door. Pass up the elevator and escalator and take the stairs. Instead of letting the dog out, take him for a walk (with your children). There will be less overweight dogs in America, as well as creating a pattern of activity in our children.

Remember, children are excellent observers. The more they see an active lifestyle, the more active they will be. Help children make exercise and regular physical activity a part of their lifestyle, and bequeath them the priceless gift of health.

STRESS MANAGEMENT

Most of us tend to think of stress as being a condition that only adults have to deal with. Unfortunately, this is another problem we are passing on to our children. A child's schedule in the

21st Century tends to be as over-scheduled as a parents. Our children are becoming victims of the adult tendency today to over-achieve, multi-task, and cram all that's possible into a single day. The following example is a case in point.

One of my close friends recently outlined the plans for her nine-year-old son for the upcoming summer. Before school was even out, summer plans were finalized and calendared. This boy was scheduled for a series of different camps. He had two weeks each of soccer and basketball camp, followed by a week of Spanish camp and, finally, two weeks away at a camp in the mountains. Although it was summertime, this child was just as scheduled as he was during the school year. He was up early and gone all day with little time to just be at home with neighborhood friends, do some summer "fun" reading, or go swimming at the local pool. The family vacation occurred in early August, after all the camps were completed. The family spent a week in Southern Florida rushing from Disney World to Sea World to Epcot Center to the Kennedy Space Center. They came home completely exhausted, where everyone came down with a cold.

During the school year, many children today spend time in an after school program or daycare setting. Then they are rushed off to ballet, piano, or soccer. Homework is being finished at 9:30 or 10:00 at night, a good hour later than most children should be up. I have lived a life like this with my children. It is easy to be drawn into over-scheduling the entire family's life. I urge you to stop and take a look at your family's schedule. If children are missing more than a few days of school a year because of illness and if a child has headaches or "stomach pains" that a doctor can't explain, take a long look at the family schedule.

Another aspect of stress management is getting adequate sleep. How much sleep do children need? Elementary school-aged children require at least nine hours of sleep per night and pre-adolescents (ages 11-13) should ideally have 9-10 hours of sleep per night. This means that if children have to be out the door by 7:45 a.m. to catch the bus or be driven to school, they should be in bed no later than 9 p.m. to allow them 15 minutes to relax and fall asleep. Is this happening at your house?

Teens also need more sleep than they are getting on average. Most teenagers, to function optimally, require eight to nine hours of sleep per night. So, when a 14-year-old daughter is moody and irritable, it may not be hormones, but rather a lack of sleep!

Overscheduling of a child's life, getting less than optimal sleep, and normal childhood stresses—a teacher yelling or a friend being unkind—add up to a very stressful lifestyle. A stressful lifestyle contributes to the development of weight problems. Some children who are under stress will turn to food, such as candy bars, Twinkies, and/or a big bowl of ice cream to help them feel better. Stress eating, coupled with our fast food oriented diets and high fat, low fiber school lunches, is a significant contributor to the obesity epidemic in today's children.

A recent study, published in the Journal of the American Medical Association, gave "Quality of Life" questionnaires to a group of obese children and a group of children with cancer. Sadly enough, the children who were obese clearly had higher levels of stress, lower levels of satisfaction with life, and were more likely to express symptoms of depression than the children with cancer.

The study's author, Dr. Jeffrey B. Schwimmer, an Assistant Professor of Pediatrics at the University of California, San Diego, said that the findings suggest that "severely obese children really are suffering in a way that is perhaps greater than people recognize. We need to, as parents, physicians, teachers, be aware of just how bad things are for many of these children, particularly because it's often difficult for them to talk about some of these issues."

While both obese children and young cancer patients may experience teasing and have trouble keeping up with peers due to their conditions, the author notes, obese children are usually "not exposed to the intense medical interventions" that cancer patients go through. Thus, Schwimmer and his team felt that the similar health-related, quality-of-life scores were "an unexpected and important" finding.

As part of this study, Schwimmer and his team surveyed 106 children and their parents. The children ranged in age from five to 18 and had an average body mass index (BMI) of 34.7. BMI is a measure of weight in relation to height. 20-25 is considered healthy, 25-29 is considered overweight, while 30-35 is considered obese. These children were all in the obese to "morbidly obese" category (BMI is greater than 35). To illustrate, a child with a BMI of 35, if he is five feet tall, weighs between 175-180 pounds.

Comparing the results to past surveys of children of normal weight, the researchers found that the obese study participants were five times as likely as their healthy peers to have impaired physical functioning. In fact, the obese children's quality-of-life scores were lower than that of their healthy peers in every area assessed, including physical, psychosocial, emotional, and learning development. For example, obese children missed an average of four days of school in the month before their evaluation, whereas their healthy peers missed less than one day of school. About 65% of the youngsters in the study had an obesity-related health problem, such as diabetes, sleep apnea, or elevated cholesterol, and 13% had psychiatric problems, such as anxiety or depression. However, neither the physical nor mental problems were responsible for the differences in health-related quality of life, according to the report. Obese youngsters, even without those types of health problems, had a poor quality of life compared with normal weight peers.

If you have a child who is suffering from a weight problem, now is the time to do something about it. Work alongside your child to eat better and be more active. And, don't ever forget that your child needs a chance to be a child. Don't add to the stresses already inherent in his life. Give him opportunities to relax, unwind, and play. Help him to utilize stress management techniques (as suggested in chapter 8). As you help de-stress your child's life, you will be giving him valuable tools to deal with the challenges of life and reduce his risk of developing stress and weight-related problems.

What kind of legacy do you want to leave your children? Do you want them to have a poor quality of life, riddled with health problems because of obesity or do you want to join with your child and embrace a healthier lifestyle? Remember, the responsibility rests with you. You can be part of the problem, or you can be part of the solution.

FOLLOW-UP PREVENTIVE PERSCRIPTION

GOAL SETTING FOR A HEALTHY FAMILY—STARTING TODAY.

A healthy family = A happy family

Make the incorporation of healthy lifestyle changes a family-based decision. This will not only increase the likelihood of success, but will also immediately begin the process of making everyone aware of how to create a healthy lifestyle. Don't try to take on too much change at once. Even positive changes will bring some stress—human beings really do not like change. Take it one day, and one change, at a time.

Guidelines for Moving the Family to a Pathway of Health and Vitality

1. Limit fast food meals to once per week (ultimately once per month).
2. Take stock of the pantry and refrigerator, while keeping the following guidelines in mind:
   a. Chips are not a necessity of life and there is no recommended daily allowance for them.

    b. Dessert fare is not limited to cake, ice cream, cookies, and pie. Desserts can consist of low-fat pudding or, better yet, fresh sliced peaches sprinkled with nutmeg.

    c. Children older than toddlers do not need whole milk. Transition to skim or soy milk. Toddlers are the exception as they need the fat for brain development. However, 2% milk rather than whole milk, is better for younger children.

    d. Stock plenty of fresh vegetables. Experiment with different ways to cut up carrots, celery, red bell peppers, and cucumbers. Make a dip out of plain yogurt, lowfat cottage cheese, and some fresh basil.

3. Start eating breakfast. It really is the most important meal of the day. Send children off to school with a healthy balance of protein, dairy, and fruit. Studies validate this combo for jump-starting metabolism, circulation, and brain function. A yogurt or soy protein-based smoothie is quick and easy, especially for time-constrained families. Hot oatmeal with a handful of raisins, or a poached egg on whole-wheat toast with a glass of skim or soy milk is pretty quick and easy as well. Make a commitment to not buy cereals that have more than five grams of sugar per serving, and aim for cereals that have at least three to four grams of fiber per serving. (This means no more Cocoa Puffs or Trix.)

4. Make a weekly menu. Use this as a teaching lesson (after you reading Chapter 5 again) about healthy eating.

5. Plan a Family Date and let nothing interfere. Incorporate some type of activity, such as rollerskating or going to the batting cages. If there is more than one child, have occasional "one parent, one child" activities (or even an entire weekend). The quality of your relationship with your children, as well as their health, will improve.

6. Create a tradition of reading to children every night before bedtime. My children enjoyed my reading to them even when they could read perfectly well on their own. As they reached ages five and six, they would read a page, and then I would read a page. We followed that routine until they were 10 to 12 years old. After that, we had "talk time"—first with my daughter who was four years younger than her brother, and then with my son. I am sure both of them will establish those same traditions with their children.

7. Turn off the television on weeknights and limit the time on computers to what is necessary for school work, with 30-45 minutes maximum "video game time." Have a "set in stone" time for lights out.

8. Review the "total activity" of the family. Think about balance and reserve some time to read and just "be" together. Consider eliminating some of the activity load of the family, if necessary.

9. And last, but not least, cherish the time you have together. In this fast-paced world, we grow up and away from each other all too quickly. Make memories now to last a lifetime.

CHAPTER 18

HEALTHFUL AGING
It's Never Too Early to Begin or Too Late to Slow Down Your Aging

Points to ponder as you read:

- ✓ What are the current theories about aging?
- ✓ Why can people look significantly older or younger than their actual chronologic age?
- ✓ What are the safe ways to slow the natural aging process?
- ✓ Is it lifestyle, genetics, or both that "rule" aging?

As America became increasingly gray over the second half of the 20th century, a furor of research was unleashed looking for scientific answers to the mysteries of aging. Since Ponce de Leon, human beings have been fascinated with the possibility of preserving youth and delaying the aging process. As modern science has previously discovered solutions to many of the common "scourges" that killed prematurely, such as pneumonia, polio, tuberculosis, and the plague, we are now looking for solutions to diseases that have become more of a problem as we are living longer.

Today, we are faced with unprecedented numbers of people who are living with chronic diseases that are due in part, if not totally, to unhealthy aging. Coronary artery disease, also known as heart disease, is caused by inflammation in the arterial walls (due to pro-inflammatory oils in our diets), build-up of cholesterol deposits in these inflamed arterial walls (due to excessive intake of saturated fats and inadequate intake of certain vitamins, minerals, and soluble fiber), and increased platelet stickiness (due to dietary factors). These three factors eventually result in the blockage of blood flow to the artery (arteries) and cause myocardial infarction, also known as a heart attack. All of these conditions, which take many years to occur, ultimately lead to having a heart attack that could have been prevented with dietary changes.

In addition to diet, the major risk factors for the development of atherosclerotic heart disease are 1) elevated cholesterol, 2) obesity, 3) sedentary lifestyle, 4) smoking and 5) genetic predisposition. In other words, five of the six reasons why or why not athersclerosis will develop are in your personal control. Other diseases of aging include cancer, stroke, hypertension, osteoporosis, osteoarthritis, dementia, Parkinson's disease, and Alzheimer's. Are these actually preventable? Modern epidemiology and science tell us they are.

We'd all like to blame our genes for our health, as well as other aspects of our lives, but the reality is that about 80% of all health challenges are related to diet and lifestyle, and 20% or less are related to genetics. The good news is our lives and our health are really up to us. The bad news, of course, is that there is no passing the buck on this one.

Here in the beginning of the 21st Century, we live almost twice as long as just 100 years ago. A little girl born today in America is expected to live about 80 years. The "weaker sex" not only gives birth to the next generation, but lives approximately six years longer than her male mate! And while 41 countries have life expectancies longer than the United States, essentially all of the top 50 countries have life expectancies within seven years of each other. But there is a small island in the Japanese archipelago where the life expectancy is 12 years longer than any other country in the world.

The men and women of Okinawa live, on average, 95 years. What is their secret? Are they genetically different than the rest of Japan, whose average life expectancy is 81 years? The answer lies with diet and lifestyle, not genetics. Okinawans eat even more fish, fruits, and vegetables than the rest of Japan. They walk more, ride in cars and buses less, and have a "laid back" philosophy towards life.

What all of this comes down to is that it is possible to slow, and even reverse, the aging process. Sounds far-fetched, but I promise it is not. Modern science is giving us a better understanding of why we age and how we can slow that process. Aging may not be inevitable. Living longer is the new promise of the coming century.

But anti-aging has to be more than just living longer. I am personally not interested in just living longer. If I am going to live to be 110 years old, then I want to feel great, be active, be in charge of my mental faculties, and be able to live a full life.

But, before discussing how to stop or reverse aging, let's understand the process of aging.

The four main theories of aging are: the Free Radical Theory, the Wear and Tear Theory, the Neuroendocrine Theory, and the Genetic Theory.

FREE RADICAL THEORY

The Free Radical Theory of aging is based on cellular damage that occurs due to free radicals, which are generated in the body by the metabolism of food, as well as exposure to external sources such as air pollution. These free radicals are unstable molecules that bombard cell membranes, leading to disruption of the actual membranes and/or disruptions to functions on the membranes themselves. Antioxidants (from fruits, vegetables, and other plant foods) are the "fighters" against free radical damage. Antioxidants give up an electron that neutralizes the free radical so that it passes out of the body without damaging cell membranes.

Unfortunately, modern diets are extremely deficient in antioxidants. The increase in incidence and prevalence of cancer is a sign of this theory in action. Much research has been done in this area. Nobel Laureate Dr. Linus Pauling, who discovered the functions and properties of vitamin C, and Dr. Lester Packard, who did valuable work on the networking and synergistic effects of multiple antioxidants, are two famous scientists who have brought understanding about the functions of free radicals and antioxidants.

WEAR AND TEAR THEORY

The Wear and Tear Theory is easy to understand. The body just gradually slows down its many functions so that, over time, we do not process nutrients as well, we don't heal as quickly, we don't incorporate "bone growing" cells at the proper ratio compared to "bone breakdown" cells, and so on. A complete and balanced diet is the best defense against this theory of aging.

NEUROENDOCRINE THEORY

The Neuroendocrine Theory has received lots of attention since the mid-1990's. As the first Baby Boomers began turning 50, there was a burst of interest in anti-aging. Baby Boomers have sparked tremendous growth in certain sectors of the economy and have been the determinants of the major trends of the past 20 years—fitness gear, baby joggers, computers, stock market choices, SUVs—and now, the wellness and anti-aging industry.

The Neuroendocrine Theory of aging says that as we age our production of certain hormones—especially growth hormone and the sex hormones (estrogen, progesterone, testosterone, DHEA)—declines. This results in a gradual loss of muscle mass, increased fat deposition, loss of libido and sexual function, graying of hair, etc. Baby Boomers, as a group, are fighting hard against these losses occuring. Consequently, there is a resurgence of interest in the use of HGH (human growth hormone) and DHEA (testosterone precursor). Our natural production of growth hormone begins to decline at age 25 and continues to decline about 14% per decade. For the most part, HGH has had to be supplied by injections, which are expensive and inconvenient. Very recently, however, there have been a variety of products developed that are natural stimulants of HGH. Preliminary data indicates promise in that people may be able to support sagging growth hormone levels without the need for injections.

GENETIC THEORY

The Genetic Theory, is one of the hottest areas of medical research. We are still mapping the human genome (our genetic makeup). An entire new area of science, called genomics, is the study of genetic material and its functions and actions. From the study of genomics, we will be able to better diagnose disease, develop more targeted treatments, and eventually find ways to eliminate many diseases that plague us today. DNA research is currently looking at telomerase, a substance that controls the number of cell divisions. When we run low on telomerase, the cell begins to age—sometimes quite quickly. This may be a major key to anti-aging—learning how to keep the telomere from shortening, which will keep the cell from dying.

The theories of aging are important because they give us the information we need to get practical help in the aging process. The basis of these theories answers the question: Why is it that one person who is 45 years old will look like they are 55 and another 45 year old could pass for 37? The answer to that question is that there are two types of aging—chronological and biological. Just 25 years ago, most scientists believed that aging was 50/50 genetics and lifestyle. We now know that this is not true. We have scientific proof that aging is at least 80% lifestyle factors.

This means that what you eat, whether you are overweight or not, whether you exercise or not, whether you smoke or not, and other lifestyle factors largely determine how gracefully you will age and how likely you are to develop the diseases of aging—arthritis, cancer, heart disease, and kidney failure.

We tend to look at the outside only. We notice how wrinkled someone is or how much their skin sags. We need to keep in mind, however, that there is a parallel process going on internally. How young or old someone looks on the outside definitely correlates with internal aging.

The "old" 45 is, most likely, a smoker who spends a fair amount of time in the sun, exercises little, and eats a typical American processed food diet, high in saturated fat and sugars and low in whole foods. The "young" 45, on the other hand, exercises at least an hour, three times a week, is a partial vegetarian, has never smoked, and uses sunscreen faithfully. Notice, we haven't given any family history data at all. All the aging factors listed relate totally to diet and lifestyle. Therefore, we are almost totally in control of how gracefully (or not) we age but, of course, we don't get to blame our parents (or inherited genes) for the end results.

Personally, I am thrilled about this new scientific data, because only one of my four grandparents lived beyond age 73. My paternal grandmother died at age 61 of colon cancer. She was overweight, smoked, and ate a high fat diet. My paternal grandfather died of heart problems, secondary to emphysema, at age 73. He was a smoker and had a history of tuberculosis. My mother's father died at age 57 from lung cancer. He was a heavy smoker and drinker. I'm hoping, genetically-speaking, that I take after my maternal grandmother who died quite recently at the advanced age of 96! She ate a simple, healthy diet, maintained a normal weight throughout her lifetime, walked regularly until her late 80's, and always said whatever was on her mind, a "stress management" technique that surely contributed to her longevity.

My children, ages 19 and 23, have all four of their grandparents, whereas I lost two of my four grandparents by age 21. My children's paternal grandparents are in their early 80's and doing well. They still travel, and Grandma has an amazing garden that she tends. My parents are 73 and 74. They work out at their local gym three to four times a week, walk regularly, and have modified their diets over the past 10 years to exclude all meat except fish (they live in the Pacific Northwest where the fresh fish is unbelievable), and eat plenty of fresh fruits and vegetables every day. I am proud of you, Mom and Dad!

So, now let's focus on you. How do you want to age? Do you want to take steps now that will allow you the very best chance to age gracefully and live a long, healthy life with the ability to do what you want when you want—at ages 50, 60, 70, and beyond? I am planning on jogging, hiking, and tromping around the pyramids of Egypt or visiting the Greek Isles when I'm 85—how about you?

If you not only want to live an extended life, but also make it a life worth living, here is a plan worth following. In the "Follow-up Preventive Prescription," is a simplified approach to graceful aging and it is far better than simply covering gray hair or having Botox injections. The plan begins with making a commitment to living on a—"Personal Pathway to Health and Vitality"—starting today. It is eating a colorful diet with plenty of fresh produce. It is controlling caloric intake to maintain a healthy weight, being active every day, making time for family and friends, and pursuing relaxing activities. It is prioritizing life to have time to keep your brain active, as well as your body.

There is no longer any doubt—diet and weight are the two most important keys to minimize aging. Science has clearly validated that eating an unhealthy, unbalanced diet and being overweight accounts for at least 60% of all cancers and 70 to 75% of increased biological aging. In countries where at least a pound of fruits and vegetables are eaten every day, there is a 50% reduction in cancer risk. The antioxidants in fruits and vegetables clearly protect our DNA from damage; and the diseases of aging—heart disease, stroke, diabetes, and most cancers—are essentially due to DNA damage. These diseases are the cause of 80% of all deaths in America each year and the basis of life-limiting challenges for over 100 million Americans.

The healthcare budget is reaching one trillion dollars. It is estimated that by the end of this decade, one out of every three dollars spent in this country will go towards treating disease and keeping chronically ill people alive for a year or two longer. This does not have to be our future. Each one of us can make a commitment today to eat right, achieve a healthy weight, walk every day, and focus on happiness. Essentially, the future is truly yours. What do you want your future to be?

FOLLOW-UP PREVENTIVE PERSCRIPTION

DEVELOP A PLAN TO AGE GRACEFULLY AND WELL

"Apple" and "Pear" Dietary Recommendations

People can be divided into two basic categories—those who tend to be insulin resistant and those who do not. Those with an "apple" body type, which includes most men and about 25% of women, tend to gain excess weight primarily around their waist. If they are overweight, they have a high incidence of heart disease and Type 2 diabetes. The "pear" body type, which describes most women and 15-20% of men, tends to gain excess weight around the hip and buttock area. They do not have a significant increased risk of heart disease or diabetes unless they are obese or morbidly obese.

Apple body types: Limit starchy and refined carbohydrates to 1 or 2 servings per week. This means white bread, pastries, pasta, crackers, white rice, and potatoes. Eat 5-7 servings of vegetables and 2 servings of fruits (no fruit juice). Aim for about 100 grams of high quality protein (up to 150 grams for men) per day. To achieve this and keep calories low, use soy protein powders to make shakes or smoothies for 1 to 2 meals per day. Grocery stores are now stocked with low carb alternatives from bars to soups to cereals. Be sure to check labels to make sure these products are not high in saturated fats and have reasonable calorie amounts.

Pear body types: Diet is easier for you. Find the calorie range that you need to maintain a healthy weight. Do not count calories, but rather incorporate fresh foods, at least 7-9 servings of fruits and veggies every day, and eat healthy types of fats and proteins in reasonable portions. You will never be overweight, will have plenty of energy and look younger than your chronological age.

Colorize Your Diets

Dr. David Heber, founding director of the UCLA Center for Human Nutrition and one of the nation's leading experts in nutrition, has developed a color wheel of foods that has put science behind what this book teaches. See the chart below, make a copy of it and put it on the refrigerator for a daily reminder of healthful eating!

THE RED GROUP	Tomatoes, pink grapefruit, and watermelon. Lycopene is the main phytonutrient, known to decrease the risk of prostate cancer.
THE RED-PURPLE GROUP	Grapes, red wine, berries of all sorts, and red apples. These contain anthocyanins, antioxidants that lessen the likelihood of blood clot formation which may reduce your risk of heart disease and stroke.

THE ORANGE GROUP	Carrots, apricots, cantaloupes, winter squashes, and pumpkin. These are sources of alpha- and beta-carotenoids which are overall powerful antioxidants.
THE ORANGE-YELLOW GROUP	Oranges, peaches, papayas, and nectarines. These are a source of beta-cryptoxanthin, as well as an excellent source of vitamin C.
THE YELLOW-GREEN GROUP	Spinach, mustard and collard greens, peas, avocado, and honeydew melon. These provide excellent sources of lutein and zeaxanthin, and carotenoids that have been shown to reduce the risk of age-related macular degeneration and cataracts.
THE GREEN GROUP	Broccoli, brussel sprouts, cabbage, and kale. These provide compounds that stimulate the liver to produce enzymes that break down cancer-causing chemicals. This is especially important in the colon, and regular consumption of this type of vegetable may reduce the risk of colon cancer.
THE WHITE-GREEN GROUP	Garlic, onions, pears, and white wine. These foods contain a variety of antioxidants that have been shown to have anti-tumor activity.

Eat Fatty Fish at Least Three Times Per Week

Fatty fish provide important omega-3 fatty acids which lower the risk of heart disease, stroke, and prostate cancer. Omega-3 fatty acids are also potent anti-inflammation mediators that help to protect our colon, brain, and joints. These are all locations where poor diet, pollution, and other factors can lead to inflammatory bowel disease, Alzheimer's, and various types of arthritis.

Avoid Fried Foods And Foods Containing Saturated Fats

Cancer and aging-causing chemicals are released in the deep frying process so minimize the intake of fried foods (Ok—maybe French fries once a month). Look for the new labeling of trans-fatty acids, a type of saturated fat that greatly contributes to the development of atherosclerosis. This also means a limit on the intake of high fat red meat to two or less servings per week. Choose lean cuts of red meat (e.g. top round) or, better yet, eat the white meat of chicken and turkey.

Have a Handful Of Almonds Once a Week

Studies show that women who consume almonds on a regular basis have a lower risk of stroke. Almonds are a great source of natural vitamin E, omega-3 fatty acids, and many important minerals. Pay attention to portions. A serving of 10 almonds is plenty and contains about 100 calories.

Eat Whole Grains

Consider white flour to be "poison." Adults require 25-30 grams of fiber per day, according to the Institute of Medicine guidelines, but most Americans average less than 10 grams per day. Whole grain breads and cereals, and brown and whole grain rice are the easiest ways to get fiber needs taken care of, while also getting essential minerals and other nutrients. Fiber helps to control cholesterol and triglyceride levels and is essential for healthy colon function. Fruits and vegetables are also great fiber sources.

Supplement Suggestions

Fish oil capsules—Look for a fish oil capsule that provides EPA and DHA; you need a minimum of two grams per day, including at least 500 mg EPA. Capsule should be clear and contain essential oils to minimize the fish taste and potential aftertaste.

- Natural vitamin E—200-400 IU
- Vitamin C—500-1000 mg per day

- Magnesium—250-400 mg per day
- Balanced multivitamin-mineral containing at least 2 times the RDA of B vitamins with 15 mg zinc
- Calcium—1000 mg per day for women; 500-800 mg for men
- Chromium—150-200 micrograms per day
- Lutein—3 mg per day
- Coenzyme Q10—5-10 mg, especially if heart disease or Alzheimer's are in the family history
- Gingko biloba—100-200 mg per day—take in divided doses
- Ginger—100 mg per day
- Genistein—isoflavone from soy, red clover—50 mg per day

Activity and Exercise Choices

There is no doubt that active people live longer than sedentary people, and there are a variety of reasons why this is true. Regular exercise helps maintain normal blood pressure, lowers the risk of heart disease, diabetes, and most cancers, is the best anti-depressant known, and increases circulation to the skin to lessen aging changes. The great preponderance of evidence recommends at least 45 minutes of activity per day. The good news is that this 45 minutes can be cumulative and not accomplished at one time. So, take the stairs and park the car at the far end of the parking lot instead of circling until you get a close space. Walk the dog every night—borrow a neighbor's if you don't have one. Instead of sitting and watching kids play at the park—play with them!

We need both aerobic and anaerobic types of exercise to slow aging. Aerobic activity helps keep insulin production normal, which helps lessen fat deposition as well as preventing Type 2 diabetes. Weight training (aerobic) supports muscle mass, at least in part, by increasing growth hormone and testosterone. So, walk briskly to stay slim and lift weights to stay strong.

Other Considerations

Probably the most significant "other" aspect of anti-aging is the mental and emotional aspects of health. Most of what we have focused on thus far, relates to the physical aspects of slowing aging. However, if we don't protect our brains and our emotions, we cannot truly age gracefully. We will look young, but will not have our full mental capacity. It is estimated that at least 50% of people over the age of 80 have some degree of mental impairment. This can be stopped.

Following the diet and exercise guidelines, and suggestions discussed above will provide at least 70% of the protection needed for mental functions. Additionally, keep exercising your brain as well as your body. Read every day. Try new activities. Don't be afraid to attempt to learn a new craft or sport activity—even if you are 75 years old. Take adult education classes at the community college or check out the possibilities online. University of Phoenix and others provide distance learning that can be accomplished right at home.

Meditation, relaxation strategies, and yoga are all helpful in reducing cortisol levels (stress hormones that increase aging) and lowering cholesterol and blood pressure. Laugh frequently and heartily. Laughter has been shown to be a potent stimulator of the immune system. Choose to be happy!

I wish you a long life full of vitality and happiness.

CHAPTER 19

MAKING YOUR PHYSICIAN A PARTNER
in Your Health Journey

Points to ponder as you read:

- ✓ How can you better communicate with your doctor?
- ✓ What are some responsibilities your doctor has in connection with your health?
- ✓ What are your responsibilities regarding your health?

As I progressed through my medical school and residency days, I was frequently struck by how frightened and intimidated many patients were by the overall experience of being in the hospital. As medical students and residents, the great majority of patient contact is in the hospital setting, whereas once physicians are in practice, most of them see patients in an office setting. This training process involving hospitalized patients, who are usually quite ill or in need of some sort of acute treatment (surgery, for instance) probably contributes to the "god-like" perception that many people have of doctors. The result of this perception is that people tend to take what the doctor says as the gospel truth, advice not to be questioned, but accepted with complete faith. But is this how it should be?

I will never forget an experience I had as a third-year medical student when I was just beginning my clinical experiences and training. We were on morning rounds. This is a process where by the medical student, intern (one year after medical school), and resident (2nd year and beyond, after medical school) update the attending staff physician. This physician is charged with providing guidance and education regarding the proper care for each patient, while, at the same time, overseeing student, intern, and resident care to prevent medical errors. On this particular morning, our team consisted of two medical students (one of whom was me), an intern, and one resident who supervised us all. We were presenting the case of Edward, a 62-year-old gentleman who had been admitted the previous night to our attending physician due to a progressive shortness of breath. Edward had had surgery to remove a cancerous lung tumor six months previously and had been told by the surgeon that "it looked good." Edward interpreted that statement to mean "you are cured," and asked no further questions of his doctor.

After Edward was admitted, a chest x-ray was taken. When I looked at that x-ray, I had a sinking feeling. Edward's tumor had recurred and was now quite large. Additionally, there was fluid from the tumor that was filling up one side of his lungs, which was responsible for the shortness of breath that brought him to the hospital. After we presented the history and physical findings, including the chest x-ray and a lung tap to examine the fluid, we ended with our assessment and recommendations.

The options were dismal for Edward, but the intern and I, who were treating him, had not discussed that there were no curative options and had certainly not informed Edward of the amount of time he had left. (Remember, he believed the surgery six months before had cured him.) Our attending physician, who had never met Edward, said to him at the end of our presentation, "So, Edward, do you have your affairs in order?" Edward was silent and just looked at us. He finally muttered "Doctor, what do you mean?" Without ever making eye contact with the patient, our attending physician responded, "I hope that you have your affairs in order, as you have a very short time to live." I will never forget the look on Edward's face that day or the feeling in my heart. Our team exchanged looks of horror, but we were afraid to say anything to our attending physician, because he was, unfortunately, the Chief of Medicine in our hospital.

I vowed on that day to always listen intently to my patients, to always make eye contact with them, and always put myself in their situation, especially when a serious diagnosis or life-changing event was being discussed. I will not claim to have been perfect. Doctors are highly trained, well-educated and, generally, quite intelligent people, but we are still human beings.

However, I learned early on that my patients could often tell me what the diagnosis was if I took the time to ask the right questions and gave them a chance to talk. I also learned early on that one-on-one connection was the most therapeutic intervention I could provide. This might involve a hand on the shoulder as I talked out a treatment plan for dealing with their back pain. It could be a sympathetic look as they recounted various stresses in their lives that factored in with recurring headaches. And it always included the questions, "Do you understand what I am saying?" (if a new diagnosis was being discussed) and "Do you have any questions?"

I can always learn from my patients, as well as they can learn from me. I am not in their body; and I am not with them as they go through the day dealing with pains, worries, stresses, and cravings for certain foods, cigarettes, or alcohol. My philosophy is that my patients and I form a partnership with a mutual goal—their good health. This is, however, an uneven partnership because 98% of the day-to-day running of this concern is accomplished by one partner, and that would not be the doctor!

It is critical to your health to have a physician tuned in to your needs, fears, concerns, and beliefs. A physician should be a partner in creating a healthy existence for you. But a physician cannot possibly know all there is to know about your body. In fact, he or she cannot know as much as you know. You are one of many patients that a doctor sees, and there are good days and bad days for doctors, just like everyone else. That said, however, it is certainly possible to develop a working partnership with a physician. If a connection cannot be made with your doctor, it is time to consider looking for a new one. Or, it might be time to look at yourself and determine if you need to be more assertive. Doctors in today's world of managed care are so incredibly time-strapped, you must go at least 50% of the way to create the kind of partnership described. Physicians are trained to be paternalistic, to be "all-knowing," and most patients are conditioned to accept, without question, the diagnosis and treatment plan prescribed by their doctor. One of the major problems with this, of course, is that our modern medical model focuses on disease treatment, and not on health preservation. A change is long overdue and you can make it happen. Be proactive and take control of your health!

Let's create a new paradigm with the foundation being a successful partnership.

A SUCCESSFUL HEALTH PROTECTION PARTNERSHIP

In your Health Protection Partnership, you are the CEO (aka the Big boss) and your physician is the Executive Vice President in charge of Information and Therapeutic Options. Despite the fact that the two of you are partners, one person must have the final say. In business, that person is the CEO, and in your Health Protection Partnership, that person is you. With that foundation established, let's examine some guidelines for making a doctor-patient partnership a successful one.

EACH PARTNER MUST BE COMMITTED TO THE SUCCESS OF THE PARTNERSHIP. Each partner sees the needs of the partnership overriding individual needs. As required, each partner is willing to sacrifice personal convenience or wants for the success of the partnership. Remember that the goal of seeing a physician is good health and not diagnosis of disease. Therefore, the success of a Health Protection Partnership is your physical, mental, and emotional well-being. The first step is to find a physician who is equally committed to the same goals.

EACH PARTNER PULLS THEIR OWN WEIGHT. No one in the partnership can coast. Each member of the partnership is willing to work hard and fulfill their responsibility. The doctor is expected to utilize his training and skills to find answers to medical concerns and to safeguard your health. He must provide you with the proper diagnosis and all reasonable options of treatment (not just the conventional ones). He must alert you to potential health risks, so adjustments can be made (diet, exercise, and stress management) to help prevent those risks from becoming a reality.

Be prepared when you go to the doctor. Be able to give a detailed history of current symptoms, whether this has occurred before, and the necessary details about what you are experiencing. Take responsibility for your own health care. Be willing to do some research and study about medical problems or conditions you may have. Be prepared to ask the doctor specific questions to get the appropriate answers needed.

EACH PARTNER HAS INDIVIDUAL STRENGTHS AND SKILLS. The partnership is successful because of the individual strengths of each. A doctor's strength is a medical degree and skills, based on education and experience. But your strength is in knowing yourself, the body you're walking around in. You have intimate knowledge of medical conditions, surgeries, and allergic reactions. You also know what medications or supplements you've been taking. You may also know what genetic susceptibilities you have toward a disease or condition. For instance, if your grandmother had breast cancer, your mother had breast cancer, and your older sister had breast cancer, you doctor needs to know this. Despite a doctor's medical background, he can't know every question to ask to get all the information needed. Communication between the knowledge and the reality of you is essential for the right outcome—a quick recovery or prevention of disease.

YOU AND YOUR DOCTOR MUST BE WILLING TO PUT ASIDE PERSONAL FEELINGS TO FOCUS ON THE PURPOSE OF THE PARTNERSHIP—YOUR HEALTH. No matter how many patients a doctor has sitting in the waiting room, he needs to give you full attention when he meets with you. And you need to be willing to pay attention to the medical advice that he gives. For instance, let's say you have a significant weight problem. You have been in to see the doctor numerous times for sinus infections, flu, or bronchitis. The doctor can just keep prescribing antibiotics, or he can (and should) talk to you about the need to improve your diet and lose weight, suggesting that your immune system will function better if you change your eating habits, focusing on plenty of fresh fruits and vegetables, plenty of rest, and possibly suggesting the use of Echinacea and vitamin C at the first sign of a cold, so it doesn't progress to sinusitis. And, if he does talk to you about losing weight, you can choose two paths. You can think, "how rude!" and make a commitment to never come back or, you can take the advice in the spirit it was given and give thoughtful consideration to making some lifestyle changes to safeguard future health, as well as improve your health today!

One of the biggest stumbling blocks to forming a partnership with a doctor is intimidation. Have you ever gone to the doctor with a list of questions, only to find you didn't have the courage to ask them? If so, you're not alone. Most people have experienced the inability to talk with their doctors. But, to be an active part of this partnership, you must find the necessary information and take an active role in all of the decisions made concerning your healthcare. Research has shown that the patients who have the best relationships with their doctors are the ones who are also most satisfied with their care—and have better results. Her are some specific tips to cement your partnership with your physician in your health care journey.

Give information. Do not wait to be asked!

- You know the important things about your symptoms and health history. Tell the doctor everything you think he or she needs to know. It is important to tell your doctor relevant personal information—even if it feels uncomfortable or embarrassing.

- Bring a health history with you, and keep it up to date. Make a health history form for all family members that you are involved in the care of (children, parents, and even friends). Be sure that these health histories are stored in a safe place where another family member has access.

- Always bring the medicines you are taking, or at least an up-to-date list of medications, including the strength, how you take it, etc. Don't forget to include over the counter medications, such as Tylenol, aspirin, Benadryl, Claritin, etc. and note how often you are using them. Also bring any supplements you are using. I strongly advise bringing the actual supplements so the physician can see them. Doctors know about medicines and they have a Physician's Desk Reference (PDR) to check on any details they may not be familiar with regarding a particular drug. The great majority of physicians today, however, do not have a good understanding of, or are comfortable with, nutritional and herbal supplements. There is a PDR for Herbal Medicines and a PDR for over-the counter medications and Nutritional Supplements. The latter is quite small and not all-inclusive of the many supplements available. Because there is a cost to having products listed in these books, not all companies choose to spend money on it. But if you are using supplements, it is very important that your physician know this. If your physician is not comfortable with your use of herbal and/or nutritional supplements, and you have had a positive benefit from taking these supplements, then you have two choices: 1—Insist that your physician learn about the supplements (they can usually call the company, check out information on the company website, or read their own sources), or 2—find a new physician who is willing to be your partner.

- Bring all other medical information, such as x-rays, test results, and previous medical records.

Get the information you need.

- Ask questions. If you don't, the doctor may assume you understand, when you don't.
- Write down questions before your visit. List the most important questions first, in case the doctor is in a rush. (If they seem rushed, nicely point out to them that this is very important to you).
- Ask the doctor to draw pictures to illustrate something you may not understand—such as what a hiatal hernia looks like or where exactly an ovarian cyst is located.
- Take notes or bring a tape recorder. Let the doctor know, in advance, you are planning to this.
- If you run out of time and questions have not been answered, ask if you can speak with a nurse or other physician assistant regarding your questions. If this is not an option, ask the doctor (or his nurse) to call you later at home to finish answering your questions.
- Ask the doctor if he has washed his hands before examining you. Research is very clear that hand

washing can prevent the spread of infections. If you are uncomfortable asking this question, you could say, "I've noticed that doctors and nurses always wash their hands or wear gloves when examining people. Why is that?" Hopefully, the doctor washes his hands in front of you, then there will be no need for this concern.

Take information home.

- Ask for written instructions.
- Ask for brochures, audiotapes or videotapes if dealing with a new diagnosis or condition. If the doctor does not have these in the office, ask where materials can be obtained.

Once you leave the doctor's office — follow up.

- If you have questions, call.
- If symptoms get worse or if there are problems with medication(s), call.
- If you had blood drawn or other tests ordered and you don't hear from the doctor's office in a reasonable period of time (say, a week after the tests were done), call for the results.
- If the doctor ordered tests that you must make an appointment for, make the appointments and have the tests done. If you do not understand, once you are home, why these tests were ordered, call the doctor and ask for an explanation.
- If the doctor recommends seeing a specialist, make the appointment.

Some additional hints for helping you and your physician work together are:

- Talk to the doctor before consulting a complementary medicine practitioner. Don't assume your doctor will be negative. There are many physicians now who are comfortable with the concept of integrative medical care and may even be able to suggest a chiropractor, naturopathic doctor, or an acupuncturist that they have worked with.

- Ask the doctor about a specific remedy, or supplement, that you may want to try for a condition you are dealing with. See what the doctor knows about this particular remedy and listen carefully to what he says.

- If your doctor is negative about this particular remedy, ask for a detailed explanation why.

- If your doctor doesn't know about the therapy you wish to try, offer information from the sources where information was obtained. Alternatively, the doctor can do his own research. As stated above, if you believe in a particular type of approach, insist on a full discussion of the whys and why nots.

- If the doctor approves of an alternative or complementary therapy, ask for a prescription or referral. The therapy may be covered by your health insurance if your doctor prescribes it.

- Expect the same cooperation and information from the complementary medicine professional that you expect from your regular physician.

Also, in working with your doctor, keep in mind that the more you know, the better off you are, when it comes to taking medication. So, if your doctor wants to prescribe something for you, be sure you're more than just a good listener. Here are important questions to ask:

1. What are there potential side effects?
2. Are there alternatives to this medicine and how long has it been in use?
3. What should I do if I experience side effects?
4. How long before the drug starts working?
5. What should I do if I miss a dose?
6. Are there any special instructions for taking this

medication?

7.   Is a generic version of this drug okay?

Besides actively listening and questioning the doctor about medication, there are some things you need to tell him before the prescription gets filled.

- The names of all drugs and supplements you are currently taking
- If you are pregnant, may become pregnant, or are breastfeeding
- If you drink alcohol
- Any medical problems you have in addition to the one(s) he is treating you for
- If you're allergic to or have had any type of adverse reaction to a drug

My final advice to you is to be alert to the possibility of medical errors. Medical errors are one of the nation's leading causes of death and injury. A report by the Institute of Medicine (part of the NIH), published in JAMA in 1998 estimated that as many as 98,000 Americans die in U.S. hospitals as a result of medical errors. This means that more people die from medical errors than from motor vehicle accidents, breast cancer, or AIDS.

What are medical errors?

Medical errors occur when something planned to be part of the medical care doesn't occur (as in someone forgets to do it), something in the medical care plan is not done properly, or the wrong plan is chosen in the first place. Medical errors can occur anywhere in the health care system:

- Hospitals
- Clinics or doctor's offices
- Outpatient surgery centers
- Nursing homes
- Pharmacies
- Patients' homes

Errors can involve:

1. Medicines
2. Surgery
3. Diagnosis
4. Equipment
5. Lab reports

Errors can occur during even the most routine tasks. For instance, a patient who has just had an acute heart attack and has congestive heart failure is given a high-salt meal, instead of the salt-free meal that was ordered. The errors can be minor and not impactful of the person's successful treatment. Or, the error can be major, such as the wrong kidney being removed.

Most errors occur because of the complexity of today's healthcare system. But errors can also happen when doctors and patients don't communicate. A recent study supported by the Agency for Healthcare Research and Quality (AHRQ) found that doctors often do not do enough to help their patients make well-informed decisions. Uninvolved and/or uninformed patients are less likely to accept the doctor's choice of treatment and less likely to be compliant in doing what they need to do to make the treatment, surgery, etc. work as planned.

The key to preventing medical errors from happening is to be involved in your health care.

1. Take part in all decisions. Understand why a treatment, therapy, medicine, surgery is suggested.

Regarding medicines:

2. Make sure your doctors know about all medicines, both prescription and over-the-counter medications, you are taking. Be sure to include dietary supplements and herbs.

3. Make sure your doctor knows about any allergies or adverse reactions you have had.

4. Make sure you can read any prescription the doctor

writes.

5. Ask for any information needed. Some sample questions are:

    a. What is the medicine for?

    b. How do I take it and for how long?

    c. What are the side effects that may occur and what should I do if they occur?

    d. Are there any other medicines, dietary supplements, or herbal supplements that I should avoid while using this medication?"

6. When picking up the medicine from the pharmacy, ask: "Is this the medicine that my doctor prescribed? Can you please check the prescription for me?" A study done by the Massachusetts College of Pharmacy and Allied Health Sciences found that 88% of all medical errors involved the wrong medicine or the wrong dose.

7. Ask for written information from the pharmacist, if not offered, regarding side effects. Also, ask the pharmacist how to measure a liquid medicine, should you be prescribed one. If possible, ask the pharmacist to provide you the appropriate measure.

Regarding hospital stays:

1. If you have a choice, choose a hospital where many patients have had the procedure or surgery you are having. You must ask these questions and insist on answers. If you are not given the information, seek it out yourself.

2. If you are in the hospital, ask all healthcare workers who have direct contact with you whether they have washed their hands. A recent study found that when patients checked whether healthcare workers had washed their hands, the workers washed their hands more often and used more soap.

3. When being discharged, make sure the doctor or other
    member of your treatment team carefully explains the
    treatment plan your will use at home.

Regarding surgery:

Make sure you and your surgeon have discussed all aspects of
the impending surgery. The American Academy of Orthopedic
Surgeons urges its members to sign their initials directly on the
site to be operated on before the surgery.

If the above guidelines and suggestions are followed in your
partnership with the physician, it will be successful. In the final
analysis, you are responsible for your own wellness. Be proactive
and take control of your health.

FOLLOW-UP PREVENTIVE PERSCRIPTION

FINDING A NEW DOCTOR

If you have decided your current doctor will not work in the
partnership, find a new one. Ask friends and colleagues who their
doctors are. If they have a good relationship, one of trust and cooperation, with their doctor, chances are you will too. There are
also numerous physician referral sources to utilize. Oftentimes,
the referral agencies can match you with a doctor that will meet
your specific needs.

Never settle for below par medical care. There are good doctors everywhere. Don't give up until you find the one who com-
patible.

CHAPTER 20

PUTTING IT ALL TOGETHER
Creating Your Own Wellness Plan

Points to ponder as you read:

- ✓ How is climbing a hill like achieving wellness?
- ✓ What are the five components that make up a healthy lifestyle?
- ✓ What are the various aspects of wellness?
- ✓ Why are you the best person to create your own wellness plan?

Imagine that you are climbing up a rather steep hill. The trail consists of a series of diagonal, zig-zag pathways with switch-backs. You start at the bottom right of the hill, taking a gradual pathway that climbs towards the left side of the hill; then you curve back the other direction, going gradually upward toward the right side.

As you climb each diagonal section of the path, you are only able to see to the end of that section. It isn't until you reach the top of the hill that your view broadens. From this position, your outlook is no longer limited; you have a panoramic view. Rather than just seeing details of the section you are climbing, you are now able to see the whole picture.

In essence, the climb described parallels your reading of this book. The first 19 chapters were like 19 diagonal sections of path-way. As you read each chapter, you focused on one particular element of wellness. But, now, in this final chapter, I want you to get the big picture. See how each element connects together, leading you to ultimate wellness.

Climbing a hill as a metaphor for the process of creating ultimate good health—it is not a spontaneous event. If you don't move, expend energy, you won't make it to the top of the hill.

Wellness requires effort, too. You are the one in charge of your health and you must be willing to make necessary changes become as healthy as possible. Realize that the one person responsible for your health is YOU.

Here is a panoramic perspective of wellness.

Now reexamine the chart from Chapter 2, "Personal Pathway to Health and Vitality." Note how the elements of wellness flow together.

PERSONAL PATHWAY TO HEALTH & VITALITY

Having a healthy lifestyle includes the five important components shown above. Focus on all five of these components to have a healthy life. If nutrition is improved, including a commitment to minimize fast foods, weight control will be easier. In turn, losing weight will provide more energy for physical activity, which, completes the cycle to help with weight control. When the body is fed all the nutrients needed and there is regular physical activity, the stresses of daily life are easier to deal with.

Social health is improved by strengthening relationships with parents, children, and spouse and by reaching out to others, developing friendships, and being involved in the community. Spiritual health is especially important in times of high stress. Prayer, meditation, worship, faith, and commitment can strengthen you to face tough times when they inevitably come.

Social and spiritual health will keep stress levels in check.

When stress levels are managed, the body is less adversely affected by the "ups and down" of life. And, when you are less stressed, you are better able to focus on the nutrients, weight control, and exercise that your body needs.

Wellness requires being aware of the different dimensions in your life and having them flow together in balance.

Here are some additional aspects of wellness to keep in mind when creating your own wellness plan.

Wellness is about BALANCE.

Wellness is the active process of keeping your life in balance, which, in turn, will enhance the quality of life. This process is ongoing. Finding balance in life requires self-responsibility and involves making choices based on personal values and attitudes.

For example, John can have an autoimmune disease and still be well if he focuses on the five components of wellness: eating a nutritional diet, keeping his weight under control, getting plenty of exercise, managing stress levels, being involved in the community, and increasing his spiritual strength.

Wellness is about VARIETY.

Keep a balance in life by including variety.

- Choose a variety of food to eat. The best way to get all the vitamins, minerals, and nutrients needed is to eat a variety of fruits and vegetables.
- Choose a variety of activities for exercise. Don't get in a rut of doing the same workout video 79 days in a row until you have all the songs, moves, and lame sayings of the instructor memorized. Use a variety of videos, or better yet, intersperse a workout video with a vigorous walk with a neighbor, swimming laps with the kids, or a 10-mile bike ride with your spouse.
- Have a variety of family members and friends to rely

on. Extend your social circle and reach out to others. Enlarge the sphere of your social community.

- Have a variety of resources to use when you are stressed out or feeling blue. Turn to Chapter 8 and get some ideas on how to relieve stress. Maybe relaxation exercises will help you sleep, or soothing music help with the ride home through rush hour.

Wellness is about ACCEPTANCE.

Almost everyone has at least one area of wellness that can be improved. There are many reasons why you may have habits that do not support overall wellness. But practicing wellness is not about guilt. Do not harangue yourself over an area that needs improvement. Simply obtain the best information that will encourage and support the necessary changes and put them into practice.

Accept the fact that wellness is not about perfection. If you got up early and walked every day for three weeks, and then you wake up late one morning and had to forego walking in order to get to work on time, don't think of yourself as a failure. Realize you are only human. Get up the next morning and get back on track.

Wellness is a process. It's a matter of making long-term choices and changes. It's being healthier a month from now than you are today.

Wellness is about HEALTHY CONTENTMENT.

Wellness encompasses being "hale and hearty," in good physical shape, fit, and vigorous. It is about feeding the mind, body, and soul with things you enjoy that will improve your outlook on life.

Wellness is as flexible or regimented as you want or need it to be. Some people can make healthy food choices every day, increasing the amounts of fruits and vegetables in their diet, and eat very nutritiously. Others need to have meals, snacks, and water-drinking planned out and written down to achieve good nutrition. Everyone is different. Find out what works for you.

Wellness is about LIVING IN THE PRESENT MOMENT.

If you think living in the present moment means eating a double-sized portion of rich, chocolate brownie, piled high with vanilla ice cream, and drizzled with chocolate sauce, you're wrong! Living in the present moment does not mean ignoring the consequences of your actions.

Living in the moment means accepting where you are and recognizing it is primarily your choice of where you go and what you need to do to improve daily living.

Let's say you have to lose 50 pounds. If the future is the focus, thinking about how many days and weeks it will take to lose the weight or, if you constantly focus on the past—berating yourself for being such a pig and eating non-stop until you had 50 pounds to lose—you are setting yourself up for failure. On the other hand, if you learn to enjoy the present, doing the best you can do today, the past will resolve itself and the future will be a success.

Living in the present moment, involves choosing to be happy. Negativity is destructive and has no place in any wellness plan. Look for positive things every hour of the day and savor those times and moments. Remember the quality of life is really up to you and your attitude. Abraham Lincoln said, "Most people are about as happy as they make up their minds to be."

Wellness is positive PERCEPTION.

People who perceive themselves as healthy are more likely to be healthy, while people who think they are unhealthy are more likely to have health problems. Have you ever been around a hypochondriac? With each ache and pain, they begin planning their funeral and ordering their coffin. The more they focus on how bad they feel, the sicker they become.

I know a woman who battled cancer. She did not think about dying. She didn't concentrate on what the illness might be doing to her body. She was determined to die only once. She perceived herself as a healthy person who needed to go through radiation and chemotherapy treatments. She always perceived herself as successfully defeating this disease . . . and, she did.

Wellness is about EXPERIENCING CONNECTIONS.

Wellness is about connecting mind, body, and spirit. It is ultimately about finding the answers in and for yourself. You know yourself better than anyone else. Educate yourself and discuss your ideas about maintaining a healthy body with your doctor. Remember, wellness is also about enjoying the journey, as well as the destination.

Well, my friends, you are almost at the end of this final chapter on my first volume of wellness advice. I hope this information has opened your eyes and thoughts to the world of possibilities and responsibilities related to your health. In a modern world that focuses on treatment and management of disease, I hope you have found enlightenment and inspiration to take control of your future—do not leave your destiny to chance. Achieving and maintaining health is up to you, not your doctor. A doctor can give great advice, or may be too busy to spend the time necessary to determine your needs and provide the necessary information. I hope this book (and future volumes) can be a guide, a reference, and an inspiration.

If you are well—guard that health fiercely! If you have health challenges, learn all that you can to lessen the progression of disease, or even reverse its progress. For over 25 years, I have pursued knowledge about prevention of disease and maintenance of health. The human body is truly amazing. It is a powerhouse of physical, mental, spiritual, and emotional capabilities just waiting to be explored, but it is also a powerhouse that requires the best of care.

Eating a balance of nutrients in adequate amounts is a must. Learn the signals the body gives about hunger and satiety, so maintaining a healthy body weight for life can be established.

Avail yourself of supplements for nutritional assurance and to assist with particular health challenges or genetic predispositions that may be present.

Make being active a priority. Find a way to walk, even when it is snowing or raining (try a shopping mall, for instance). Walk your dog every day—he deserves a morning and an evening walk.

Incorporate stress management techniques, until they become a healthy habit.

Find ways to give back to society—volunteer for activities, charitable donations, or community theater. It is a great world to live in and the future depends on each and everyone of us!

Use the chapters in this book as a guide to explore changes to achieve a healthier lifestyle. Use the medical and health advice found to complement what you learn from your personal physician. Question the use of medications prescribed by a doctor that is too busy to talk about other options.

If you feel hopeless, because of a chronic disease diagnosis such as fibromyalgia or multiple sclerosis, bolster your comfort and hope with this sound advice regarding herbs and nutritional supplements.

Health begins with desire to be healthy and well, followed by a commitment to a wellness-enhancing, health-preserving life style. It requires a daily commitment—one you must think about regularly until it becomes a way of life. This book will give you a great start on the wellness path, and if you're already on this pathway, current, science-based information will help you stay there.

I have been referred to as a "health nut" since my twenties— before ever entering the world of medicine. This is a fact that I am both proud of and mystified about. Shouldn't we all be health nuts? Shouldn't we all be conscious of our bodies and protective of our health? Shouldn't we look for healthy, long-term solutions rather than quick fix superficial approaches, such as liposuction, Botox injections, and one fad diet after another? Be mindful of the needs of your body. It is where your mind, your emotions, and your soul resides. It is the vehicle in which you enjoy and explore the world and spend time with the people in your life.

Thank you for taking the time to thoughtfully read this book. I hope you have been inspired to begin or enhance a wellness lifestyle and will use this book as a resource to keep you on that pathway. I am honored to play a part in helping you create *Your Personal Guide to Wellness*.

Warm wishes for health and happiness,

Dr. Jamie

FOLLOW-UP PREVENTION PERSCRIPTION

DEVISE YOUR OWN WELLNESS PLAN.

The five components of wellness are listed below. Write down some goals to get started today on your personal journey to wellness.

Nutrition Goal

What I want to accomplish: ————————————

————————————————————————

————————————————————————

How I will accomplish this: _____

_____

_____

_____

When I will do this: _____

_____

Weight Control Goal

What I want to accomplish: _____

_____

_____

How I will accomplish this: _____

_____

_____

_____

When I will do this: _____

_____

Exercise Goal

What I want to accomplish: _____

_____

_____

How I will accomplish this: _____

_____

_____

_____

When I will do this: ————————————————————————————

——

Stress Management Goal
What I want to accomplish: ————————————————————————

——

——

How I will accomplish this: ——————————————————————

——

——

——

When I will do this: ————————————————————————————

——

Community/Spirituality Goal
What I want to accomplish: ————————————————————————

——

——

How I will accomplish this: ——————————————————————

——

——

——

When I will do this: ————————————————————————————

——

It might be helpful to go ahead and set goals in all five areas. Some goals will be easy to work on concurrently, however, don't try to change so much all at once that you become frustrated and throw in the towel. It's okay to set 5 goals, but it might be best to work on just one at a time. Experts tell us that it takes 30 days for an action to become a habit. As healthy behaviors become habits, wellness is within your grasp – one goal and one day at a time.

GLUTEN-FREE FOOD CHART

Food Categories	Foods Recommended	Foods To Omit	Tips
Breads, cereals, rice, and pasta: 6-11 servings each day			
Serving size = 1 slice bread, 1 cup ready-to-eat cereal, ½ cup cooked cereal, rice, or pasta; ½ bun, bagel, or English muffin	• Breads or bread products made from corn, rice, soy, arrowroot corn or potato starch, pea, potato or whole-bean flour, tapioca, sago, rice bran, cornmeal, buckwheat, millet, flax, teff, sorghum, amaranth, and quinoa • Hot cereals made from soy, hominy, hominy grits, brown and white rice, buckwheat groats, millet, cornmeal, and quinoa flakes • Puffed corn, rice or millet, and other rice and corn made with allowed ingredients • Rice, rice noodles, and pastas made from allowed ingredients • Some rice crackers and cakes, popped corn cakes made from allowed ingredients	• Breads and baked products containing wheat, rye, triticale, barley, oats, wheat germ or bran, graham, gluten or durum flour, wheat starch, oat bran, bulgur, farina, wheat-based semolina, spelt, kamut • Cereals made from wheat, rye, triticale, barley, and oats; cereals with added malt extract and malt flavorings • Pastas made from ingredients above • Most crackers	Use corn, rice, soy, arrowroot, tapioca, and potato flours or a mixture instead of wheat flours in recipes. Experiment with gluten-free products. Some may be purchased from your supermarket, health food store, or direct from the manufacturer.

Food Categories	Foods Recommended	Foods To Omit	Tips
Vegetables: 3-5 servings each day			
Serving size = 1 cup raw leafy, ½ cup cooked or chopped, ¾ cup juice	• All plain, fresh, frozen, or canned vegetables made with allowed ingredients	• Any creamed or breaded vegetables (unless allowed ingredients are used), canned baked beans • Some french fries	Buy plain, frozen, or canned vegetables and season with herbs, spices, or sauces made with allowed ingredients.

Food Categories	Foods Recommended	Foods To Omit	Tips
Fruits: 2-4 servings each day			
Serving size = 1 medium size, ½ cup canned, ¾ cup juice, 1/4 cup dried	• All fruits and fruit juices	• Some commercial fruit pie fillings and dried fruit	

Food Categories	Foods Recommended	Foods To Omit	Tips
Milk, yogurt, and cheese: 2-3 servings each day			
Serving size = 1 cup milk or yogurt, 1 ½ oz natural cheese, 2 oz processed cheese	• All milk and milk products except those made with gluten additives • Aged cheese	• Malted milk • Some milk drinks, flavored or frozen yogurt	Contact the food manufacturer for product information if the ingredient is not listed on the label.

Food Categories	Foods Recommended	Foods To Omit	Tips
Meats, poultry, fish, dry beans and peas, eggs, and nuts: 2-3 servings or total of 6 oz daily			
Serving size = 2-3 oz cooked; count 1 egg, ½ cup cooked beans, 2 tbsp peanut butter, or 1/4 cup nuts as 1 oz of meat	• All meat, poultry, fish, and shellfish; eggs • Dry peas and beans, nuts, peanut butter, soybean • Cold cuts, frankfurters, or sausage without fillers	• Any prepared with wheat, rye, oats, barley, gluten stabilizers, or fillers including some frankfurters, cold cuts, sandwich spreads, sausages, and canned meats • Self-basting turkey • Some egg substitutes	When dining out, select meat, poultry, or fish made without breading, gravies, or sauces.

Food Categories	Foods Recommended	Foods To Omit	Tips
Fats, snacks, sweets, condiments, and beverages			
	• Butter, margarine, salad dressings, sauces, soups, and desserts made with allowed ingredients • Sugar, honey, jelly, jam, hard candy, plain chocolate, coconut, molasses, marshmallows, meringues • Pure instant or ground coffee, tea, carbonated drinks, wine (made in U.S.), rum • Most seasonings and flavorings	• Commercial salad dressings, prepared soups, condiments, sauces and seasonings prepared with ingredients listed above • Hot cocoa mixes, nondairy cream substitutes, flavored instant coffee, herbal tea, alcohol distilled from cereals such as gin, vodka, whiskey, and beer • Beer, ale, cereal, and malted beverages • Licorice	Store all gluten-free products in your refrigerator or freezer because they do not contain preservatives. Remember to avoid sauces, gravies, canned fish and other products with HVP/HPP made from wheat protein.

GLYCEMIC INDEX

Beans

baby lima	32
baked	43
black	30
brown	38
butter	31
chickpeas	33
kidney	27
lentil	30
navy	38
pinto	42
red lentils	27
split peas	32
soy	18

Breads

bagel	72
croissant	67
Kaiser roll	73
pita	57
pumpernickel	49
rye	64
rye, dark	76
rye, whole	50
white	72
whole wheat	72
waffles	76

Cereals

All Bran	44
Bran Chex	58
Cheerios	74
Corn Bran	75
Corn Chex	83
Cornflakes	83
Cream of Wheat	66
Crispix	87
Frosted Flakes	55
Grapenuts	67
Grapenuts Flakes	80
Life	66
Muesli	60

NutriGrain	66
Oatmeal	49
Oatmeal one-min	66
Puffed Wheat	74
Puffed Rice	90
Rice Bran	19
Rice Chex	89
Rice Krispies	82
Shredded Wheat	69
Special K	54
Swiss Muesli	60
Team	82
Total	76

Cookies

Graham crackers	74
oatmeal	55
shortbread	64
Vanilla Wafers	77

Crackers

Kavli Norwegian	71
rice cakes	82
rye	63
saltine	72
stoned wheat thins	67
water crackers	78

Desserts

angel Food Cake	67
banana bread	47
blueberry muffin	59
bran muffin	60
Danish	59
fruit bread	47
pound cake	54
sponge cake	46

Fruit

apple	38
apricot, canned	64
apricot, dried	30

apricot jam	55
banana	62
banana, unripe	30
canteloupe	65
cherries	22
dates, dried	103
fruit cocktail	55
grapefruit	25
grapes	43
kiwi	52
mango	55
orange	43
papaya	58
peach	42
pear	36
pineapple	66
plum	24
raisins	64
strawberries	32
strawberry jam	51
watermelon	72

Grains

barley	22
brown rice	59
buckwheat	54
bulger	47
chickpeas	36
cornmeal	68
couscous	65
hominy	40
millet	75
rice, instant	91
rice, parboiled	47
rye	34
sweet corn	55
wheat, whole	41
white rice	88
wh. rice, high amylose	59

Juices

| agave nectar | 11 |
| apple | 41 |

grapefruit	48
orange	55
pineapple	46

Milk Products

chocolate milk	34
ice cream	50
milk	34
pudding	43
soy milk	31
yogurt	38

Pasta

brown rice pasta	92
gnocchi	68
linguine, durum	50
macaroni	46
macaroni & cheese	64
spaghetti	40
spag. prot. enrich.	28
vermicelli	35
vermicelli, rice	58

Sweets

honey	58
jelly beans	80
Life Savers	70
M&M's Choc. Peanut	33
Skittles	70
Snickers	41

BIBLIOGRAPHY

Bray, G. A. and D. S. Gray. "Body Mass Index (BMI) Chart." Obesity, Part I, Pathogenesis. West J. Med., 1988.
Online. http://www.consumer.gov/weightloss/bmi.html.

"Digestive Disorders Disease at Griffin Hospital." Griffin Hospital. Online, August 2003. http://www.griffinhealth.org/GI.html.

Ebbeling, Cara B. PhD. Marketing of Fast Food and Sugar-Sweetened Beverages to Children: Is it Promoting Obesity? Online, June 2003.
http://www.commercialexploitation.com/articles.html.

Fast Food Facts. Brochure published by the consumer division of the Minnesota Attorney General's Office. Online. http://www.olen.com/food/book. html.

"Fiber Chart." United States Department of Agriculture (USDA) Nutrient Database for Standard Reference. Online, August 2003. http://www.nal. usda.gov/fnic/foodcomp.html.

"Finding/Evaluating a Theraptist." Eating Disorder Referral and Information Center.
Online. http://www.edreferral.com/finding therapist.html,
June 2003.
Information adapted from K. Grold and C. Hartline. 1-800-THERAPIST, 1999.

"Gluten-Free Food Chart from the American Dietetic Association." Patient Education Materials: Supplement to the Manual of Clinical Dietetics. 3rd ed., 2001.

Heber, David. What Color is Your Diet? The 7 Colors of Health. New York: Regan Books, 2001.

Hellmich, Nanci. "Obesity Explodes from Teens to 20s." USA TODAY 13 Oct. 2003: A01.

Holmes, Thomas and Richard Rahe. The Social Readjustment Rating Scale." Journal of Psychosomatic Research, II. Published 1967.

"Laughter and Health." How Stuff Works. Online, March 2004. http://people.howstuffworks.com/laughter.html.

Lazarou, J., B. H. Pomeranz and P.N. Corey. " Incidence of Adverse Drug Reactions in Hospitalized Patients." Journal of the American Medical Association (JAMA). 1998, 279:1200-1205.

Nagy, Diana Karol & Stephanie Nagy. "There's Five More Things: Living Well with Fibromyalgia." About.com. Online, January 18, 2003. http://www.about.com/health/fibromyalgia articles.html.

Pilzer, Paul Zane. The Wellness Revolution New York: Wiley & Sons, 2002.

"Quick Tips—When Talking With Your Doctor." Agency for Healthcare Research and Quality. Online, January 15, 2004. http://www.ahrq.gov/consumer/doctalk.html.

Schwimmer, Jeffrey, M.D., Tasha M. Burwinkle, and James W. Varni. "Health-Related Quality of Life of Severely Obese Children and Adolescents." Journal of the American Medical Association (JAMA). 9 April, 2003, 289:1813-1819.

The American Medical Women's Association. The Women's Complete Healthbook. Ed. Susan Cobb Stewart and Roselyn Payne Epps. New York: Delacorte Press, 1995.

"The Hidden Health Costs of Meal Deals." American Institute for Cancer Research (AICR) Quarterly Newsletter. No. 80, Summer 2003.

"Updated Compendium of Physical Activities" from the American College of Sports Medicine. Medicine & Science in Sports & Exercise. September 2000.

Walch, Tad. "Undergo Therapy—Avoid Doctor?" Deseret Morning News 30 Jan. 2003: A01.

"Watching Out for Skin Cancer." American Institute for Cancer Research (AICR) Quarterly Newsletter. No. 80, Summer 2003.

Whyshak. Grace. "Teenaged Girls, Carbonated Beverage Consumption, and Bone Fractures." Archives of Pediatric and Adolescent Medicine. June 2000 Issue, Vol. 154, No. 6: 542-640.

JAMIE F. MCMANUS, M.D., FAAFP

EDUCATION
B.S., Biological Sciences, Cum laude; University of California, Davis 1973

- Postgraduate Studies in Microbiology and Nutrition; University of California, San Francisco 1974-1975
- M.D. with Honors; University of California, Davis 1979
- Family Practice Residency; U.C. Davis Medical Center 1979 – 1982

PROFESSIONAL EXPERIENCE

January 1997 to Present
Sr. Vice President, Medical Affairs and Nutrition Education
Medical Advisory Board
Herbalife International of America, Inc., Century City, CA
- Speaking engagements in 40 countries
- Nutrition product development
- HBN (Herbalife Broadcast Network) Live International shows
- Contributing writer, multiple global publications
- Established Doctor – Distributor Network

August 1994 – January 1997
Lead Physician
Providence Harbor Village Clinic, Mukilteo, WA

May 1993 – June 1994
President
Wellness Center, Citrus Heights, CA

July 1992 – August 1993
Staff Physician, Urgent Care
Sierra Doctors Medical Group, Auburn, CA

July 1982 – July 1992
Senior Physician, Family Practice Department
Founder, Teen Clinic
Kaiser Permanent Medical Group, Roseville, CA

June 1979 – July 1982
Family Practice Residency
UC Davis Medical Center, Sacramento, CA

June 1973 – June 1975
Research Associate/Project Manager, Biochemistry Department
Family Appointment
University of California at San Francisco School of Dentistry

1987 – 1995
Assistant Clinical Professor, Dept. of Family Medicine
University of California at Davis

HONORS AND PROFESSIONAL MEMBERSHIPS

- Named in-Best Doctors in America
- Alpha Omega Alpha Medical Honor Society
- Fellow, American Academy of Family Practice
- American Medical Women's Association
- California Medical Association
- California Academy of Family Practice

MEDICAL LICENSE
California - # G043579

BOARD CERTIFICATION
American Board of Family Practice